WHAT THE BEST MBAs KNOW

WHAT THE BEST MBAs KNOW

How to Apply the Greatest Ideas Taught in the Best Business Schools

Edited by

PETER NAVARRO

Graduate School of Management
University of California—Irvine

McGraw-Hill

New York   Chicago   San Francisco   Lisbon   London
Madrid   Mexico City   Milan   New Delhi   San Juan
Seoul   Singapore   Sydney   Toronto

1 2 3 4 5 6 7 8 9 0   FGR/FGR   0 9 8 7 6 5

ISBN 0-07-142275-7

McGraw-Hill books are available at special quantity discounts to use as premiums and sales promotions, or for use in corporate training programs. For more information, please write to the Director of Special Sales, Professional Publishing, McGraw-Hill, Two Penn Plaza, New York, NY 10121-2298. Or contact your local bookstore.

This publication is designed to provide accurate and authoritative information in regard to the subject matter covered. It is sold with the understanding that neither the author nor the publisher is engaged in rendering legal, accounting, or other professional service. If legal advice or other expert assistance is required, the services of a competent professional person should be sought.

> —*From a Declaration of Principles jointly adopted by a Committee of the American Bar Association and a Committee of Publishers.*

> This book is printed on recycled, acid-free paper containing a minimum of 50% recycled, de-inked fiber.

Library of Congress Cataloging-in-Publication Data

What the best MBAs know : how to apply the greatest ideas taught in the best business schools / edited by Peter Navarro.
    p. cm.
    ISBN 0-07-142275-7 (hardcover : alk. paper)
    1. Business education.   2. Master of business administration degree.
I. Navarro, Peter. II. Title.

    HF1106.W55 2005
    658--dc22   2004018239

CONTENTS

As editor, I would like to dedicate this book to the wonderful mentors in my life: At Tufts University, during the turbulent 1960s, Professor Alan Lebowitz gave me focus as he eloquently introduced me to the writer's craft. At Harvard University, during the energy crisis and stagflationary times of the 1970s, Thomas R. Stauffer taught me much of what I know today about the myriad intersections between business, economics, and politics. Finally, also at Harvard, as I pursued my doctorate in economics in the 1980s, I was exceedingly fortunate to develop under the watchful eye of Professor Richard E. Caves. No student ever had a more dedicated teacher and advisor.

Peter Navarro
Laguna Beach, California
www.peternavarro.com

CONTRIBUTORS

Charles P. Bonini   *Graduate School of Business, Stanford University.*

Leslie K. Breitner   *Daniel J. Evans School of Public Affairs, University of Washington.*

Jeffrey F. Jaffe   *The Wharton School of Business, University of Pennsylvania.*

Richard J. Lutz   *Warrington College of Business Adminstration, University of Florida.*

Steven L. McShane   *Graduate School of Management, University of Western Australia.*

Steven Nahmais   *Leavey School of Business, Santa Clara University.*

Peter Navarro   *Graduate School of Business, University of California, Irvine.*

Steven A. Ross   *Sloan School of Management, Massachusetts Institute of Technology.*

Daniel F. Spulber   *Kellog School of Management, Northwestern University.*

Mary Ann Von Glinow   *Florida International University.*

Barton Weitz   *Warrington College of Business Adminstration, University of Florida.*

Randolph W. Westerfield   *Marshall School of Business, University of Southern California.*

The Big MBA Picture

Who Should Read This Book?

Each year, from the ivy-covered halls of Harvard and Wharton and the sun-drenched campuses of Stanford and USC to the intellectual vineyards of France's INSEAD, the fabled London School of Business, and the teeming campus of Hong Kong University of Science and Technology, more than 100,000 students graduate from full or part-time regular and executive MBA programs. As Table 1-1 indicates for a typical year, this is more than *three* times the number of law degrees, more than *four* times the number of engineering degrees, and more than *seven* times the number of medical degrees.

There is a very good reason why the Masters of Business Administration (MBA) degree is so popular. The big questions that are addressed, the key concepts that are taught, the skills that are honed, the tools that are developed, and indeed the wisdom that is conveyed in the core MBA curriculum provide business executives from all walks of life and in every layer of management with the most powerful arsenal of analytical weapons ever assembled to fight the corporate wars.

The purpose of this book is to attempt the near impossible: compress these questions, concepts, tools, skills, and wisdom into one of the most useful and eminently readable management books ever assembled.

T A B L E 1-1

Professional Degrees Conferred Annually

Professional Degrees	Conferred Annually
Business	116,475
Engineering	26,250
Law	37,904
Medicine	15,403

Source: National Center for Education Statistics.

Ultimately, you will be the judge as to whether the crack team of business school professors that I have assembled to write this book are up to the task. But my promise to you is this: we are going to give you our absolutely best effort in illustrating, in the most practical of terms, just how useful the core curriculum elements of the MBA degree can be in your everyday business life. As for who should read this book, we have at least four different audiences in mind.

First, you may be considering pursuing an MBA degree and may want to learn more about the degree. This book will show you how the typical MBA curriculum is organized along "bread and butter" functional areas such as accounting, finance, and marketing, "toolbox" topics such as managerial economics and decision modeling, leadership topics such as organizational behavior, and the broader strategic areas of macroeconomics and corporate strategy.

Secondly, you may have already applied and been accepted to an MBA degree program. Accordingly, you may want to get a leg up on your classroom competitors by familiarizing yourself with the subjects you will be studying as well as the style in which the material will be presented. In fact, this book absolutely excels at this task because of its "big picture" approach to the core curriculum and coursework.

Thirdly, you may be close to graduating or have already graduated from an MBA degree program. However, you may now realize that many of the concepts, tools, and skills that you acquired during your studies have begun to grow a bit fuzzy. This book can serve as both a capstone to your MBA experience as well as a handy little reference volume to keep near your desk.

Finally, you may already be a busy and seasoned business executive who has always wanted to go back and get your MBA degree but never had the time. You may have pressing family commitments. You may have too many responsibilities within your company to afford the time to go back to school. Or, no doubt in some cases, you simply do not want to incur what is typically a very hefty expense. If any of these particular shoes fit you, the good news here is that this book can serve as a very able substitute for the physical classroom. In this regard, the always down-to-earth and often entertaining conversational lecture style of each chapter will get you as close to being in an MBA classroom as you can get without actually sitting in a seat!

That said, I want to be lightning quick in pointing out that this book can *never* be a perfect substitute for the MBA *experience*. Indeed, there are at least two main benefits that every good business school serves up to its students. The first, of course, is the set of key concepts, tools, and skills that we hopefully will convey quite ably in this book. The second, however, is the *invaluable set of networks* that most students develop as part of their MBA experience. For many MBA graduates, these networks turn out, over time, to be almost as valuable as the knowledge embedded in the degree itself.

With that caveat, I now urge you to plunge into these pages with the greatest enthusiasm and intellectual curiosity that you can muster. Indeed, I hope you will be as excited about reading these pages as the absolutely top-notch professors within these pages have been motivated to bring you this book.

CHAPTER 2

The Big Picture—An Overview of the MBA Curriculum

In both business and in life, I have always found it useful to first look very carefully at the forest before examining each of the individual trees. That is precisely the philosophy we are going to use in this book as we begin, in this chapter, with a big picture overview of the MBA core curriculum. Then, in succeeding chapters, and with the help of some of the top business professors from schools around the world, we will look much more closely at each of the courses in that curriculum.

USING A "CONCEPTUAL FRAMEWORK"

Let us start, then, by looking very carefully at the list of core MBA courses in the *conceptual framework* in Table 2-1. The conceptual framework is one of the most common learning devices you will encounter in business school.

This particular conceptual framework provides an overview of the MBA core curriculum at the "Top 50" business schools in the United States. The data for this table was developed from an extensive analysis of the curricula of each of the Top 50 schools listed in Table 2-2.

Note that in Table 2-1, the left-hand column conceptually groups the courses offered in the typical MBA core curriculum into five separate—but highly interrelated—categories. These categories range from the "Strategic MBA" and "MBA Toolbox" to the "Functional MBA," "Organizational & Leadership MBA," and "Political & Regulatory MBA." Note further that in the right-hand column of the table, there is a percentage listed for each course. This is the percentage of the Top 50 schools that include the particular course in the core curriculum.

Now, there are two things that are quite interesting about these percentages. First, as you can see, there are only two courses that are taught at every single school so that the percentage is 100: Corporate Finance and Marketing. Secondly, you may find the coverage—or lack thereof—for some subjects to be quite surprising.

T A B L E   2-1

The MBA Core Curriculum at the Top 50 U.S. Business Schools

Categories and Courses	Percentage of Top 50 Schools Requiring Course
The Strategic and Tactical MBA	
• Management Strategy	92%
• Macroeconomics	66%
The MBA Toolbox	
• Quantitative Analysis (Statistics, Decision Analysis, and Modeling)	94%
• Managerial Economics	92%
The Functional MBA	
• Operations Management	96%
• Marketing	100%
• Financial Accounting	98%
• Managerial Accounting	66%
• Corporate Finance	100%
• Information Technology	50%
The Organizational and Leadership MBA	
• Organizational Behavior and Leadership	90%
• Human Resource Management	28%
The Political and Regulatory MBA	
• Business and Govenment	28%
• Corporate Ethics	40%

Source: Compiled by Darlene Carver from an Internet survey of the Top 50 Schools.

T A B L E   2-2

The Top 50 Business Schools

1. Harvard University
2. University of Pennsylvania (Wharton)
3. Stanford University
4. University of Chicago
5. Northwestern University (Kellogg)
6. MIT (Sloan)
7. Columbia University
8. Dartmouth College (Tuck)
9. University of Michigan
10. Duke University

11. New York University	31. Arizona State University
12. University of Virginia (Darden)	32. University of Minnesota
13. University of California, Berkeley	33. Pennsy lvania State
14. Cornell University	34. Rice University
15. Yale University	35. University of Rochester
16. University of California, Los Angeles	36. Vanderbilt University
17. Carnegie Mellon University	37. University of Wisconsin, Madison
18. Emory University	38. BostonUniversity
19. University of North Carolina	39. University of Iowa
20. University of Southern California	40. Brigham Young University
21. Ohio State University	41. Southern Methodist
22. Washington University	42. Wake Forest
23. Indiana University	43. Notre Dame
24. University of Texas, Austin	44. Babson College
25. University of Illinois, Urbana-Champaign	45. University of California, Irvine
26. University of Maryland	46. University of Pittsburgh
27. Purdue University	47. College of William and Mary
28. Michigan State University	48. Georgia Tech
29. Georgetown University	49. University of Arizona
30. University of Washington	50. University of Georgia

Source: Compiled from the annual rankings of *Business Week*, the *Financial Times*, and *U.S. News & World Report*.

For example, in a post-Enron world that has sometimes seemed to be absolutely inundated with corporate scandals, well *less than half of the Top 50 schools require a course on corporate ethics.* Equally astonishing, in an increasingly global economy where movements in the business cycle, inflationary spikes, and currency movements can have a tremendous impact on business, fully one-third of the Top 50 schools do *not* require macroeconomics.

The broader point of these observations is that there is no "standard" MBA core curriculum taken from a "cookie cutter." Rather, there are material differences across schools. This means that if you have a particular interest in a set of subjects, you will want to look very carefully at what a given school chooses to emphasize in its core. That said, let us use our conceptual framework to take a little deeper look at each of the categories and courses.

The Strategic and Tactical MBA

The first category is that of the "Strategic and Tactical MBA." It includes what I like to call the two "grand chess master" courses: *Management Strategy* and the aforementioned *Macroeconomics*.

Management strategy teaches you both *how* and *why* to make the big decisions every corporation faces—from market entry and market positioning to product diversification and mergers and acquisitions. In a very complementary way, **macroeconomics** is all about the "when" or *timing* not just of these strategic decisions but of many of the business cycle-sensitive tactical and functional decisions of the organization as well—from production and inventory levels to the tone of the marketing messages.

Consider, for example, the executive team that can use macroeconomic forecasting to more accurately anticipate an approaching downturn in the business cycle. This team will begin to cut production and trim inventories, even as rivals are upping theirs. The team may also better be able to "right size" their company through more timely layoffs, even as their rivals continue to add workers at premium wages. Nor will such an executive team embark on an overaggressive capital expansion program at a time when the cash flow is soon likely to begin falling and borrowing costs are at their highest.

Note that in many business schools, the strategy and macroeconomics courses are taught at the *back end* of the curriculum in the second year as "capstones" to the rest of the curriculum. In some sense, that is certainly appropriate. On the other hand, in this book, I am going to introduce you to these two courses *first*. This is because, as I indicated earlier, I prefer that you always work from the forest to the trees—the big picture to all of the little ones.

The MBA Toolbox

The second category of core courses includes two that will fit neatly into your MBA "tool box": *Quantitative Analysis* and *Managerial Economics*. The hallmark of these integrative courses is that they provide a set of concepts, skills, and (yes) tools that you can apply and use *across* the traditional functional disciplines as well as the broader tactical and strategic decisions of the corporation.

For example, when you learn about quantitative analysis and decision modeling, you will see that its applications are ubiquitous across the corporation. Supply chain managers can use linear programming models to improve production and distribution efficiencies while marketing executives can use regression analysis to determine the level of expenditures on their next promotion.

Similarly, as you are introduced to various concepts in managerial economics such as marginal cost, price elasticities, and opportunity costs, you will quickly understand just how every manager across every strategic, tactical, and functional area may find such tools useful at one time or another.

The Functional MBA

The third category is that of the "Functional MBA." This category is, in fact, the long-time "bread and butter" of the traditional MBA curriculum. It includes those courses in functional disciplines ranging from the dynamic duo of *Corporate Finance* and *Accounting* to *Operations Management* and *Marketing*.

In these courses in the Functional MBA, you will learn how to find and manage the funds for your company's capital facilities and activities. You will learn how to produce, distribute, market, and sell your products and services. You will also learn how to count your revenues, costs, and profits properly—both for external and regulatory purposes when you learn about *Financial Accounting* and for internal decision-making purposes when you learn about *Managerial Accounting*.

The Organizational and Leadership MBA

As for the fourth category of courses, this includes the suite of courses that address questions of *Organizational Behavior and Leadership* and *Human Resource Management.** In this suite of courses, you will learn just why and how managing a successful business is very much a "team" sport. You will also see why even the best strategies that a company may pursue will ultimately crash and burn IF the *structure* of the organization is ill-designed to implement the strategy or the company has severe "people issues."

The Political and Regulatory MBA

The final category includes several courses that have very spotty coverage across the top schools. These courses have to do in one way or another with effectively managing within the broader business and regulatory environment in which all businesses must operate. They include courses that are alternatively labeled such as the *Governmental and Legal Environment of Business, Ethics and Responsibility in Business, Business and Government, Business Law,* and just simply, *Ethics.* With respect to these courses, you may find it interesting that even though the government can do your business far more good or damage than any ten competitors, these types of courses are most likely to be ignored by many business schools.

Because of their spotty coverage in the MBA core curricula of many business schools and because of space constraints in this book, regrettably, I am not going to include chapters on any of these courses in the Political MBA category. I do hope, however, that the Top 50 business school deans would at some point recognize the importance of these courses and then give them their due in the core curriculum.

APPLYING THE CASE STUDY APPROACH

Okay, let us stop and assess where we are in this chapter so far. We started by using one common business school device—the *conceptual framework*—to take a first cut at the MBA core curriculum. Using this framework, we sorted the various core courses in that curriculum into five basic categories: the

---

*Sixty percent of the Top 50 schools also include *Business Communications* in the core, but many schools only offer this subject as a half course or workshop. For this reason, we do not cover this subject in this book.

Strategic & Tactical MBA, the MBA Toolbox, the Functional MBA, the Organizational & Leadership MBA, and the Political & Regulatory MBA.

Now, let us use another device that is equally common in business schools to take a second and slightly deeper cut at this core curriculum. This device is the all-hallowed and, in most business schools, the ever-ubiquitous *case study*.

In this particular case, what I am going to do (with your help) is create a purely fictional product and an equally fictional company. Our goal together will be to illustrate in a bit more detail how each of the courses in the MBA core curriculum can be applied in an everyday business context.

Starting Your Own Business From the Ground Up

Suppose, then, that you are a young Bill Gates with a hot piece of software or, better yet, a young Steve Jobs with an even hotter piece of hardware. By using this software or hardware, you and several business school buddies have come up with what you believe is the next "killer application" in the world of high technology. This "killer app," which you have already patented, is so astonishing that [*YOU fill in this blank with your own imagination!!!*].

Now, if you are going to develop this product properly, the first step you will want to take is to create a *business plan*. Such a plan will precisely define your business and identify its goals and include such *financial accounting* tools as a current and pro forma balance sheet, an income statement, and a cash flow analysis. The plan will also describe what service or product your business will provide, what needs in the marketplace it will fill, as well as who your potential customers are, how you will reach them, and why they will purchase it from you. Armed with such a business plan, you and your partners can then go about the business of trying to raise enough "venture capital" to get the project up and running.

Now, if your company is successful over time, you will constantly be raising additional funds to build new facilities, modernize old ones, and maybe even acquire some of your rivals to consolidate your position in the industry. All of this will take money and it will be your *corporate finance* team that will help you determine whether you will finance your growth by issuing new stock or new bonds, or drawing on retained earnings, or, most realistically, using some optimal combination of all three of the forms of capital financing.

Assuming all goes well with this fundraising phase of the business and that you have enough capital to get your venture off the ground, here are just some of the questions you will be asking your other teams of MBA-equipped experts that you necessarily will assemble to help run your company.

For starters, although your product seems like a sure winner, you may still want your *management strategy* team to examine the question as to whether or not you should even enter the market. Is there room in this market for another competitor? Perhaps not. Are there rivals out there who can bury you with their deep financial pockets, reputational capital, and established marketing and distribution chains? Perhaps so.

If you get the green light from your strategy team to enter the market, you will also want to know which part of the market you want to attack—for example, the high-end, high-quality, high-margin end versus the low-end, lower quality, tight-margin end. In consultation with your *operations management* team, *managerial economists*, and your *marketing* team, your *strategy* team will also want to consider whether the company should actually produce the product or outsource production and simply distribute it. And if your company is going to produce the product, just where should the facilities be located? Should you produce locally or perhaps in a state like Tennessee or Texas with a more business-friendly climate? Or should you seek an international location like India, Indonesia, or Malaysia where wages are cheap but political upheaval is more of a risk.

Let us next suppose that, after reviewing all of the information, you do in fact decide that you will produce your own product and will do so locally. At this point, you will want to discuss with your *operations management* team how to design a production process that is most efficient. This, of course, will entail a detailed examination of your "supply chain," which is the chain of various inputs such as energy and raw materials that you will need in your production process.

Of course, once you have produced your product (hopefully, very efficiently), the next step will be to sell it. This will be the bailiwick of your *marketing* team. It will be the role of this team to figure out the most appropriate distribution channels. Should you sell wholesale to the big chains like Wal-Mart or Costco? Or open your own line of retail stores? Or just sell the product Amazon-style over the Internet?

Your marketing and sales team must also figure out an advertising strategy and the most appropriate message around which to build this strategy. With considerable input from your firm's *managerial economists*, the marketing and sales team will also determine a pricing structure.

Of course, your product will be wildly successful, so the money will start to pour in. As it does so, it will be the job of the *financial* and *managerial accounting* teams to carefully track both the cost and revenue flows. Essentially, this team will be your "scorekeepers," who will be able to tell you whether you are making it, or will soon be broken. This team will account for the various cost and revenue streams, calculate your profits, distribute earnings to shareholders, and pay your taxes—and internally use such information to improve decision making.

The Business Grows Up!

From an *organizational behavior* and *human resource management* point of view, in the early stages of the company, you and your entrepreneurial partners will likely know all or most of the employees and you together will make most of the decisions. And, like a lot of entrepreneurs, you may manage your company mostly from your gut and your hip rather than in the manner taught in the management textbooks.

Note, however, that as your company grows and prospers, you will likely notice that not only does it become increasingly difficult to keep track of everyone, but any flaws in your personal management style will likely also be magnified. Accordingly, once your fledgling corporation reaches a certain critical mass, it will become absolutely essential that you pay more and more attention to how your company is actually organized and what incentive structures you have in place to make sure it operates efficiently and to its full potential. At such a point, you will come to rely more and more on your *organizational behavior* and *human resource management* teams to appropriately staff the corporation, put procedures in place to ensure best management practices, and, perhaps most importantly of all, create a management culture in which morale is always high, productivity is maximized, and efficiency rules.

Once your corporation reaches a certain critical mass, it will also become more and more important to manage the company in a scientific rather than purely intuitive way. Although your *quantitative analysts* will be important from the very start, this team will take on more and more responsibility as the corporation grows. At this stage in your corporation's development, it will become equally important that you become more and more aware of the political and regulatory environment within which your firm operates. This is where your *business and government* team will show their worth. Want to locate a new plant in a particular state? You may have to lobby the local city council or state legislature for the appropriate permits.

Make your money primarily from the Internet? Some states, and even the Federal government, may be trying to impose stiff new taxes on the Internet that your industry may want to fight. Would a bigger capital investment tax credit allow you to build a new plant locally and thereby help keep jobs in the country? That might be a nice argument that your corporate lobbying team could pitch to a congressman or a committee.

At this stage in your corporation's development, it will likewise be important that you come to better understand the global economic environment—at least if your firm is going to produce and/or sell its products in other countries. That is again where your *management strategy* team can help you wade through any cultural, geopolitical, or logistics minefields.

Of course, throughout this whole process in which your company grows from a small seed in your consciousness to an "IPO" on the Nasdaq and then finally into a "large cap" stock on the New York Stock Exchange, you and all of your employees will want to conduct yourselves in a manner consistent with both the law and certain ethical canons. However, during this ongoing process of wooing consumers, on the one hand, and fighting competitors, on the other, you will soon learn that at least in some cases, the law will allow you to do things that may not, in fact, be quite up to your own ethical standards.

In such cases, will you serve your shareholders or your own moral consciousness? And how, buffeted by these ethical crosswinds, will you determine the "right thing" to do? Hopefully, with the help of both your lawyers and other advisors, you will figure that out—but a solid grounding in the concepts and lessons of *corporate ethics* will surely help.

From these two different cuts at the MBA core curriculum apple, I hope I have given you an eye-opening big picture overview of where we will be heading in this book. I also hope that I have given you the drive and motivation to dive deeply into the content herein.

In this regard, if you are *truly* interested in answering the Big Questions and mastering the Key Concepts taught in business school, I can assure you that you have certainly come to the right place. For you will learn from some of the very top business school professors and leading textbook authors in the world.

What I have done with each of these authors is help them distill from their leading textbooks the truly essential lessons of their respective fields— and to do so for you in a most entertaining and accessible way. So how about we roll up our sleeves, dust off our laptops, and really get started!

PART TWO

The Strategic and Tactical MBA

CHAPTER 3

Management Strategy— Five Steps to Successful Strategic Analysis

Daniel F. Spulber*

In the real world of business, "perfect" strategies are not called for. What counts...is not performance in absolute terms but performance relative to competitors.

Kenichi Ohmae
The Mind of the Strategist: The Art of Japanese Business
(New York: McGraw Hill, 1982)

INTRODUCTION

When Ed Zander became CEO of communications giant Motorola, he did *not* start out by announcing a strategy or taking any specific actions. Instead, he observed that the important thing was to "talk to customers, listen, learn, and develop a plan in the first several months."[1] Although Zander brought a wealth of experience from his earlier positions at Sun Microsystems and elsewhere, he knew each company was different. That is why he would wait and review each of the many businesses operated by the company before formulating his strategy.

During this review, Zander's intention was to scrutinize every aspect of Motorola's massive organization. This included a dizzying array of products

*Daniel F. Spulber is the Elinor Hobbs Distinguished Professor of International Business and Professor of Management Strategy at the Kellogg School of Management, Northwestern University. This chapter is abstracted from his textbook *Management Strategy*, Irwin-McGraw Hill, 2004.

1. Dave Carpenter, "Ed Zander Takes Over as New Motorola CEO," *USA Today*, January 5, 2004, *http://www.usatoday.com/tech/techinvestor/techcorporatenews/2004-01-05-mola-zander_x.htm*

ranging from mobile phones, microchips, television set-top boxes, and cable modems to home theater equipment, wireless communications infrastructure, networking equipment, and automotive electronics.

Chief among the challenges Zander faced in this product line was the decline of Motorola's mobile phone business. This was a bitter irony because this was a business that Motorola had itself invented through its early work on wireless communication. However, the company had now fallen from market leader grace well behind the tough Scandinavian duo of Finland's Nokia and Sweden's Ericsson.

In preparation for what would be a major strategic overhaul of Motorola, Zander knew that it would be necessary to "look at whether to buy new businesses [or] eliminate some others."[2] His ultimate decisions about what businesses to buy or sell would depend critically on whether each particular business could offer a competitive advantage over rivals. Then, Zander would have to make sure that each new or remaining business in the company developed consistent plans for its competitive activities. How would Ed Zander go about developing such a strategy? The answer lies in Figure 3-1. It depicts the Big Questions and Key Concepts of the field of management strategy within the context of a five-step process of *strategic analysis* that you will learn about in your MBA strategy course.

In Step One, strategic analysis must invariably begin with *goal selection.* The big question here is: "What business should your company be in?" To answer this, you will learn key concepts such as market-driven versus organizational-driven goals and value-driven strategies.

Step Two involves two types of analyses: an *external analysis* of customers, suppliers, competitors, and partners together with an *internal analysis* of the firm's structure, performance, abilities, and resources. The big questions range from "who are our current and prospective customers, suppliers, competitors, and partners" and "are the firm's goals and strategies are actually feasible for the organization."

Step Three involves answering questions such as: How do you select activities to obtain a competitive advantage? And which factors should be emphasized to achieve superior market performance? To answer these questions, you will learn the important difference between the three types of

---

2. Roger O. Crockett, "Memo to: Ed Zander. Subject: Motorola," *Business Week Online,* December 29, 2003, *http://www.businessweek.com:/print/magazine/content/03_52/b3864038.htm?tc*

FIGURE 3-1

The Big Questions and Key Concepts of Management Strategy

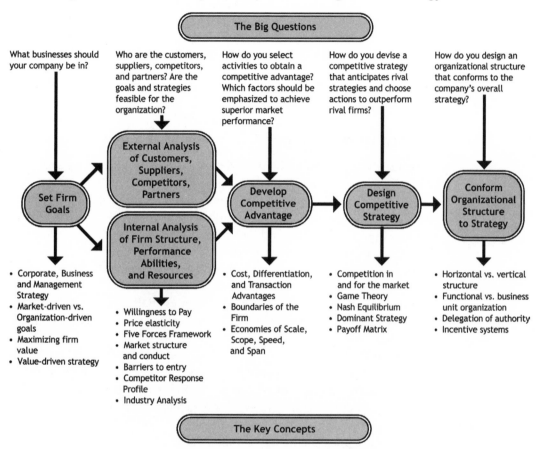

The Big Questions

What businesses should your company be in?

Who are the customers, suppliers, competitors, and partners? Are the goals and strategies feasible for the organization?

How do you select activities to obtain a competitive advantage? Which factors should be emphasized to achieve superior market performance?

How do you devise a competitive strategy that anticipates rival strategies and choose actions to outperform rival firms?

How do you design an organizational structure that conforms to the company's overall strategy?

Set Firm Goals

External Analysis of Customers, Suppliers, Competitors, Partners

Internal Analysis of Firm Structure, Performance Abilities, and Resources

Develop Competitive Advantage

Design Competitive Strategy

Conform Organizational Structure to Strategy

- Corporate, Business and Management Strategy
- Market-driven vs. Organization-driven goals
- Maximizing firm value
- Value-driven strategy

- Willingness to Pay
- Price elasticity
- Five Forces Framework
- Market structure and conduct
- Barriers to entry
- Competitor Response Profile
- Industry Analysis

- Cost, Differentiation, and Transaction Advantages
- Boundaries of the Firm
- Economies of Scale, Scope, Speed, and Span

- Competition in and for the market
- Game Theory
- Nash Equilibrium
- Dominant Strategy
- Payoff Matrix

- Horizontal vs. vertical structure
- Functional vs. business unit organization
- Delegation of authority
- Incentive systems

The Key Concepts

competitive advantage: cost advantage, product differentiation, and transactions advantage.

Once you have set your goals, performed your external and internal analyses, and determined your competitive advantage, it is time for Step Four—the critical task of *designing your competitive strategy*. This entails answering big questions such as: How do you devise a *competitive strategy* that anticipates rival strategies and how do you choose actions to outperform rival firms? Which markets should be contested or conceded? When should new products be announced or prices changed?

Finally, in Step Five, you must undertake a step that many firms unfortunately ignore. This is to answer questions like: How do you design the organization to conform to your company's overall strategy? And how do you delegate authority to employees and provide incentives to implement the strategy?

In the remainder of this chapter, we are going to systematically work through each of these five steps. Before we do that, however, I introduce some useful terminology for the topic of strategy.

Corporate, Business, and Management Strategy

Corporate strategy refers to the overall strategy of a multibusiness company. For example, when Ed Zander came to Motorola, the company operated six sets of businesses: Broadband Communications, Commercial, Government and Industrial, Global Telecom Solutions, Integrated Electronic Systems, Personal Communications, and Semiconductor Products. Zander's primary job was to come up with a game plan or corporate strategy for this set of businesses—which businesses to keep, which to cut, which to expand, which to contract. In this context, one of Zander's strategic goals was to choose that collection of individual businesses that would determine the scope of the firm's activities and then effectively coordinate those businesses.

In contrast, *business strategy* is the overall strategy of a particular business unit of a large corporation—say, for example, the broadband communications division of Motorola. It can also be that of a standalone business. As such, business strategy refers to the plans of an established firm for serving existing markets or new markets as well as to the plans of an entrepreneur contemplating entry into a market.

In this chapter, I use the more general term *management strategy* to include both corporate strategy and business unit strategy. I rely on the convention in this book that refers throughout to the "executive team" as the business leader (although in my own text, I use the term "manager"). Let us turn now to an examination of the five-step strategic process.

STEP 1: SETTING THE FIRM'S GOALS

Before all else, the executive team must first specify the company's *goals*. One way to frame such goals is to do so within the context of the specific market(s) the company serves. The following business activities represent different possible goals for differently positioned companies:

- Operate hair care salons in Japan
- Manufacture electric power tools for household use
- Produce sportswear for sale in North American retail outlets
- Conduct basic research in biotech for pharmaceutical companies
- Provide a complete line of financial services throughout Europe
- Serve the market for electric power generation in Brazil
- Create and supply specialized designs of microprocessors
- Operate supermarket chains in many countries around the world

These goals are as simple as they are diverse. The far more interesting question is: How should executive teams choose the goals that fit best, that is, *what are the businesses they should be in*? Surely the process cannot be accidental—a dart thrown at a chart on the wall will not do. Interestingly enough, there is no easy answer, and finding the "right" strategic process sparks considerable debate among both strategy professors and practitioners. (See Snapshot Application 3-1 for how the legendary Jack Welch set goals at General Electric.)

Market-Driven versus Organization-Driven Goals

Because the issue is hotly debated, you may well encounter any one of a number of different approaches in your MBA strategy classes. For example, some strategists argue that the company's goals should be *market-driven*—based only on the best market opportunities. Such *market-driven goals* require discovering original market opportunities characterized by growing customer demand and relatively limited competition.

In some markets, however, the executive team may find that a market-driven strategic approach will only get them into trouble! Consider the video game market. It may look attractive to a company, but other companies might be better at designing or marketing games. In such a case, the company's goals must adapt to the abilities of the organization relative to its competitors.

This alternative *organization-driven* approach serves as an interesting counterpoint to a market-driven strategy. From this *organization-driven goals* perspective, some strategists argue that the organization should only engage in those tasks that reflect the company's unique skills and *core competencies*,

S N A P S H O T   A P P L I C A T I O N   3-1

JACK WELCH SETS GENERAL ELECTRIC'S GOALS

In 1981, Jack Welch became chairman and CEO of General Electric (GE)—a sprawling company with 350 different businesses and 43 Strategic Business Units.[a] Welch quickly spelled out his "number one, number two" strategy. He would continue to operate or to acquire only those businesses that would be number one or number two in their market. Those businesses that did not perform or could not be improved would be divested. Those businesses remaining would either be the "lowest-cost worldwide producers" or those that had a clear technological edge or clear advantage in a market niche.[b]

Welch observed: "I'm looking at the competitive arena. Where does the business sit? What are its strengths vis-à-vis the competition? And what are its weaknesses? What can the competition do to us despite our hard work that can kill us a year or two years down the road? What can we do to them to change the playing field?"

As the second part of his strategic plan, Welch also reoriented GE toward services. When Welch became CEO, the company was composed of 15 percent services and 85 percent products. As the company began the twenty-first century, it was almost *exactly the reverse*, with a mix of 25 percent products and 75 percent services, including financial services and medical systems.[c]

Third, Welch embraced globalization. Operating in more than 100 countries, GE now has about 45 percent of its 293,000 employees outside the United States and approximately the same share of revenues earned outside the country. Welch's choices of what businesses to maintain, improve or to exit together with the orientation toward services and the decision to enter into international markets, established GE's *goals*.

---

[a]Robert Slater, *The New GE: How Jack Welch Revived an American Institution*, Irwin Business One, Homewood, IL, 1993, p. 80.
[b]Slater, *The New GE*, p. 78.
[c]General Electric, Annual Report, 1998.

particularly those that are hard for others to copy. Such organization-driven goals are based on recognizing unique organizational abilities and resources that will help the company prevail over its competitors.

Again, however, as with the market-driven approach, organization-driven goals can get a company into trouble if, as in some cases, there is little demand for the things the company is best able to do. For example, the company may be very good at designing and producing wooden tennis rackets when the market has switched to composite materials or the company makes VCRs when DVDs are the rage.

Value-Driven Strategy

As a third analytical approach that I embrace in this chapter and my own textbook, there is the *value-driven* method of goal and strategy selection. With a *value-driven strategic approach*, the executive team only chooses those goals and strategies that *maximize the total value of the firm* for its owners or shareholders.

What do I mean by *maximizing the value of the firm*? This is a key concept that you will encounter in several of your MBA courses, most notably, corporate finance and managerial economics—and I leave the finer details and mathematics of this key concept to these other courses. For now, let me simply illustrate the concept in Figure 3-2.

We see that the *total value of the firm* is the *present value* of the stream of profits over the long term (where *present value* is a key concept explained fully in the finance chapter). Therefore, maximizing the value of the firm requires that the executive team obtain the greatest present value of economic profit, where *economic profit* refers to the revenues of the firm net of all costs—including the costs of labor services, resources such as land and energy, services, manufactured inputs, technology, capital equipment, and capital investment.

F I G U R E   3-2

Maximizing the Total Value of the Firm

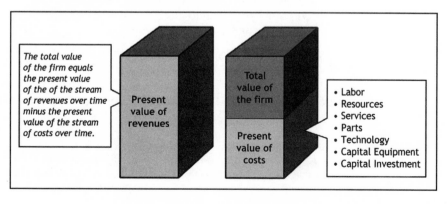

Please note that maximizing the value of the company is *not* the strategic goal in and of itself. Instead, the executive team uses the value of the company as a way of evaluating alternative goals and as a tool to measure potential success. Accordingly, "making money" is not a goal either. Establishing and operating a successful business that serves customers is. This means that a company's goals are, in effect, specific business objectives such as in the bulleted list presented earlier.

To maximize the total value of the firm, the executive team will choose *goals that make the best match between organizational abilities and market opportunities.* The path to success is choosing the value-maximizing *combination* of market opportunities and organizational strengths. The executive team will need to integrate information from both the external analysis and the internal analyses when choosing the company's goals.[3]

Why a Value-Driven Strategy is Appropriate

As for why the total value of the firm is the right way to evaluate the company's goals, here are five good reasons. First, companies that fail to be profitable go out of business so that activities that do not maximize the company's total value are likely to result in bankruptcy.

Secondly, executives of publicly traded companies that do not maximize shareholder value will often be replaced either by boards of directors or through takeovers.

Thirdly, in using the value-driven approach, the executive team takes into account the cost of natural resources, manufactured inputs, and labor services. This promotes productive efficiency and avoids wasting resources.

Fourthly, maximizing the value of the firm means that the company will only serve those markets that earn the greatest profit. This allows the executive team to respond to market forces and be guided by customer needs.

Finally, by embracing a value-driven strategy, the executive team is able to easily reconcile the often conflicting signals of market-driven versus organization-driven goals. Put simply, with a value-driven strategy, the executive team need not necessarily chase the most attractive market opportunity. Nor will it necessarily employ the best skills of its organization.

---

3. This key insight is developed fully in my book *Management Strategy.* My approach agrees with Kenneth R. Andrews (*The Concept of Corporate Strategy*, Irwin, Homewood, IL, 1971) who argued that managers looking at opportunities and threats in the market should take into account the company's strengths and weaknesses.

Instead, the executive team's path to success—as specifically defined by the goal of maximizing firm value—lies in choosing the best combination of market opportunities and organizational strengths. This is illustrated in Figure 3-3.

F I G U R E   3-3

Market Opportunities, Organizational Abilities, and Value-Driven Strategies

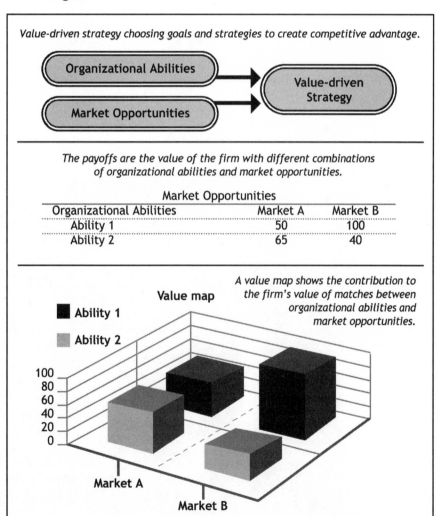

Value-driven strategy choosing goals and strategies to create competitive advantage.

Organizational Abilities

Market Opportunities

Value-driven Strategy

The payoffs are the value of the firm with different combinations of organizational abilities and market opportunities.

Market Opportunities

Organizational Abilities	Market A	Market B
Ability 1	50	100
Ability 2	65	40

Value map

A value map shows the contribution to the firm's value of matches between organizational abilities and market opportunities.

- Ability 1
- Ability 2

100
80
60
40
20
0

Market A

Market B

STEP 2: CONDUCT THE EXTERNAL AND INTERNAL ANALYSES

The executive team's choice of the company's goals and strategy depends critically on information. That is why in the second step of the strategic analysis, the executive team is responsible for gathering information about both the company's external markets and internal organization. This is where the key concepts of *external analysis* and *internal analysis* come into the strategic picture.

The External Analysis

As illustrated in Figure 3-4, the *external analysis* identifies and evaluates the "Four Market Dynamics" of the firm: its prospective *customers, suppliers,*

F I G U R E   3-4

The Market Dynamics and the External Analysis

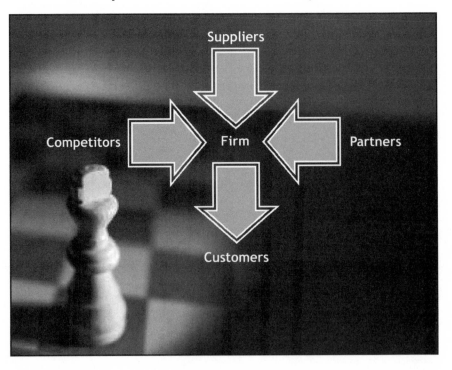

competitors, and *partners*. Note that the connections between the firm and its customers and suppliers are referred to as *vertical market relationships*, while competitive and cooperative interactions with other companies in the industry are referred to as *horizontal relationships*. Table 3-1 illustrates the wide range of big questions involved in the external analysis. From the table, we see that these questions revolve around evaluations of both the current market and the prospective market and range from "who are the current customers and suppliers" to "who are our potential competitors and partners?" *Please look this table over carefully before reading onward as it provides an excellent overview of the process!*

T A B L E   3-1

Conducting an External Analysis

	Evaluate Current Market	**Evaluate Prospective Market**
Prospective customers	Who are our current customers and how are their preferences and income changing?	Which customers do we want to retain? What new customers should we try to attract? What are the characteristics of customers in markets we seek to enter?
Prospective suppliers	Who are our current suppliers and how are their technologies and opportunities changing?	Which suppliers do we want to retain? What new suppliers should we try to attract? What are the characteristics of suppliers that will be needed to carry out our entry plans?
Prospective competitors	Who are our current competitors and how are their technologies and opportunities changing?	Which competitors will we face as our firm enters new markets? What competitors will we face as companies develop substitute products, new production processes, new types of transactions, and new combinations of products, services, and transactions?
Prospective partners	Who are our current partners and how are their technologies and opportunities changing?	Which partners do we want to retain? What new partners should we seek among customers, suppliers, and makers of complimentary and substitute products? What new partners should we attract as we enter new markets and develop new products?

The Customer is Always King

The external analysis always begins with an analysis of the firm's customers. Customers are the foundation of any business, and a company can only earn its revenues by providing products to satisfy customer needs.

In each of your strategy, marketing, and managerial economics MBA courses you will acquire a number of very valuable tools and key concepts to analyze customer preferences. One such concept is that of the consumer's *willingness to pay* for the firm's goods and services. This key piece of information identifies the maximum amount the customer is willing to pay for the firm's product and reflects the benefits received relative to the best alternatives.

Another key concept is the *price elasticity of demand*, which informs the executive team as to how sensitive the customer is to changes in prices. In the chapter in this book on managerial economics, for example, you will learn why raising prices to increase your profits can sometimes have just the opposite effect! This can happen if price is highly "elastic," that is, very sensitive to price changes.

Understanding such key concepts is useful because the ability of the firm to earn revenues depends on the extent of customer willingness to pay and price responsiveness. By understanding consumer preferences, the executive team can improve the combination of features of company products. It can also adjust the variety of products that are offered as well as determine the firms' best pricing strategies. *All of this adds up to competitive advantage.*

The Suppliers are Also Important

Let us turn briefly now to the external analysis of suppliers. While customers define the business, the company's suppliers are its foundation. That is why the executive team's external analysis identifies the company's suppliers with almost as much care as it gives to understanding its customers.

Indeed, the quality of the company's suppliers often makes the difference between success and failure in delivering customer satisfaction. This is because no company is an island. Instead, companies must rely on others for financing, services, manufactured inputs, and technology.

Consider manufacturers like Ford or GM or Applied Materials. They depend on the quality of their parts and the cooperation of their suppliers. So, too, do retailers like Nordstrom and Circuit City depend on the quality of the products they can resell. That is why those executive teams that understand their companies' suppliers better than their competitors do and adjust purchases accordingly can likewise gain a competitive advantage.

Evaluating the Competition

The next step of the external analysis, which evaluates competitors, is one of the most interesting and important. Business history is replete with examples of firms that were blindsided by new competitors.

Despite its pioneering retail experiences, Sears did not accurately foresee the new type of retailing threat that Wal-Mart represented. Despite its technological leadership, IBM did not fully understand the implications of the personal computer and the Apple–Dell–Microsoft invasion. Moreover, many traditional retailers and wholesalers have taken too much time to come to understand the impact of electronic commerce and incorporate the technology into their sales strategies—a phenomenon, by the way, you will learn much more about in the chapter in this book on Information Technology.

In this regard, effective strategy requires competing in markets that highlight your company's strengths relative to its potential competitors. Consider Webvan, an Internet-based grocery delivery service, which did just the opposite. Webvan went bust trying to take on the major grocery chains. Despite its large warehouses, Webvan was not able to achieve lower costs than the supermarkets since it did not generate enough orders to benefit from economies of scale.

On the plus side, consider also Toshiba. Its executive team abandoned the manufacture of commodity memory chips where it did not have an advantage over low-cost producers. Instead, the team chose to focus on custom-designed chips where Toshiba's technological strength might give them an edge over competitors.

More broadly, in your MBA strategy class, you will learn about how challenges from new competitors arise in many ways. Entrepreneurs start up new firms. Established companies diversify into related markets. Start-ups expand to become regional, national, or global competitors. Mergers and acquisitions can change both the direction and focus of a business. Locating all of these possibilities on the radar screen is all part of the *external analysis* of competitors.

The executive team begins its evaluation of the competition by *defining the relevant market* in which the company will operate. In this effort, the team will focus on the *conduct* of its competitors, that is, on their behavior and competitive strategies, as well as their demand and cost characteristics.

In addition, market *structure* is also important because the number and size of firms within the industry provide useful summary information about the identity of competitors. In this regard, the executive team should clearly understand how market structure is affected by the conduct of competitors—a point I will return to shortly.

As for actually identifying competitors, this process begins with a clear understanding of the firm's customers and suppliers. What services does the firm provide to its current and prospective customers? What benefits does the firm derive from its current and prospective suppliers? How do the firm's activities coordinate its relationships with customers and suppliers?

But this is only part of the story. To get the complete picture, it is useful to introduce you to a key concept in strategy called the *Five Forces*— Customers, Suppliers, Established Rivals, Substitutes, and Potential Entrants. This framework was first put forth in 1980 by one of the most influential thinkers in corporate strategy, Professor Michael Porter of the Harvard Business School. By being aware of each of these drivers of competition, the executive team can better understand the industry context in which the firm operates and thereby develop a competitive edge over rival firms. Key questions implied by this framework include: How hard or difficult is it for new entrants to compete? How easy and cheaply can a product or service be substituted for? How strong is the position of the suppliers? Is there strong competition between existing players?

Porter's highly valuable checklist emphasizes that the executive team should not restrict attention to obvious competitors but also consider producers of *substitute goods* that compete for customer attention and expenditures. Moreover, the executive team must be aware of any opportunities for the market entry of potential competitors who will pose future challenges. These include the firm's established rivals, suppliers of substitutes, and potential entrants.

In this regard, Porter outlines four questions to ask: What drives the competitor? What is a competitor doing and what can it do? What assumptions does the competitor hold about itself and the industry? What are the competitors' strengths and weaknesses?

By answering these questions, the executive forms a *competitor response profile*, which consists of the competitor's goals, assumptions, strategies, and capabilities. Such a profile attempts to infer whether the competitor is satisfied with its current position, what likely moves or strategy shifts the competitor will make, where the competitor is vulnerable, and what will provoke the greatest and most effective retaliation by a competitor.

Porter's external analysis of competitors' strengths and weaknesses includes many of the factors that you will learn about not just in your strategy course but also in other of your MBA courses—from managerial economics and operations management to marketing and corporate finance. These factors range from the competitor's product quality, distribution channels, marketing and sales techniques, and supply chain management to its research and engineering, financial strength, general managerial ability, and corporate portfolio. In addition, an external analysis examines the competitor's core capabilities, its ability to grow, quick response capability, ability to adapt to change, and staying power.

The point of using concepts such as Porter's Five Forces Framework is that "know thy competitor" is one of the most important rules of strategic analysis, and the key concepts and tools of corporate strategy that you will learn to master in your MBA class will show you just how to do that.

Industry Analysis and Market Definition

Industry analysis is a key ingredient of the competitor external analysis. It provides the executive team with summary descriptions of the competition that are useful for strategic decision making by identifying the relevant markets that the company is serving. Then, it attempts to characterize the extent of competition using this definition.

The rub here is that *market definition* is actually a very difficult process that is closely related to defining the nature of the company's business. In this task, the executive team should try to identify the relevant market from the perspective of customers. The executive team must ask: What problems or needs are the customers trying to address and what benefits will consumers receive from the product?

Importantly, in this industry analysis, the executive team must continually reevaluate the product definition to determine whether it is too narrow or broad. If the executive team uses a product description that is too narrow, the market definition will be too narrow as well and the company will miss the threats posed by many potential competitors. On the other hand, if the team uses a definition of the product that is too broad, the team may be distracted by perceived threats from many false competitors.

Once the market is defined, the executive team can evaluate market structure, that is, the number and size of firms in an industry. This, too, is a key concept you learn more about in managerial economics as well as your strategy course. For now, let us just say the market is said to have a "concentrated" market structure if there are only a few large firms. Market structures range from monopoly to a fragmented industry with many small firms.

Although market structure provides a quick and useful snapshot of the industry, what matters more is the nature of competition. This requires understanding *conduct*, which refers to the behavior and competitive strategies of companies in the industry. The big questions here are: Do firms compete on price, product features and quality, service, choice of distribution channels, or technological innovation? Other important questions include: Do firms respond slowly or quickly to competitor moves? Is competition primarily from established companies or is the primary challenge from potential entrants? This means that market structure, the number and size of firms in an industry, depends on the conduct of firms, so that structure and conduct are interdependent.

In this regard, another key concept that is closely tied to market structure and conduct is that of *barriers to entry*—a concept absolutely essential to understanding how markets evolve over time. Barriers to entry reflect the competitive advantages of incumbent companies relative to new entrants. Figure 3-5 lists the four main sources of such competitive advantage—including cost advantage, product differentiation, transactions costs, and government regulations and subsidies—and their relationship to industry conduct and market structure. It also lists the four main types of market structure, which you will encounter later in more detail in the chapter in this book on managerial economics.

The concept of barriers to entry has strategic importance because when entry barriers are low, companies can cross industry boundaries with relative ease. Moreover, entrepreneurial start-ups can establish beachheads and challenge incumbents. That means markets with low entry barriers tend to be much more competitive.

Note, however, that because entry barriers have the potential to shield established firms from competition, the executive team must be aware of any specific barriers. If the entry barriers are effective, they can be important determinants of industry attractiveness. In general, the greater the size of the barriers, the lower the return to entrants and the higher return to incumbents. However, as we will see in Step Three of the strategic analysis, there are competitive strategies that can be used to overcome perceived entry barriers.

Partners and Alliances

The executive team concludes the external analysis by identifying prospective partners, which may be found on both the customer and

F I G U R E   3-5

Effects of Entry Barriers on Industry Conduct
and Market Structure

Type of Barrier to Entry	Source
Production Cost Advantage	Efficiencies in plant and equipment, sunk costs
Product Differentiation Advantage	Product development and design, marketing and brand equity
Transaction Cost Advantage	Procurement and contracting, sales, market information
Government Regulations and Subsidies	Lobbying regulations that grandfather incumbents, licensing and government franchises, trade protections such as tariff and non-tariff barriers

Conduct

- Strategies of established companies
- Strategies of potential entrants

Market Structure

Number and size of companies

- Monopoly (one firm)
- Oligopoly (a few firms)
- Competition (many firms)
- Monopolistic Competition

supplier sides. They also include manufacturers of *complementary goods* with whom the company can coordinate product features, promotion, and pricing.

Figure 3-6 illustrates three different varieties of such partnerships, which are formed to share costs, to set up sourcing and distribution networks, and/or to establish technological standards.

From the top and bottom of the figure, we see that companies can enter into either formal contractual arrangements or informal strategic alliances.

FIGURE 3-6

Varieties of Partnerships

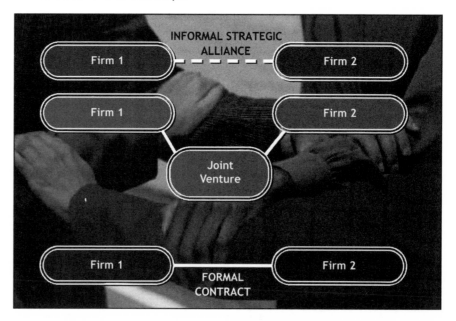

As an example of an informal alliance, there is the classic partnership between Hewlett-Packard and the Japanese company Canon, which invented the laser printer. Canon supplied the printer engine, and Hewlett-Packard provided the software, control technology, branding, marketing, and sales. This relationship was built on trust rather than on any formal long-term contract such as is illustrated in the bottom third of the figure.

As for the joint-venture arrangement in the middle of the figure, this occurs when a separate organizational unit is formed by two or more companies. Joint venturing facilitates cost sharing because the executive team can avoid duplicating investment and production capacity. The team can also reduce the risks associated with large-scale investment.

Partners to a joint venture can be any type of firms, from small entrepreneurial businesses to multinational corporations. In the joint venture arrangement, companies may choose to pool capital investment to manufacture products. Alternatively, distribution joint ventures share marketing and sales and knowledge while research and development joint ventures share scientific knowledge and technical personnel.

The takeaway point is that in the external analysis, the executive team is always looking for partnering opportunities and examining the various ways such partnering can be achieved.

The Internal Analysis

Let us finish Step Two of the strategic analysis process by touching briefly on the *internal analysis*. This is a topic, by the way, which will be looked at in considerably more detail in the chapter in this book on *organizational architecture*.

Table 3-2 provides a useful summary of the internal analysis. Take a bit of time to study this in detail before reading further—particularly because we do not have time to examine this topic very closely in this chapter.

T A B L E   3-2

Conducting an Internal Analysis

Aspects of the Organization	Analysis of Current Conditions	Analysis of Prospective Conditions
Structure	What is the company's current organizational structure, including activities, divisions, decentralization, efficiency, and delegation of authority?	How should the company's structure change to carry out its strategies and achieve its goals?
Performance	How is the company performing relative to industry and financial benchmarks?	How can the company's performance be maintained or improved? What new measures of performance should be applied?
Abilities	What are the company's current tangible and intangible assets? What are its unique skills in productive technologies and operating processes?	How do the company's abilities match up with market opportunities and constraints? Can they be applied to realize market opportunities? What new abilities should be developed?
Incentives	What are the company's incentive mechanisms? What types of performance are rewarded by the company's incentives?	What types of performance measures are used as the basis for the company's incentives? How should incentives be changed for employees to carry out the company's strategies

The purpose of the internal analysis is to support the decision-making process by determining: (1) whether the company's goals and strategies are feasible for the organization, and (2) whether the design of the organization should be modified to adapt to the company's strategy.

From the table, we see that some of the big questions include: "What is the company's current organizational structure?" and "How should the company's structure change to carry out its strategies and achieve its goals?" "How is the company performing?" and "How can the company's performance be maintained or improved."

The internal analysis examines the company's organizational structure, performance, abilities, and resources, where the company's *organizational structure* refers to its boundaries, divisions, lines of authority, management practices, and incentives.

The company's *performance* is evaluated in terms of the total value of the firm, which the executive team is seeking to maximize. Remember our emphasis on a value-driven strategy!

The company's *abilities* include the capabilities and competencies of the company's employees as they work together to achieve the company's goals.

Finally, the company's *resources* encompass tangible assets such as plant and equipment, inventories, and accounts receivable as well as less tangible assets such as intellectual property, technological knowledge, product brands, and goodwill.

As part of the strategy-making process the executive team evaluates how the company's organization must change as a result of any change in the company's strategy. In this regard, the market opportunities identified through the process of setting goals and examining market dynamics can suggest the need for changing the company's organizational structure.

STEP 3: DEVELOPING COMPETITIVE ADVANTAGE

Let us turn now to Step Three of the strategic analysis, that of developing competitive advantage. To begin our discussion, we must first connect the dots between the process of maximizing the value of the firm and developing a competitive advantage. In particular, we can say that to obtain a competitive advantage, the executive team must create a greater total value for the firm than its competitors and then be able to capture the incremental value that the firm brings to the market.

Such value has three different aspects: the benefits received by customers, the costs incurred by the company and its suppliers, and the particular combination of customers and suppliers. *Achieving a competitive advantage therefore means that the firm must either increase customer benefits, lower supplier costs, or discover innovative transactions.*

Accordingly, there are three main sources of competitive advantage that an executive team can seek: cost advantage, product differentiation advantage, and transaction advantage. Since we do not consider nonmarket strategies in this chapter, we leave aside advantages that stem from government intervention. These three main types of competitive advantage, which are closely related to our discussion of barriers to entry earlier, are illustrated in Figure 3-7.

Before we discuss each of these three sources of competitive advantage in more detail, let me first comment briefly on how industry conditions can affect the process of value creation. In this regard, the potential for value

F I G U R E   3-7

The Three Sources of Competitive Advantage

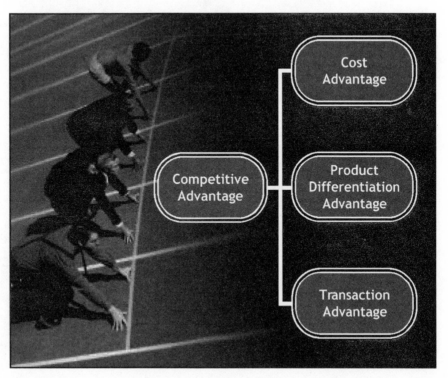

creation depends critically on how the growth of market demand compares with the growth of industry capacity. There are two main scenarios, which are illustrated in Figure 3-8.

In the first scenario, if market demand outruns industry capacity, practically all companies can operate profitably and add value to the market.

FIGURE   3-8

Growth and Value Creation—The Two Main Scenarios

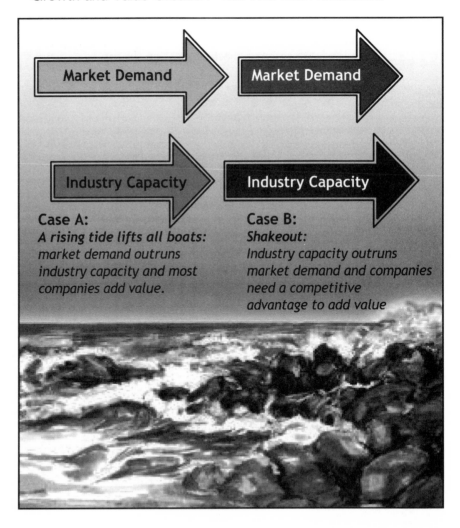

If, on the other hand, industry capacity outruns market demand, some companies may not be profitable, and the company must have a competitive advantage just to survive.

Cost Advantage

A company has a cost advantage if cost efficiencies allow it to consistently outperform competitors and earn greater economic profits. By producing the same products and services at lower cost than competitors, companies can gain additional profits and still attract customers with lower prices. In the presence of a production or service cost barrier to entry, the big question the executive team of a prospective market entrant must evaluate is whether the company will be able to achieve costs that are at or below that of the incumbent firms. If that cannot be done, your promising new company is likely to be quickly driven out of the industry in a price war.

In analyzing cost advantage in your strategy course, you will need to focus on the four *boundaries of the firm.* The key concepts that define these boundaries are quite interesting and are summarized in Table 3-3. They include economies of both scale and scope as well as economies of both span and speed.

Economies of Scale and Scope

Economies of scale are reductions in unit costs associated with higher levels of output production per unit of time. In your managerial economics class, you will look at production functions to determine the existence of such economies and also analyze their origins.

T A B L E   3-3

Four Potential Cost Economies Associated with the Boundaries of the Firm

Types of Cost Economies	Definitions	Expansion of the Firm
Scale	Size of capacity	Growth
Scope	Product variety	Diversification
Span	Production sequence	Vertical integration
Speed	Rate of innovation	Accelerated innovation

Economies of scope are more subtle but no less important. The firm achieves economies of scope if it can produce two or more products or services at a lower cost than if separate firms produce them. Examples of economies of scope may be found in the joint production of, say, cars and trucks by auto makers, as well as kerosene and gasoline by oil refiners.

Note that even if two companies have similar technologies, the presence of scale and scope economies allows a company with greater output or more products to have a cost advantage over the other. That is why the executive team often seeks a *virtuous cycle* in which lower costs allow lower prices, leading to higher sales, allowing the firm to produce a higher output and achieve returns to scale and scope.

Economies of Span and Speed

While economies of scale and scope are achieved by reducing higher output or greater variety of products, cost advantage can also be achieved by more fundamentally restructuring the company or remaking its technology through innovation.

For example, *economies of span* are achieved through greater vertical integration of activities along the value chain. A key strategic decision here is to carefully evaluate the trade-off between increased coordination resulting from in-house production versus the increased flexibility from outsourcing.

Wal-Mart is a great example of a company with economies of span. As you will learn more in the chapter on Operations Management, when you look at supply chain efficiency, Wal-Mart has become a master at moving most of its products through a complex distribution system, making it a vertically integrated wholesaler and retailer.

As our final comment on firm boundaries, *economies of speed* refer to cost efficiencies that arise as a return to the scale of the company's R&D processes. Put simply, the more research and development some companies engage in, they faster they are able to carry out and apply technological innovations—often giving them a leg up on their "R&D-lite" competitors.

As an example of how executive teams must learn the trade-offs between these various economies, consider how Cemex—the largest cement company in the Americas—uses sophisticated modeling techniques to analyze the trade-off between economies of scale and span.

Headquartered in Mexico, Cemex has operations in more than 33 countries. Its executive team uses computers and the company's information technology system to continually monitor the company's worldwide operations.

Because cement is very costly to transport, one method of reducing the total costs of delivered cement is to locate the company's many plants based on customer location. With this strategic problem, the company faces a trade-off between manufacturing economies of scale at the plant and the cost of transporting cement. That is why the company monitors the total production and transportation costs in its network of manufacturing facilities.

Product Differentiation Advantage

Product differentiation is a key concept that you will encounter repeatedly in your MBA courses, from marketing and managerial economics courses to strategy. That is because product differentiation is a very important source of competitive advantage. By producing products that are different from those of competitors, companies can gain additional revenues that exceed the higher costs of the enhanced features.

For example, an established firm may benefit from brand loyalty, such as consumer preferences for Campbell Soup or Oreo cookies. Alternatively, customer loyalty can be a result of the high costs of brand switching, such as the time involved in learning the features of a new type of consumer computer software or changing cell phone service.

In fact, there are a number of strategies the executive team can adopt to achieve a differentiation advantage. In one strategy, the company will position its products and brands based on comparison with existing and anticipated brands of competitors, and may spend a lot of money on advertising and marketing doing so.

In a second and possibly complementary strategy, the company may provide customers with information that affects their purchasing decisions and the way they evaluate the product after purchase, again through heavy advertising and promotions.

Finally, the company or its partners can supply *complements* that provide enough benefits to customers to distinguish the company's products. A case in point is the bundling of software and online applications by Microsoft to carve out its commanding competitive advantage.

Note that I am not going to spend a lot of time talking about product differentiation in this chapter, as important as it is. This is because you will encounter it so often in your other courses. Nonetheless, I can recommend that you take a quick look at Snapshot Application 3-2. It tells an interesting product differentiation story about the rivalry between Boeing and Airbus

AIRBUS VERSUS BOEING IN THE COMPETITIVE ADVANTAGE SWEEPSTAKES

The rivalry between Boeing and Airbus offers an excellent example of how companies can jockey for competitive advantage in the area of product differentiation through innovation. To enter the super-jumbo jet category, Airbus spent over $10 billion to develop a completely new design embodied in its A380 aircraft. This double-decker carries anywhere from 481 to 656 passengers and five different passenger configurations.

In contrast to Airbus's "new design" strategy, Boeing went merely for a "stretch" and revamp of its older 747 aircraft—for less than half the cost. Boeing's underlying strategy was to counter Airbus's product differentiation and production innovation with a cost advantage. Interestingly enough, Airbus wound up eating Boeing for lunch.

Within months, Airbus got over 60 orders for its innovative super-jumbo. In the same time interval, Boeing's stretched old plane dressed up in new clothes got zero orders. In response, Boeing quickly discontinued the project and then tried to leapfrog Airbus with a totally new design that would not compete on size but rather on energy efficiency—the Boeing 7E7 Dreamliner was launched.

and the two competing strategies that each adopted with respect to product innovation.

Transaction Advantage

Let us turn now to the third source of competitive advantage, namely, *transaction advantage.* I coined this term to describe sources of advantage that derive from the many creative ways that executive teams structure transactions with their customers and suppliers. A company has a transaction advantage if innovative transactions allow the company to consistently outperform competitors and earn greater economic profits.

Transaction advantage allows the firm to discover new combinations of customers and suppliers that create greater value. Established firms may derive advantages from existing transactions that create loyal suppliers. Or new entrants may not be able to deal easily with suppliers of key services, manufacturing components, and raw materials that have a contractual relationship with established companies and limited capacity to supply new customers.

Such transaction advantages go well beyond production cost advantages and product differentiation. In this dimension, the executive team must coordinate the company's demand-side distribution, supply-side procurement, and enterprise systems—all the while increasing convenience for customers and suppliers.

In thinking about transactions costs, note that, while they are subtle, they are often the most important types of costs for certain industries. This is because customers regularly encounter the high costs of searching and shopping, learning about product features, finding out prices, negotiating the terms of exchange, placing orders, keeping track of payments and receipts, and arranging for delivery.

One traditional way to reduce these transactions costs is for the executive team to explore ways to increase customer convenience. Often this involves reducing the time buyers need to complete a purchase. This can be done, for example, by improving store layouts and increasing the speed at the checkout counter.

In a new age of technological change, the Internet has also proved to be a tremendous driver of transaction advantage. A case in point is offered by the airline computer networks. Their computer reservation systems coordinate a staggering amount of transactions. They are quite literally capable of handling millions of flights and all the details of passenger reservations on those flights. This substantially cuts communications and search costs for both customers and travel agents.

STEP 4: CHOOSING THE COMPETITIVE STRATEGY

Let us turn now to Step Four of the strategic analysis—choosing the competitive strategy. In this regard, a *competitive advantage* based on the advantages of cost, product differentiation, or transactions is far from a guarantee of success. The executive team must also have a *competitive strategy* to outperform its rivals in the marketplace. Indeed, *many companies with lower costs, better products, or more creative transactions have been soundly defeated by more nimble competitors with better strategies!*

Competitive Strategy Defined

Competitive strategy refers to the actions of the firm that are best responses to the observed or anticipated actions of competitors. It is a critical component of the company's overall strategy since it specifies the company's market moves. Should the firm try to move before or after competitors. Should the firm emphasize prices or distinctive product features? How should the firm carry out market entry? What market segments should be targeted?

In this regard, competitive strategy spells out the specifics of pricing, products, and technology needed to surpass competitors. It also requires the executive team to choose the key market segments to be contested and those to be conceded to competitors. Any attempt to dominate all segments of the market can strain the company's limited resources and increase costs, putting the company at a disadvantage resulting in losing the overall strategic objective.

Importantly, such strategic analysis must be suited to the market context; that is, the choice of strategic moves depends on industry conditions such as the number of competing firms and their market power, the extent of product differentiation, and the rate of technological change. Moreover, the executive team must anticipate the potential for entry of new competitors. That is why the team chooses its competitive strategy by building on market information from the external analysis.

Competition "In" and "For" the Market

Note that competitive strategy can also depend strongly on the number of competitors faced by the firm. There are two important situations: competition *in the market* and competition *for the market*.

Companies competing in the market face a known set of rivals. The outcome of the competition is defined in terms of strategic moves. Companies pay close attention to the number and size of competitors. As noted earlier, the number and size of firms in the market is referred to as *market structure*.

In contrast, when companies compete for the market, the number of competitors constantly changes. New competitors may choose to enter the industry or established companies may choose to exit the industry. Established companies plan for the entry or exit of competitors or the possibility that they may be forced from the industry. Moreover, potential entrants make plans to establish their companies in anticipation of the reaction of incumbent firms.

Game Theory and the Greatest Unknown

In crafting a competitive strategy, the greatest unknown for the executive team is what competitors will do. Through this prism, the whole goal of competitive strategy is to devise actions that anticipate the actions of competitors—and *an effective competitive strategy is one that converts a competitive advantage into a successful market outcome.*

One of the most important key concepts and tools in this process is that of *game theory.* Game theory provides a method for the executive team to identify the objectives and potential strategies of competitors. It does so by encouraging managers to think ahead, particularly with respect to the sometimes inscrutable task of determining how competitors will choose their strategic responses. Game theory also helps managers determine how their company strategy should respond to those planned by their competitors.

In thinking about what rival firms are likely to do, consider these words of wisdom from the Roman nobleman Flavius Vegetius Renatus. In his analysis of military strategy, he observed that "it is essential to know the character of the enemy and their principal officers—whether they be rash or cautious, enterprising are timid, whether they fight on principal or from chance."

Putting this insight in a more modern corporate context, it is therefore useful to ask questions like: Is the executive team of your key rival risk averse? If so, this will rule out many possibilities.

And are they ardent competitors? Are they obsessed with details and internal control, or do they delegate effectively to focus on the big picture? And what is the functional background of the CEO—is it finance, marketing, or perhaps operations? Such information can be very useful in determining the type of strategies the company may lean towards. At the same time, the pay-offs of competing firms from alternative actions provide useful clues to their future actions. For example, by understanding how competitor revenues and costs vary with sales it is possible to make some predictions about future pricing and other strategic behavior.

The overriding strategic principle is that the executive team must adjust its company's strategy as the best response to future actions of competitors, not necessarily to their past actions. In this endeavor, it is essential to know the goals and strategies of competing firms. It is equally essential to know the character of competing firms' top managers because this will be useful in predicting their strategy.

In this effort, companies try to identify the types of strategies available to their rivals. Are competitors most likely to vary their prices, productive capacity, or product features? The choice of strategic instruments can change the outcome of the game significantly.

In addition, the *timing* of moves is fundamental to the firm's interaction with its competitors. When should a new venture be launched? When should new products be announced and when should they be introduced? When should a price change be put in place? When should a promotion begin? Should the company respond immediately to a competitor's price cuts or a targeted marketing campaign? Should the company introduce products to the market before their rivals or try to leapfrog over competitors' products after they are introduced? In seeking to answer these questions, competitive strategy takes into account trade-offs such as that between *first mover advantages* and second mover technological improvements.

These observations indicate why game theory provides a very powerful arsenal of analytical weapons to examine these kinds of strategic implications. In fact, you will encounter game theory in a number of your MBA courses. It will certainly be featured in your strategy course. It is also often taught as a prominent feature of both your decision modeling and managerial economics courses. Because of space constraints, I cannot get into the very rich variation of games here. I will, however, give you a quick overview of how the typical game works and how it relates to management strategy.

The Method of Game Theory

To apply game theory to corporate strategy, the executive team must answer three basic questions. First, who are *the players*? The team must consider their own firm and current competitors including makers of products that buyers can substitute and potential entrants into the market. Of course, if the executive team has performed its external analysis carefully, identifying the players will be a fait accompli.

Secondly, the executive team must ask what available *actions or strategies* the firm and its competitors can choose from? In this effort, the team must take care to identify the range of possible choices. Moreover, it is useful to apply a common time frame when considering the strategies of the firm and its competitors.

Thirdly, and perhaps most importantly, the executive team must assess the pay-offs to each of the players from the actions that they and the wrong other players can take. These payouts, generally speaking, are defined using the very same metric we used to measure the total value of the firm, namely, the net present value profits.

Typically, in the game format as it is applied to business, players are presumed to be *rational* and take actions that maximize their payouts given what they expect the other players to do. Note, however, that both irrationality and human error occasionally must be taken into account.

The solution to the game—the result one observes once the players have chosen their actions—is called the *equilibrium*. In an equilibrium, each player is satisfied with his or her choice of moves, at least given the information they have at the time the move is taken. Of course, as the game unfolds and players acquire more information about their opponents, they may be far from satisfied with their choices.

There are a number of very powerful concepts that you will learn about in your strategy class. Perhaps the most important is called the *Nash equilibrium*, named after Princeton mathematician and Nobel prize winner John Nash.

A Nash equilibrium represents a set of strategies for each of the players under the assumption that the players have given the best responses to the specific strategies that the other players are expected to follow. Note that in some games there is only one Nash equilibrium while in others there may be multiple Nash equilibria.

A key concept closely related to the Nash equilibrium is that of the *dominant strategy*. In a dominant strategy equilibrium, each player chooses his most preferred move regardless of what his opponents will do. In this case, a player's best move is *not* affected by the expected move of the opponent.

A Game Theory Example

To illustrate a dominant strategy that is also a Nash equilibrium, consider a very simplified version of competition between Southwest and United Airlines. In this game, Southwest Airlines offers a low-end, point-to-point service in regional markets. In contrast, United Airlines offers higher-end service and a complete route network with long-haul flights and a hub-and-spoke system.

The question the executive team of United faces is whether or not to add a "no-frills" service to compete head-to-head with Southwest in the short-haul markets, beginning with the West Coast. Southwest's executive team similarly confronts the choice of remaining in its niche or taking on United in its own territory.

Suppose, then, that Southwest is not flying at all. How would United's executive team make its decision? Most probably, the team would do so on purely *economic* grounds. That is, the team would simply compare revenues and costs from adding the additional service and determine whether net revenues would increase.

Moreover, Southwest's executive team, for its part, would make a similar calculation under the assumption that United was not there. Specifically, the team would ask whether a route expansion would create more revenues than costs, including a boost to business on its existing routes from feeding in additional traffic.

Now, let us next ask how this calculus changes when we allow each of these two airlines to face each other as potential opponents. This is where *strategic*—as opposed to purely *economic*—issues enter the picture for both airlines. The matrix in Table 3-4 provides the various scenarios and associated pay-offs of this market entry game.

Note that to construct this matrix, we have assumed that neither airline knows whether it will face entry by the other airline, and that each airline must make a decision about whether or not to enter the other's market. The key strategic factor, then, would seem to be what each airline expects the other airline to do. However, as we now analyze the scenarios and outcome of this game, the structure of the pay-offs for the two airlines leads to quite a conclusion.

In scenario one, if neither takes action, each airline will remain a leading company in its market niche, and each will continue to earn profits of $3. In direct contrast, in scenario two, if both decide to enter each other's markets, they wind up competing head-to-head in *both* markets. This drives up costs, drives down prices, and each only earns $1.

In scenario three, if United adds the no-frill service and Southwest does not expand, it will compete directly only in Southwest's regional market niche. To arrive at a set of pay-offs here, we can assume that Southwest just breaks even, while United's expansion yields profits of $4.

Symmetrically, in scenario four, if Southwest expands and United stays out of basic service, the two airlines will meet only in United's niche. But this time, it is Southwest earning $4 and United only breaking even.

T A B L E   3-4

A Market Entry Game

Southwest	United	
	Stay Put	Expand
Stay Put	3,3	0,4
Expand	4,0	1,1

Now take a few minutes to study Table 3-4 and the three main ingredients of the competition as I have described it—the players, the strategies, and the pay-offs. The question is: How do you think this game will end? That is, what will be its equilibrium?

Looking at the pay-offs, it should become quickly apparent that each airline would prefer to enter the other's market without experiencing entry into its own. Moreover, the worst-case scenario for each airline is that it stays put as the other airline expands. Finally, total profits are highest when the two stay put and keep out of each other's niche. So what moves do the two airlines make?

Well, no matter what United does, Southwest would rather expand. It does better by expansion if United stays put, making $4 instead of $3. It also does better by expansion if United expands, since it makes $1 instead of $0. Since this game is symmetrical, it is easy to see that the same holds true for United. That is, no matter what Southwest does, United would rather expand and conversely. As a result, in this game, both sides will choose to expand their business, and head-to-head competition ensues. Each airline earns a profit of $1 in equilibrium. Thus, we see that expansion is the *dominant strategy* for both carriers no matter what the other carrier does.

And note, here, that IF the two carriers had been allowed to cooperate, that is, collude, neither would have entered each other's markets and both would have earned higher profits—although consumers would have been worse off with such collusion—a situation that may call for government involvement. These types of issues are addressed in MBA courses on the regulatory environment of business.

The broader point of the airline example is that game theory can be used to help the executive team formulate its competitive strategy. In MBA courses in economics and strategy, you will likely encounter more complex games about market entry and exit, price competition, quality competition based on product differentiation, and capacity decisions.

STEP 5: DESIGNING THE ORGANIZATIONAL STRUCTURE

Let us turn now to the fifth and final step of the strategic analysis. This involves designing or redesigning the appropriate organizational structure to conform to the company's strategy.

SNAPSHOT   APPLICATION   3-3

MICROSOFT REORGANIZES IN RESPONSE TO A CHANGE IN STRATEGY

Prior to 1999, Microsoft was organized in three technology-oriented divisions: operating systems for personal computers, applications such as word processing and spreadsheet programs, and Internet-related businesses. In March of that year, Microsoft reorganized the company into five units to better reflect its five core businesses: (1) the Windows operating system for consumers, (2) applications for small business and home office knowledge workers, (3) software for information technology use by large organizations, (4) tools for software developers, and (5) e-commerce applications including Internet portals and access service.[a] Microsoft's goal was to maintain or achieve a winning position in each of these businesses. After this reorganization, Microsoft's five main divisions mirrored its five core businesses.

---

[a]John Markoff, "Microsoft Will Reorganize Into 5 Units," *New York Times*, March 30, 1999, p. C2.

As a guiding principle, the executive team should choose the organizational form that best implements the company's strategy. After all, companies operate in the realm of the possible. The organizational form cannot be chosen arbitrarily since the company is limited by many constraints, including the availability of qualified personnel, the costs of travel, telecommunications and information systems, and legal and regulatory restrictions. (See Snapshot Application 3-3 for an example of how Microsoft changed its organizational design in response to a change in its strategy.)

If a company is already established, its executive team may not be able to redesign the organization from scratch because there are significant costs of adjustment. These costs of adjustment are a source of inertia and explain why some organizations are slow to adapt to market change. The executive team must also compare the costs of organizational change with the benefits of improved strategy implementation.

Because such organizational issues will be dealt with at length in these other courses and other chapters of this book, I will focus my discussion of the fifth step of the strategic analytic process on the two main forms of organizational structure: horizontal and vertical.

Designing the Horizontal and Vertical Structures

A company's *horizontal structure* refers to the scope of the company's product and service offerings and the divisions of the organization. For example, PepsiCo has three principal divisions: Frito-Lay Company, the largest manufacturer and distributor of snack chips; Pepsi-Cola Company, the second largest soft drink business; and Tropicana Products, the largest marketer and producer of branded juice.

In contrast, a company's *vertical structure* refers to what types of functional activities are performed by the organization and the degree of vertical integration. For example, Nike focuses its attention on product design, product development, marketing, and distribution. To achieve its goals, the company forms Category Product Teams that consist of their own designers, developers, and marketing specialists. These teams not only develop an athletic shoe, they also develop a marketing plan, and this is a process that the company says takes up to a year and a half. Nike then puts together a technical package consisting of designs, patterns, lasted uppers, and model shoes.

Interestingly enough, Nike does not actually produce the shoe but instead ships the technical package to manufacturing subcontractors that operate factories throughout Europe and Asia. Then, after the shoes are produced, they are shipped to Nike distribution centers and finally to independent retailers. Thus, Nike emphasizes design, development, contracting, marketing, and distribution, but does not vertically integrate significantly into either manufacturing or retailing.

In thinking about the strategic implications of a horizontal versus vertical structure, recall from the first step of the strategic analysis that the executive team's choice of goals specifies what the company's target markets are. Thus, the goals of the company determine what businesses the company wants to continue operating, to begin operating, and to cease operating. Of course, *the organization must conform to these goals*!

For example, if the company plans to enter a new market, the executive team must establish a corresponding business unit, adapt an existing business unit, or acquire an existing business. By the same token, if the company plans to exit from a market, the team must close the corresponding business unit, adapt the business unit to focus on other activities, or divest the unit. The executive team's choice of goals thus helps to specify the scope of the firm.

In addition, the executive team must ensure that there are sufficient personnel to perform the necessary tasks associated with the goals and strategy. Moreover, the strategic tasks must be somehow divided among the members of the organization. In this manner, deciding how to allocate strategic tasks across the organization guides the process of organizational design.

In determining the vertical structure of the firm, the executive team must consider the company's target markets and its product and service offerings in creating the divisions of the firm. The team next considers what functional tasks are required to execute the company's strategy. The team then chooses which of those tasks will be performed by the organization and which of those tasks will be performed by the company's suppliers. The choice of what tasks will be performed by the organization is a crucial determinant of the vertical structure of the organization.

Practically any of the company's functional tasks—R&D, finance, human resources, purchasing, marketing, sales, operations, and information systems—can be outsourced. As to what drives this decision, transaction costs are an important component. In this calculus, the executive team examines not only the direct costs of procuring a good or service from the company's suppliers, but also the indirect costs of creating market transactions. The team then examines the costs of producing that good or service within the organization, taking into account not only the direct costs but also the indirect costs of expanding management responsibilities. The activities of the organization must be selected to minimize the combined costs of managing the organization and conducting market transactions.

The executive team then must allocate functional tasks between the company's central office and its divisions. Tasks such as marketing, sales, and operations can be centralized or decentralized, that is, split up between divisions. Let us look next at the kinds of these decisions that might be made.

Organizing Along Functional versus Business Unit Lines

One way to structure the organization is along *functional* lines. This divides the organization into units responsible for areas such as finance, human resources, purchasing, and so on. A functional structure is often appropriate for a company operating a single business or a closely related collection of businesses. Note, however, that *a functional structure tends to favor central control of the organization's activities by its managers.*

For a company operating multiple businesses, another way to structure the organization is to divide the organization into individual *business units*. The company can further create strategic business units that combine multiple related lines of business. The company's divisions then contain groupings of lines of business based on related products and services or based on the provision of products and services to particular target customers. Note that *an organizational structure based on business units tends to make the company more responsive to market forces*.

In choosing whether to organize along functional versus business unit lines, the executive team must consider the trade-offs between central control of organizational activities and the market responsiveness of the organization. These decisions depend on the trade-off between the benefits of scale and coordination when functions are centralized and the benefits of market responsiveness when functions are decentralized.

Delegation of Authority and Incentive Systems

Having chosen the firm's market boundaries, the executive team must assign tasks to members of the organization. Typically, senior executives retain a major share of strategy-making functions. They devise the company's strategy, design the organization, and define projects for employees.

On the other hand, it is up to the middle layer of managers to monitor the performance of employees and to make sure that the organization is executing the company's strategy and achieving its goals. For employees to carry out their tasks, management must delegate authority to employees and provide them with the appropriate incentives to implement the strategy—a topic that will be covered very extensively in the chapter on organizational architecture.

CONCLUDING COMMENTS

I hope you have enjoyed this overview of management strategy. Obviously, the particular course that you will take in business school will differ on the range of issues covered and the emphasis, but this chapter should serve you well as a primer on the subject.

Business strategy continues to be increasingly sophisticated and the speed of competition continues to accelerate. As a corporate executive, you will face many challenges from technological developments such as electronic commerce and market developments such as the growth of global competition. Both mainstream managers and upstart entrepreneurs cannot expect to succeed with merely enthusiasm and guesswork. Effective management depends on knowing how to perform a strategic analysis, and then applying the strategy to face market competition and to lead the company's organization.

CHAPTER 4

Macroeconomics and the Well-Timed Business Strategy

Peter Navarro*

[The] brightest people in the world didn't see [this recession] coming.

John Chambers, CEO
Cisco Systems

We saw this recession coming three years ago. It was obvious the booming economic cycle couldn't continue. We tightened our belts. We focused on cash flow.

Ralph Larsen, CEO
Johnson & Johnson

INTRODUCTION

Timing is everything—in love, war, and most of all, in managing the business cycle.

Consider, for example, the corporate executive team that can accurately anticipate an approaching downturn in the business cycle. The team will begin to cut production and trim inventories—even as rivals are upping theirs. The team may also better be able to "right size" the company through more timely layoffs—even as rivals continue to add workers at premium

---

*Peter Navarro is a business professor at the Graduate School of Management, University of California-Irvine. A portion of this chapter is based on an article entitled "Principles of the Master Cyclist" that originally appeared in the *Sloan Management Review,* Winter 2004. The chapter also draws heavily on Navarro's multimedia CD-ROM textbook *The Power of Macroeconomics,* McGraw Hill, and his book *The Well-Timed Strategy: Executing Strategy Through the Business Cycle,* Financial Times/Prentice Hall, 2005.

wages. Nor will such an executive team embark on an overly aggressive capital expansion program at a time when cash flow is likely to soon begin falling and borrowing costs are at their highest.

By the same token, the corporate executive team that sees the faintest glimmer of an economic recovery on the horizon can hire earlier and thereby choose from a larger pool of unemployed talented workers and pay relatively lower wages. The team can also begin its capital expansion program sooner to take advantage of lower interest rates that typically characterize a recession as well as better position the company to seize market share when the recovery arrives. The team may even take advantage of the recessionary interlude to acquire key rivals or complementary businesses at bargain prices.

These virtues of better managing the business cycle notwithstanding, an obvious problem is this: It often seems very difficult to determine your company's place in the business cycle at any given time—much less accurately anticipate future movements in that cycle. *That is precisely where a deeper and richer understanding of the subject of macroeconomics can be so very useful*!

Management Strategy and Macroeconomics

To understand just why this is so, it is first useful to understand the critical and symbiotic relationship between macroeconomics and management strategy in the MBA curriculum. To put it most simply, strategy is about the *how* and *why* of making critical business decisions, but macroeconomics is very much about the timing or *when* of those decisions. Figure 4-1 describes the big questions and key concepts of macroeconomics along with the underlying logic of including macroeconomics in the MBA core curriculum.

As you can see from the figure, the first goal of the course is to help you master the tools, concepts, and skills of macroeconomics. In doing so, you will be able to answer big questions such as what is the best way to measure economic growth and inflation and how might fiscal or monetary policy change the course of the current business cycle, even as you master key concepts such as productivity and stagflation.

From the figure, you can also see that a mastery of these tools, concepts, and skills will help you better anticipate movements in the business cycle. The big questions in this area for managers include whether to expect an expansion or recession, or a rise or fall in interest rates. Key concepts in this

F I G U R E   4-1

The Big Questions and Key Concepts of Macroeconomics

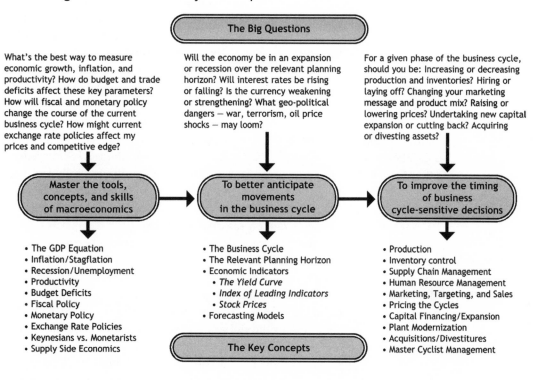

The Big Questions

What's the best way to measure economic growth, inflation, and productivity? How do budget and trade deficits affect these key parameters? How will fiscal and monetary policy change the course of the current business cycle? How might current exchange rate policies affect my prices and competitive edge?

Will the economy be in an expansion or recession over the relevant planning horizon? Will interest rates be rising or falling? Is the currency weakening or strengthening? What geo-political dangers — war, terrorism, oil price shocks — may loom?

For a given phase of the business cycle, should you be: Increasing or decreasing production and inventories? Hiring or laying off? Changing your marketing message and product mix? Raising or lowering prices? Undertaking new capital expansion or cutting back? Acquiring or divesting assets?

Master the tools, concepts, and skills of macroeconomics

To better anticipate movements in the business cycle

To improve the timing of business cycle-sensitive decisions

- The GDP Equation
- Inflation/Stagflation
- Recession/Unemployment
- Productivity
- Budget Deficits
- Fiscal Policy
- Monetary Policy
- Exchange Rate Policies
- Keynesians vs. Monetarists
- Supply Side Economics

- The Business Cycle
- The Relevant Planning Horizon
- Economic Indicators
  - *The Yield Curve*
  - *Index of Leading Indicators*
  - *Stock Prices*
- Forecasting Models

The Key Concepts

- Production
- Inventory control
- Supply Chain Management
- Human Resource Management
- Marketing, Targeting, and Sales
- Pricing the Cycles
- Capital Financing/Expansion
- Plant Modernization
- Acquisitions/Divestitures
- Master Cyclist Management

area involve the business cycle itself, as well as economic indicators such as the yield curve and Index of Leading Indicators.

We see in the figure that the pay-off for all this effort is in the third set of big questions, which focus on the timing of your business cycle-sensitive decisions—from production and supply chain management to marketing and pricing—and thereby help your company cut costs, increase revenues, improve competitive advantage, and ultimately boost profitability.

As we move through this chapter, I will use a number of case studies to illustrate these big questions and key concepts, and the importance of macroeconomics to today's business executives. And I am going to begin with this very short story about a fictional corporate executive in a painfully real situation.

MACROECONOMICS IN THE REAL BUSINESS WORLD

Jim Wells used to be the CEO and owner of a small, high-tech manufacturing business that made precision components for computer games. Every July, Jim had to decide how many components to produce for the upcoming holiday season, and every year, he had simply doubled his production. Since he never had any trouble moving the inventory, Jim decided once again in July to do the same thing—even though it meant taking out a big short-term loan to finance the expansion.

Unfortunately, Jim's college studies in engineering never included a course in macroeconomics, so, in making his decision, he missed some rather significant danger signs. For example, he had read in the *Wall Street Journal* that the Federal Reserve recently raised the bank discount rate and sold bonds in the open market, but Jim did not see this as contractionary monetary policy that might trigger a recession. Instead, he just grumbled about the higher interest rate on his business loan.

Nor did Jim see the recessionary implications of several stories on CNN and Fox News reporting a fall in consumer confidence and a slight up-tick in the unemployment rate. And even though Jim had noted a small blurb in *Business Week* about Japan's shift towards a more expansionary monetary policy, Jim did not have a clue that this would cause the value of the yen to fall relative to the dollar and give his Japanese competitors a big leg up.

So, Jim got caught with his proverbial pants down. By October, the Japanese had taken over half of a market that was already shrinking fast from the onset of a recession. By Thanksgiving, Jim found himself sitting on a huge inventory that he could not give away, and by December he was unable to pay a huge loan that would not go away. By June, he was bankrupt.

Today, Jim works as a consultant for one of his old Japanese competitors during the day and is studying macroeconomics in the evenings as part of an executive MBA program in which he recently enrolled. The tragedy, of course, is that Jim could have avoided his hardships if he had only been armed with a deeper and broader knowledge of MBA-style macroeconomics. With such knowledge, Jim might have been able to better anticipate increased competition and the coming recession, he might have halved his production rather than doubling it, and, if he had thus managed the business cycle a little better, he might still be in business today.

Macroeconomics Defined

So just what is it that Jim Wells is now learning about in his macro-economics class that is so valuable? To begin to answer this question, let me first note that the subject of economics is divided broadly into two distinct branches.

One branch is called *microeconomics*, and we will be exploring that topic in a later chapter under the heading of *managerial economics*, which is simply microeconomics for managers.

Microeconomics is the province of economists like Adam Smith, and the subject covers the functioning of *individual* markets for goods and services—from shoes and pizza to insurance. It explains how such markets are organized and how production costs and market prices are determined.

In contrast, *macroeconomics* is the world of economists like Lord John Maynard Keynes and Milton Friedman. This branch of economics focuses on movements of the business cycle and the implications of such movements for economic growth, inflation, recession, productivity, budget deficits, trade deficits, and the value of the currency.

Now here is a key policy difference between microeconomics and macroeconomics. In microeconomics, the typical presumption among mainstream economists is that the forces of supply and demand in a market will, in many cases, eliminate any shortages or surpluses in that market. Moreover, through the wonders of Adam Smith's "invisible hand," competitive markets for individual goods and services will tend to provide the most efficient allocation of society's resources. Thus, in most (but certainly not all) cases, any kind of government intervention into the market is likely to be both unnecessary and undesirable.

In contrast, most mainstream macroeconomists believe the broader macroeconomy is *not* always self-correcting. Instead, in many cases and for possibly long periods of time, an economy can suffer from chronic unemployment or galloping inflation or burgeoning trade deficits and, absent government intervention, the situation may not improve—and may even get worse! Thus, it may be necessary for the government to stimulate the economy out of a recession or purposefully rein in the economy to curb inflation or devalue the currency to improve the trade balance. This the government does through the application of discretionary policy tools such as fiscal, monetary, and exchange rate policies.

Fiscal policy uses increased government expenditures or, alternatively, tax cuts to stimulate or expand the economy. Fiscal policy can also be used to contract the economy and fight inflation by reducing government expenditures or raising taxes.

Monetary policy, on the other hand, uses control over the money supply to achieve similar goals while various exchange rate policies can be used to lower the value of the currency to stimulate the sale of exports or increase the value of the currency to attract more foreign capital.

Now here is the important point about these discretionary policies from the perspective of business executives seeking to run a company. Properly practiced, macroeconomic policies can help create a climate of prosperity and growth for business and the broader society. However, improperly applied, discretionary macroeconomic policies can actually exacerbate the problems of inflation or unemployment or slow economic growth and make it very, very difficult for businesses to maintain profitability.

Why Macroeconomic History is So Important

In teaching macroeconomics to MBA students for more than a decade, I have found that the best way to illustrate this important point is to always begin my first class with a brief outline of the historical evolution of the so-called *warring schools* of macroeconomics—from *Classical economics* and *Keynesian economics* to *Monetarism, Supply Side economics*, and so-called *New Classical economics*, with its "rational expectations" theory. In fact, my MBA students inevitably find this macroeconomic history to be very useful for several reasons.

First, this history always bring into very sharp focus the major macroeconomic problems that every economy—and business executive— must confront: from recession, unemployment, inflation, and lagging productivity to chronic budget and trade deficits.

Secondly, by reviewing this macroeconomic history, you will also be able to see how, over time, new theories like Keynesianism and Monetarism have emerged to try and cope with problems that the previous theories could not solve. This perspective is important because the outcomes of the many macroeconomic policy debates that you will witness in your lifetime as business executives will in large part be driven by which school or schools of macroeconomic thought are currently being embraced by the political leaders of your particular country.

For example, in the United States, "Supply Side" and "Monetarist" Republicans tend to favor tax cuts and monetary growth targets to restore an economy to robust growth with low inflation. On the other hand, Keynesian Democrats may prefer increased government expenditures and a monetary policy based on interest rate cuts. From a business perspective, *which* set of discretionary policy tools is embraced can have very important consequences for the operation and profitability of your business. Of course, a solid knowledge of macroeconomics and macroeconomic history can help you and your executive team sort these consequences out.

In this regard, a Republican president that chooses to fight a recession with supply side tax cuts may lower your company's tax burden in the short run. But the policy may lead to higher borrowing costs in the longer run if it leads to increased budget deficits.

In contrast, a Democratic Keynesian president that prefers to increase government expenditures to fight a recession may wind up eventually raising your corporate taxes to pay for the expenditures. However, if your company is in a sector that directly benefits from increased government spending—defense, highway construction, or other public works projects— your company may well do better under the Democratic Keynesian.

THE WARRING SCHOOLS OF MACROECONOMICS

For all these kinds of reasons, it is important that you sensitize yourself to the history of the warring schools.

The Classical Economists

Such a history always begins with Classical economics, which dates back to the late 1700s and has its roots in the *laissez faire* writings of free market economists like David Ricardo and Jean Baptiste Say. These Classical economists believed that the problems of recession and unemployment were a natural part of the business cycle, that these problems were self-correcting, and, most importantly, that there was no need for the government to intervene in the free market to correct them. And this approach actually seemed to work, albeit imperfectly, until the Great Depression of the 1930s.

The Birth of Keynesian Economics

With the stock market crash of 1929, the global economy fell into first a recession and then a deep depression. While Classical economists kept waiting for what they viewed as the inevitable recovery, British economist

John Maynard Keynes flatly rejected the Classical notion of a self-correcting economy.

Instead, Keynes believed that the global economy would not naturally rebound but simply stagnate or, even worse, fall into a death spiral. In his view, the only way to get the economy moving again was to prime the economic pump with increased government expenditures. Thus, *fiscal policy* was born and the Keynesian prescription became the underlying, if unstated philosophy of global economic recovery.

In the United States, for example, Franklin Delano Roosevelt's Keynesian "New Deal" public works programs in the 1930s together with the 1940s Keynesian boom of World War II expenditures were enough to lift the American economy out of the Great Depression and up to unparalleled heights. In the 1960s, pure Keynesianism reached its zenith with the much heralded Kennedy Tax Cut of 1964.

This Keynesian tax cut to stimulate demand helped make the 1960s one of the most prosperous decades in America as business boomed. However, this aggressive fiscal stimulus also laid the foundation for the emergence of a new and ugly macroeconomic problem that, as it would troublingly turn out, Keynesian economics would be totally incapable of solving. This problem, which would absolutely ravage the business community, was *stagflation*— simultaneous high inflation and high unemployment.

The stagflation problem had it roots in President Lyndon Johnson's stubbornness. In the late 1960s, against the strong advice of his economic advisors, Johnson increased expenditures on the Vietnam War but refused to cut spending on his Great Society social welfare programs. This refusal helped spawn a virulent *demand-pull inflation*.

Demand-Pull Inflation

The essence of *demand-pull inflation* is "too much money chasing too few goods," and that is exactly what happened when the United States tried to finance both "guns and butter"—both the Vietnam War and the Great Society. This situation is illustrated in Figure 4-2, which employs one of the typical tools you will be introduced to in your MBA macroeconomics course. This is the *Aggregate Supply–Aggregate Demand framework*.

In this framework, the price level is represented on the vertical axis and the economic output or *gross domestic product* (GDP) of the economy is represented on the horizontal line. You can see that the production side of the economy is represented by the aggregate supply or AS line. Note that it slopes upward with price—meaning, intuitively, that producers will be

F I G U R E   4-2

Demand-Pull Inflation

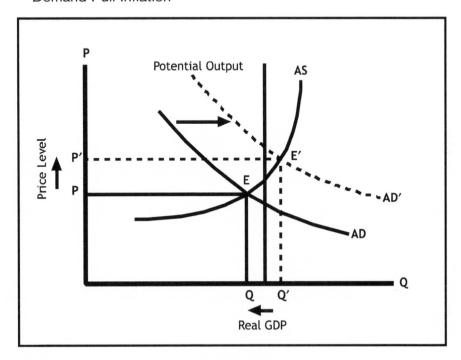

willing to supply more as the price level rises. In contrast, the demand for that production by consumers, the business community, the government, and foreigners is represented by a downward sloping aggregate demand curve, which indicates equally intuitively that demand will fall as prices rise.

Now in this example of demand-pull inflation, we can see clearly in the figure that increased government spending on both guns and butter moves aggregate demand from AD to AD', and equilibrium output increases from E to E' as real GDP expands. However, when real output rises far above the economy's *potential* output, the price level moves up sharply as well, from P to P'. This was a clear case of demand-pull inflation, and the Keynesian cure for such demand-pull inflation is quite simple: cut government spending or raise taxes to pull back aggregate demand.

Now let us contrast this demand-pull inflation with a very different kind of inflation that began to emerge in the early 1970s—one that posed a much more intractable problem for Keynesian economists. This is *cost-push inflation,* and *it is very important for business executives to be able to distinguish between demand-pull and cost-push inflation.* This is because the remedies have quite different implications for the business climate.

Cost-Push Inflation and Stagflation

Cost-push inflation occurs when factors such as rapid increases in raw material prices, oil price shocks, falling productivity, and/or wage increases drive up *production* costs. In this situation, it is the aggregate supply curve that shifts outward rather than the aggregate demand curve, as we illustrate in Figure 4-3.

Here, we see that sharply higher oil, commodity, and labor costs greatly increase the costs of doing business. These higher production costs are represented by a shift of the aggregate supply curve up from AS to AS' as the equilibrium shifts from E to E'. Note that output correspondingly declines

F I G U R E   4-3

Cost-Push Inflation

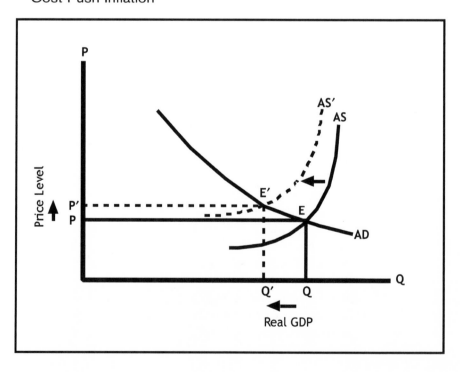

from Q to Q′ while prices rise. This is *stagflation*—recession or stagnation combined with inflation. In this situation, the economy suffers the double whammy of *both* lower output and higher prices.

Now here is the very important punch line. Prior to the 1970s, economists did not believe you could even have both high inflation and high unemployment *at the same time*. If one went up, the other had to go down. But the 1970s proved economists wrong on this point and likewise exposed Keynesian economics as being incapable of solving the new stagflation problem.

The Keynesian dilemma was simply this: using expansionary policies to reduce unemployment simply created more inflation while using contractionary policies to curb inflation only deepened the recession. That meant that the traditional Keynesian tools could solve only *half* of the stagflation problem at any one time—and only by making the other half worse.

It was this inability of Keynesian economics to cope with stagflation that set the stage for Professor Milton Friedman's monetarist challenge to what had become the Keynesian orthodoxy.

Milton Friedman and the Monetarists

Friedman argued that the problems of both inflation and recession may be traced to one thing—the rate of growth of the money supply. To Friedman's Monetarists, inflation happens when the government prints too much money and recessions happen when it prints too little.

From this Monetarist perspective, stagflation is the inevitable result of activist fiscal and monetary policies that try to push the economy beyond its so-called *natural rate of unemployment*—defined as the lowest level of unemployment that can be attained without upward pressure on inflation.

According to the Monetarists, expansionary attempts to go beyond this natural rate of unemployment may result in short run spurts of growth. However, after each growth spurt, prices and wages rise and drag the economy back to its natural rate—BUT, at a *higher* rate of inflation.

Over time, these futile attempts to push the economy beyond its natural rate of unemployment lead to an upward inflationary spiral. In this situation, Monetarists believe that the only way to wring inflation out of the economy is to have the actual unemployment rate rise *above* the natural rate. That means only one thing—which, by the way, should absolutely horrify any business executive. That is because that way to control inflation is to *purposely induce a recession*.

This is at least one interpretation of what the Federal Reserve did in the United States beginning in 1979 under the Monetarist banner of setting monetary growth targets. Under Chairman Paul Volcker, the Federal Reserve adopted a sharply contractionary monetary policy and interest rates soared to over 20 percent. Particularly hard-hit were small businesses as well as interest rate-sensitive sectors of the economy like housing construction, automobile purchases, and business investment—and if your company happened to be in one of these sectors at the time, it may not have survived the government's monetary policy "cure."

That is just one reason why while the Federal Reserve's bitter medicine worked, three years of hard economic times left a bitter taste in the mouths of the American people now hungry for a sweeter macroeconomic cure than either the Keynesians or Monetarists could offer. Enter stage right: the conservative school of Supply Side economics.

Supply Side Economics and the Reagan Revolution

In the 1980 U.S. presidential election, Ronald Reagan ran on a Supply Side platform that promised to simultaneously cut taxes, increase government tax revenues and accelerate the rate of economic growth *without* inducing inflation—a very sweet macroeconomic cure indeed.

On the surface, the supply side approach looks very similar to the kind of Keynesian tax cut prescribed in the 1960s to stimulate a sluggish economy. However, the Supply Siders viewed such tax cuts from a very different behavioral perspective. Specifically, they believed that people would actually work much harder and invest much more if they were allowed to keep more of the fruits of their labor. The end result would be to increase the amount of goods and services the economy could actually produce by pushing out the economy's *aggregate supply* curve—hence, *Supply Side economics*.

In such a scenario, the supply siders promised that by cutting taxes and thereby spurring rapid growth, the *loss* in tax revenues from the tax cut would be more than offset by the *increase* in tax revenues from increased economic growth. Thus, under supply side economics, the budget deficit would actually be reduced.

Unfortunately, during the Reagan years, that did not happen. While the economy boomed so, too, did America's budget deficit. And as the budget deficit soared, America's trade deficit soared with it.

George Bush I and the New Classical Economists

These so-called *twin deficits* deeply concerned Reagan's successor George Bush, particularly after the budget deficit jumped over $200 billion at the midpoint of his term in 1990, and the economy began to slide into recession.

To any red-blooded Keynesian, this onset of recession would have been a clear signal to engage in expansionary policy. However, in the Bush White House, Ronald Reagan's supply side advisors had been supplanted not by Keynesians but rather by a new breed of macroeconomic thinkers—the so-called "New Classicals."

New Classical economics is based on the controversial theory of *rational expectations*. This theory says that if you form your expectations "rationally," you will take into account all available information—*including* the future effects of activist fiscal and monetary policies.

Rational Expectations Theory

The idea behind rational expectations is that such activist policies might be ableto fool people for a while. However, after a while, people will learn from their experiences, and then you cannot fool them at all. The central policy implication of this idea is, of course, profound: *rational expectations render activist fiscal and monetary policies completely ineffective SO they should be abandoned.*

Accordingly, Bush's New Classical advisors flatly rejected any Keynesian "quick fix" to the deepening recession. Bush took this New Classical advice to heart, the economy limped into the 1992 Presidential election and, like Richard Nixon in 1960, Bush lost to a Democrat promising to get the economy moving again. What is perhaps most interesting about this transition of power is that the newly elected President Bill Clinton actually did very little to stimulate the economy. The mere fact, however, that Clinton *promised* a more activist approach helped restore business and consumer confidence.

The Bush II–Greenspan Hyper-Stimulus

The Clinton recovery ended with the 2001 recession—ironically under the presidency of George Bush's son, George Walker Bush. Over the next several years, the younger Bush, together with Federal Reserve Chairman Alan Greenspan, would engage in one of the most dramatic doubles doses of fiscal and monetary policy the United States has ever witnessed.[1]

In hindsight, it seems clear that the younger Bush's aggressive embrace of activist fiscal policy was in large part a reaction to the failure of his father to win re-election in 1992 because of the reluctance of his father's economic team to engage in the appropriate Keynesian stimulus. What remains unclear, however, is whether these policies will ultimately result in significant inflation brought about both by soaring budget deficits and a weakening dollar.

On the budget deficit front, such deficits must be financed either by raising taxes or selling government bonds. If the bond option is used, the government must offer higher interest rates to sell the bonds and this drives up interest rates—thus making it much more expensive for businesses to borrow. One possible result is the triggering of a recession.

On the weakening dollar front, a weaker dollar will surely stimulate exports and thereby stimulate growth in the GDP—a good thing if you do business in an export-oriented industry. However, a weaker dollar also means that imports will be more expensive so that is inflationary.

More broadly, and from the perspective of business executives, the Bush–Greenspan stimulus at the turn of the century demonstrates unequivocally the important role that the application of discretionary fiscal and monetary policies has assumed in managing the U.S. economy. Accordingly, the application of such policies will have tremendous impact on movements in the business cycle and the broader business climate within which your company operates.

In the next part of this chapter, I will describe the business cycle in more detail, discuss how the economy can get off track, and illustrate how business executives can use a deeper understanding of movements in the business cycle to better strategize and manage their companies.

THE BUSINESS CYCLE DEFINED

To begin our discussion of the business cycle, let us first more specifically define a term we introduced earlier, namely, the *gross domestic product* or

---

1. For one of the most compelling accounts of the inner workings of macroeconomic policy in a White House, see Ron Suskind, *The Price of Loyalty: George W. Bush, the White House, and the Education of Paul O'Neil*, Simon & Schuster, 2004.

GDP. A nation's GDP measures its economic output, the *real GDP* is the GDP adjusted for inflation, and the growth in the real GDP is the way macroeconomists universally measure the overall strength or weakness of an economy.

For example, a GDP growing at an annual rate of from two to three percent annually reflects modest economic growth in a developed country like the United States or Japan, while growth of the GDP in the four to five percent range indicates strong economic growth. Of course, if the GDP growth rate is negative, that means the economy is in recession.

The GDP Equation and Growth

Figure 4-4 describes one of the most important equations in economics. It shows that the GDP is calculated by adding the amount of *consumption* plus *business investment* plus *government spending* plus "*net exports*," where net exports equal the amount of *exports* a nation sells to foreigners minus the amount of *imports* it buys. The importance of this equation lies in the fact that it identifies the four important components of growth—and note that we will

F I G U R E   4-4

The GDP Equation

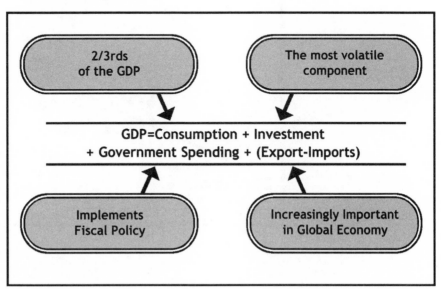

soon come back to this equation in our discussion of how business executives can use so-called *leading economic indicators* to try to forecast movements in the *business cycle*.

In this regard, it is precisely such movements of the GDP that define the business cycle, which quite literally charts the recurrent ups and downs in the real GDP over time. During this cycle, the fortunes of most corporations quite literally ebb and flow with the level of economic activity. And while individual business cycles vary substantially in length and intensity, all display common phases, as illustrated in Figure 4-5.

You can see that the cycle looks like a roller coaster. There is a "peak" where business activity reaches a maximum, a "trough," which is brought about by a recessionary downturn in total output, and a "recovery" or upturn in which the economy expands towards full employment. Note that each of these phases of the cycle oscillates around a "growth trend" line.

FIGURE   4-5

The Typical Business Cycle

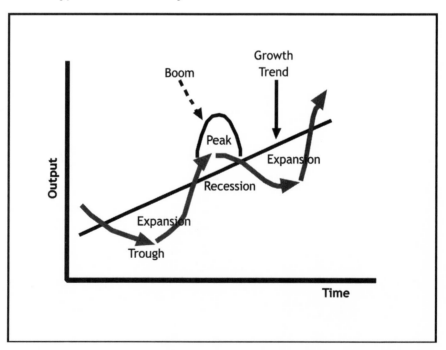

A central concern of both macroeconomists and business executives is to determine just what macroeconomic policies will be used to control or harness the business cycle—and business executives take a keen interest in the specific policies that may be adopted.

This is because a central concern of business executives is to determine whether the economy is going into a recession or expansion—with a right guess in business often being the difference between a big profit and a big loss. That is why, and we will develop this theme further below, many businesses rely on various economic forecasting services and leading economic indicators to help them plan all of the various business cycle sensitive decisions of the firm, from inventory and production to marketing and capital expansion.

To put the business cycle in perspective, Table 4-1 illustrates the various recessionary and expansionary turning points in the U.S. economy since World War II.

For example, we see in column 2 that the shortest recession has been a matter of just 6 months—January to July, 1980—and the longest recession has spanned 16 months—November 1973 to March 1975 and July 1981 to November 1982. In column 5, we likewise observe that the shortest

T A B L E   4-1

The Business Cycle Since World War II

Dates of Recessions	Duration (Months)	Maximum Negative Quarterly Growth Rate	Dates of Expansion	Duration (Months)	Maximum Positive Quarterly Growth Rate
Nov. 1948–Oct. 1949	11	−5.5	Oct. 1949–July. 1953	45	17.6
Jul. 1953–May.1954	10	−6.3	May. 1954–Aug. 1957	39	11.9
Aug. 1957–Apr. 1958	8	−10.3	Apr. 1958–Apr. 1960	24	10.9
Apr. 1960–Feb. 1961	10	−5.0	Feb. 1961–Dec. 1969	106	10.3
Dec. 1969–Nov.1970	11	−4.2	Nov. 1970–Nov. 1973	36	11.6
Nov. 1973–Mar. 1975	16	−5.0	Mar. 1975–Jan. 1980	58	16.3
Jan. 1980–Jul. 1980	6	−7.9	Jul. 1980–Jul. 1981	12	8.0
Jul. 1981–Nov. 1982	16	−6.5	Nov. 1982–Jul. 1990	92	9.8
Jul. 1990–Mar. 1991	8	−3.2	Mar. 1991–Mar. 2001	120	7.1
Mar. 2001–Nov. 2001	8	−1.6			

Sources: National Bureau of Economic Research (NBER) and Federal Reserve Board

expansion, from July 1980 to July 1981, has been just 12 months and the longest an astonishing 10 *years* during the 1990s.

One obvious conclusion to draw from this table is that, as with fingerprints, no two business cycles are exactly the same. That would seem to make it more difficult to extrapolate any future movements of the cycle based on previous patterns.

Within the context of this difficulty, the modern executive team has at its disposal a diverse set of macroeconometric forecasting models and *leading economic indicators* to help it detect movements in the business cycle. We are going to discuss just a few of the more important of these models and indicators here, but you will of course learn much more about them in your MBA program.

The Macroeconometric Forecasting Models

In the realm of macroeconometric forecasting models, business executives can choose from a wide variety—typically on a paid subscription basis. Some of these models are Keynesian by construction, others reflect Monetarist or Supply Side assumptions, still others are rooted in the theory of rational expectations or represent some synthesis of all of the competing schools of macroeconomic thought—and it will be important for you as a business executive to understand the underlying assumptions of any model in which you put your faith. Despite these differences in assumptions, however, what all of these models share are the goals of accurately predicting the future rate of economic growth and charting turning points in the business cycle.

Now here is a tip that you can begin to use right away. One of the more efficient ways for any executive team to process the available forecasting data is through a service called the Blue Chip Consensus Forecast. This Consensus Forecast is an average of more than 40 monthly forecasts that are submitted to the company as part of its Blue Chip Economic Indicators Survey.

This survey includes forecasts of 15 macroeconomic variables, including, most importantly, GDP, the Consumer Price Index, the unemployment rate, and interest rates, while survey participants range from major investment banks like Chase Manhattan and large corporations like Dupont to academic institutions such as UCLA.

Interestingly, studies have shown that the Blue Chip *Consensus* Forecast performs consistently better than any *individual* forecaster in the consensus sample. Moreover, many of the individual forecasters in the Blue Chip survey have missed important business cycle turning points.

These two observations suggest three possible conclusions: (1) it may be unwise for any executive team to rely exclusively on a single macroeconomic forecaster; (2) it may be more sensible to use the Blue Chip *Consensus* Forecast than any specific forecast; and (3) other tools, such as the various macro-economic indicators that we will now discuss, are likely to perform as well or better when it comes to predicting movements in the business cycle.

The "Macroeconomic Calendar" of Economic Indicators

In the realm of macroeconomic indicators, each month, as part of a publicly available *macroeconomic calendar*, both government agencies like the Depart-ments of Labor and Commerce and a variety of private institutions—from the Conference Board to the National Association of Home Builders—publish a variety of reports pertaining to so-called "leading," "lagging," and "coincident" indicators.

Lagging indicators include the unemployment rate and corporate profits; such lagging indicators only improve *after* the economy begins to recover from a recession. Hence, they are little help to the business executive in forecasting future movements in the business cycle.

In a similar vein, *coincident indicators* such as personal income and industrial production move *simultaneously* with the business cycle, thus indi-cating its current state; likewise they are little help in forecasting the future.

That leaves business executives with a variety of so-called *leading indicators*, which actually tend to move in anticipation of movements in the business cycle. Take housing starts, for example. They usually start to fall months before the economy actually enters a recession. They also tend to perk up several months before the emergence of a full-blown recovery. That is why they are considered a great leading indicator of recession and expansion.

Now one of the easier ways for business executives to follow the progress of the leading indicators is to keep a close watch on the Conference Board's Composite *Index of Leading Economic Indicators*. This well-known *composite indicator* seeks to forecast movements in the business cycle by charting the movements of ten individual leading indicators as they relate directly or indirectly to the conduct of fiscal and monetary policy as well as to the various different components of the GDP equation that we discussed earlier.

For example, one of the individual leading indicators in the composite is an "index of consumer expectations." This *consumer confidence* measure speaks to the likely strength or weakness of the consumption portion of the GDP equation.

Similarly, new orders for capital goods are a measure of the investment portion of that equation while the money supply is a reflection of the contractionary or expansionary nature of current monetary policy.

The broader point here is that when this composite leading indicator has turned down for three to five months in a row, that can signal a coming recession, while a sustained upturn in this indicator can signal recovery and economic expansion.

The (Almost) All-Knowing Yield Curve

Now, as our last word on the subject of leading economic indicators, there is one particularly useful indicator that I want to bring to your attention. This is the so-called *yield curve*, which measures the spread between short- and long-term interest rates.

At any given point in time, and as illustrated in Figure 4-6 with three historical examples, this yield curve can take on one of three typical shapes: normal, inverted, or steep. And please note that as we discuss these three shapes of the yield curve, what I am really trying to do beyond introducing

F I G U R E   4–6

Three Shapes of the Yield Curve

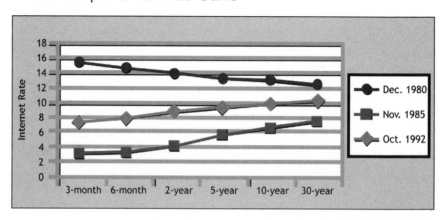

you to this particular indicator is also to illustrate more generally just how to think about the world in macroeconomic terms—a skill you will be developing in your MBA macroeconomics class.

So let us start with the *normal yield curve*. It is typically observed during a period when bond investors expect the economy to continue to expand at a healthy rate *without* fear of inflation. This normal yield curve slopes modestly upwards and is defined by an interest rate spread between the long and short ends of the curve of several hundred basis points, with the slightly higher yields on the long end compensating bondholders for the perceived modest inflationary risks associated with time.

In contrast, the *inverted yield curve* in the figure can come about from two interrelated bearish forces. At the short end, the Federal Reserve has begun to raise interest rates to fight inflation. This alone can drive the short end higher than the long end and invert the curve. However, the long end may also start to fall if bondholders believe that the Federal Reserve's contractionary medicine will trigger a recession and associated *deflationary* pressures. Bondholders might therefore be willing to lock in longer-term yields that are lower than the current short-term yields. Accordingly, the inverted yield curve is viewed as a signal of a coming recession.

Finally, a *steep yield curve* may be viewed by business executives as an expansionary signal. As a recession is ending, both short- and longer-term interest rates are relatively low, recovery is on the horizon, and businesses begin to take on more long-term debt as they engage in new capital investment. This increased capital demand pushes up long-term interest rates, even as the Federal Reserve holds short run rates steady. The result is a steep yield curve such as depicted for October 1992, which marked the start of one of the longest economic booms in U.S. history.

Table 4-2 summarizes the findings regarding the accuracy of the yield curve in predicting the six recessions and six expansions that occurred between 1966 and 2003.

T A B L E   4-2

Accuracy of the Yield Curve (1966–2003)

	True	Missed Signal	False Positive
Inverted (recession)	5	1	1
Steep (expansion)	5	1	1

You can see from the table that the inverted curve predicted fully five of the six recessions, with only one false positive and only one missed signal—the mild recession of 1990–1991. As for the steep curve, it provided five true signals of expansion while only one steep curve proved unreliable.

MANAGING THE BUSINESS CYCLE IN THEORY

So far, we have learned about the major problems any economy faces, and the different policy tools used to solve those problems as embraced by the warring schools. We have also been introduced to various forecasting tools that might be used to anticipate movements in the business cycle.

To complete this chapter, let us talk more about how the modern executive team might go about the very serious business of using a mastery of macroeconomics to better manage the business cycle. Table 4-3 presents a set of stylized management principles as they relate to the most business cycle-sensitive decisions of the firm.

T A B L E   4-3

Principles of Managing the Business Cycle

1. Inventory and production	• Cut production/trim inventories in anticipation of a recession • Increase production/build inventories in anticipation of an expansion
2. Supply chain managment	• Trim input purchases in anticipation of a recession • Use patterns of sector rotation to tactically hedge
3. Human resource management	• Prepare for layoffs before recession actually hits • Hire sooner to "cherry pick" from a larger pool of unemployed labor in anticipation of an expansion
4. Marketing, targeting and sales	• Boost marketing to trim inventories in anticipation of a recession • Change the "mood" and messages with changes in the business cycle "seasons" • Shift product line with cyclical movements
5. Pricing the cycles	• Raise prices as an expansion takes hold; lower prices as economy softents • Build revenue in good times; protect market share in bad times
6. Capital expansion	• Rein in capital expansion in anticipation of recession • Increase capital expansion in anticipation of recovery
7. Acquisitions and divestitures	• Use *corporate strategy* analysis to determine whether to acquire or divest companies • Use *macroeconomic* analysis to determine when to implement one's acquisition and divestiture plans

Inventory Control and Production

When a recession hits, it is of course costly to be caught with large amounts of product inventory. It can be equally costly—from a foregone revenue point of view—to be caught with too *little* inventory as the economy recovers. Accordingly, the executive team may begin to cut production and trim inventories in anticipation of a recession and may begin to increase production and build inventories in anticipation of a recovery.

Supply Chain Management

Large unused stockpiles of various inputs used in the production process can weigh down the bottom line as the business cycle slides from a late expansion into early recession. This is all the more costly because a company will likely have paid premium prices for these inputs at the late expansionary stage of the business cycle under conditions of robust demand. One obvious broad-tuning solution is to trim input purchases in anticipation of a recession just as the company is cutting back on production.

"Right Sizing" and Human Resource Management

Just as the executive team tries to avoid being caught with an inventory overhang, it also may want to begin to prepare for layoffs well before a recession actually hits. Accordingly, the executive team may begin to trim the work force along with inventories in anticipation of a recession—even as rivals continue to hire at premium wages. Perhaps more subtly, the team may also begin to hire sooner than competitors in anticipation of an upturn. At this point in the cycle, a company may be able to proactively "cherry pick" from the relatively larger pool of unemployed labor.

Marketing, Targeting, and Sales

As a defensive and countercyclical measure, the executive team may want to temporarily boost marketing expenditures to trim inventories in anticipation of a downturn. Once inventories are thinned, the team can, in a procyclical fashion, ratchet marketing expenditures down as the company weathers the recessionary storm.

Pricing the Cycles

A price increase in the face of "elastic" product demand will *decrease*—rather than increase—total revenues. This most basic lesson in economics often goes unheeded by desperate executives in a downturn who try to compensate for falling revenues by raising prices in the face of increasingly elastic demand. Accordingly, if the firm is in an industry where it is able to exercise any market power and short-term price elasticities are business cycle-sensitive, the executive team may want to take the lead in both raising prices as an expansion takes hold and lowering prices as the economy softens. In this way, the company builds revenue in good times and protects market share in bad times.

Capital Expansion

An aggressive capital expansion program creates the need for a large cash flow to service the expansion debt. However, with the onset of recession, revenues can fall dramatically and squeeze cash flow, leaving companies in a possible credit crunch.

To avoid such a squeeze, the executive team may want to trim its expansion plans well in advance of a recession. More subtly, because of the longer lead times often associated with capital expansion, the team may also seek to initiate capital expansion plans *countercyclically* at the perceived *trough* of the business cycle so as to have new production, operation, or retailing facilities ready for when an anticipated recovery arrives.

Acquisitions and Divestitures

While broader *strategic* considerations typically inform the executive decision as to *whether* to acquire or divest, broader *macroeconomic* and business cycle considerations can provide important guidance as to *when* to implement the decision. In this regard, stock prices typically peak in the later stages of an economic expansion and associated bull market and then begin to fall during the "early bear" phase of the stock market cycle in anticipation of a downturn in the business cycle. Accordingly, the executive team may pursue a countercyclical strategy, acquiring companies at bargain prices during downturns and divesting unwanted companies at premium prices in the late stages of expansion.

MANAGING THE BUSINESS CYCLE IN PRACTICE

Let us end this chapter with this set of very short case studies drawn from the interval surrounding the recession of 2001. These cases should help illustrate the point that proactively managing the business cycle can be very profitable, while ignoring movements in the business cycle can be disastrous. To begin, let us examine several of the recessionary signals business executives might have observed leading up to the 2001 recession, if only they were trained in macroeconomics.

Figure 4-7 illustrates the progression of the yield curve first from its fairly normal shape in June 1999 to a progressively flattening of the curve in November 1999. Then, we see that by March 2000, there was a "humpbacked" inversion of the yield curve. This not only was exactly four quarters before the official start of the 2001 recession—it also marked the peak of the stock market boom.

As for the Conference Board's Index of Leading Indicators, by September 2000, it had already turned down for five consecutive months. Studies have shown that this indicates a roughly 75 percent probability of recession within four quarters.

From this review of just two leading indicators, it seems reasonable to conclude that at least macroeconomically literate business executives could see *very discernible warning signs of a possible recession*. The question we turn to now with our examples is this: What managerial actions did select business

FIGURE   4-7

The Yield Curve from June 1999 to March 2000

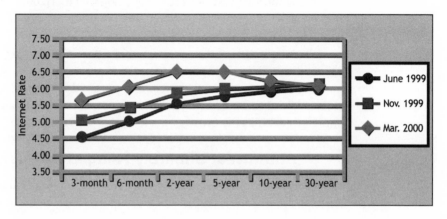

executives take that may have been consistent—or highly inconsistent—with effectively managing this coming recession?

Cisco (Mis)Manages the Supply Chain, Production, and Inventories

The Internet router market leader Cisco Systems provides an almost textbook case of a management team that rejected the use of macroeconomic forecasting to manage its production, inventory, and supply chain functions—and paid a very heavy price. By design, the company's own internal models of growth lacked the many macroeconomic variables commonly used in traditional forecasting models and this approach was rooted in the belief, as one top executive put it, that "the economy is too complex to get anything meaningful out of such broad numbers as GDP or interest rates."

Perhaps not surprisingly, Cisco got caught in the 2001 recession with a huge amount of inventory of both product and supply chain inputs. Eventually, it was forced to write off over $2 *billion* in such inventory, even as it laid off more than 8,000 employees.

In defending the company's lack of macroeconomic foresight, CEO John Chambers has stated, as we saw in the opening quotation to this chapter, that the "brightest people in the world didn't see it coming." The fact is, however, that many company CEOs *did* see that recession coming.

The "Master Cyclists" at J&J Manage Its Cash Flow

Consider the other quotation offered at the beginning of the chapter from Johnson & Johnson CEO Ralph Larsen: "We saw this [2001] recession coming three years ago. It was obvious the booming economic cycle couldn't continue. We tightened our belts. We focused on cash flow."

In anticipation of that recession, J&J cut its capital expenditures by over $100 million dollars—the first decrease in seven years. As J&J significantly built up its cash reserves, the company saw double-digit growth in both revenues and earnings, and J&J's stock got a double-digit boost in both 2000 and 2001, even as the broader stock market was collapsing.

Southwest Superbly Hedges Its Fuel Risk

As a second counterpoint to Cisco's macroeconomic failings, Southwest Airlines offers an example of a company that relies very heavily on macroeconomic forecasting to manage all phases of its business. The company' own internal model is highly sophisticated and incorporates not only various aspects of global supply and demand, monetary aggregates, and exchange rates, but also assessments of geopolitical risk. This forecasting model has proved to be particularly useful in Southwest's fuel cost hedging strategies. While almost all airline companies engage in such hedging, most typically only hedge less than *half* of their fuel needs.

Departing from this industry practice in early 2000, Southwest's executive team opted for a close to 100 percent fuel hedge for the third and fourth quarters based upon an internal forecast of a significant shortage of crude oil. As oil prices soared above $30, Southwest saved over $110 million in fuel costs and saw its earnings increase for the year by more than 30 percent—almost three times the industry average.

Duke's Countercyclical Acquisition and Divestiture Strategies

Duke Power offers an interesting example of a countercyclical acquisition and divestiture strategy. In 1999, as energy prices continued to rise and the sector prospered, Duke completed its sale of its Panhandle subsidiary to CMS Energy at a premium price. Duke then redeployed the cash to help finance its capital expansion plans elsewhere, and it is perhaps worth noting that just four years later, cash-strapped CMS would be forced to sell off the property at a $600 million loss.

CONCLUDING REMARKS

By now, I hope I have convinced you both of the importance and value of macroeconomics. We have seen that at the heart of this matter is the ability of this complex and challenging subject to arm you with a way of thinking about the world. Such a macroeconomic perspective will help you better anticipate future economic conditions and act—rather than react—accordingly.

In the next part of this book, we will move on from the Strategic MBA courses to the Functional MBA courses, including the bread and butter courses of finance, accounting, operations management, and marketing.

PART THREE

The Functional MBA

CHAPTER 5

Strategic Marketing– Delivering Customer Value

Richard J. Lutz and Barton A. Weitz[*]

INTRODUCTION

> The purpose of a business is to create and retain customers.
>
> Peter Drucker

This simple dictum by Peter Drucker captures the absolute essence of marketing management. Drucker's dictum is true whether the enterprise is a public one like the U.S. Post Office or a private one like Federal Express. It is true for a for-profit enterprise like Exxon or a not-for-profit one like the Red Cross. And it is true whether Caterpillar is selling capital equipment like tractors, Procter & Gamble is selling consumer package goods like diapers, or AFLAC is using stand-up comic ducks to sell insurance.

The fact is, without satisfied customers, no business can survive and prosper. Interestingly, however, this is a fact not always completely understood or embraced by all enterprises. Just consider this famous little story told by a former employee about Hewlett Packard:

> When I worked for HP, twenty years ago, the influence of Bill Hewlett and David Packard could still be felt. Everything from the quality of the people, the work environment, a fifty-year history of no layoffs, the initial interviewing process, contributions to society, and the quality and innovation of products made HP a unique and special place to work. My experience in the lab was that fellow engineers took incredible pride in getting things right and doing what was best for the customer.

---

[*]Richard J. Lutz is JCPenney Professor of Marketing and Barton A. Weitz is JCPenney Eminent Scholar Chair in Retail Management in the Warrington College of Business Administration at the University of Florida.

On the other hand, HP certainly had its business challenges. HP was said to stand for "High Price." Furthermore, the story went that if HP, a company started and run by engineers, were given the opportunity to market sushi, they would call it "cold, dead fish."

In this chapter, we will be guiding you through the Four Steps of Marketing Management. Our hope is that you will not ignore or downplay the marketing function as the Hewlett Packard of old once did.

As to what the "marketing function" is, in the language of business school, *marketing* is the set of activities within the enterprise designed to plan, price, promote, and distribute products to target markets. The underlying assumption is that, through effective marketing, an enterprise

FIGURE   5-1

The Big Questions and Key Concepts of Marketing Management

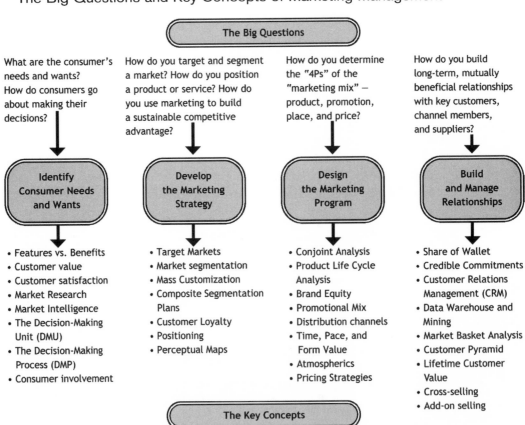

can create *customer value*. Such value is most broadly defined as the perception by the customer that what the organization is offering will satisfy—or exceed!—what the customer needs and wants.

We will talk more about customer needs and wants shortly. For now, however, please take a few minutes to study Figure 5-1. It illustrates the Four Steps of Marketing Management and their big questions and key concepts.

We see in the figure that in Step One, the enterprise uses tools like *market research* and focuses on the *decision-making unit* to identify what customers want and how they go about buying the products and services that will fulfill those wants. This information allows the executive team in Step Two to develop a marketing strategy. This revolves around key concepts such as *target markets*, *market segmentation*, and *positioning*.

Of course, once the marketing strategy is determined, the executive team must then, in Step Three, implement the *marketing program*. This involves the famous "4Ps" of *product*, *promotion*, *place*, and *price*.

Finally, in Step Four, the enterprise focuses over the much longer term in building and managing mutually beneficial relationships with key customers, channel members, and suppliers.

Before we work our way sequentially through these four steps, we would like to digress briefly to discuss two very important additional key concepts in marketing—that of a *market orientation* and the *marketing concept*.

ADOPTING A MARKET ORIENTATION

> Our basic function is to mill high-quality flour, and of course (and almost incidentally) we must hire salesmen to sell it, just as we hire accountants to keep our books.
>
> The Pillsbury Company

> For years, we thought of ourselves as a production-oriented company, meaning we put all our emphasis on designing and manufacturing the product. But now we understand that the most important thing we do is market the product.
>
> A Nike Executive

These two observations—one by the Pillsbury company circa 1900, the other from a Nike executive circa 2000—reveal an evolution in marketing that has taken place over a time frame of more than a century. In fact, marketing management truly is a "modern" phenomenon, because prior to World War II, many organizations had the kind of *product orientation* epitomized in the

Pillsbury quote or a *sales orientation* epitomized by the "high pressure salesman." However, as the Nike quote illustrates, many organizations have now embraced a *market orientation* and with it, the *marketing concept*.

A market orientation implies that the firm's decision making should be strongly outwardly focused, with a continuous inflow of information about customers, competitors, and environmental trends. This guarantees that marketing decisions are not made with blinders, but instead are firmly grounded in marketplace realities.

The related marketing concept holds that a firm should satisfy the wants and needs of its customers, while also meeting the firm's objectives. Thus, satisfying the customer does not imply sacrificing reasonable profits. Rather, this concept suggests that those firms that do not earn sufficient profits will not survive to satisfy their customers in the long run.

Note that when the executive team does not fully integrate a market orientation and the marketing concept throughout the enterprise, the results can be catastrophic. Consider the recent fall from grace of the venerable Kodak Corporation. Its executive team failed to anticipate both the rate and magnitude of the market's shift from film to digital photography, and it has seen its stock price get sliced by more than half in less than a decade.

The broader point here is that marketing management is not just a set of tools and key concepts. Much more fundamentally, it is a *corporate philosophy* that permeates *all* the firm's operations.

Succinctly stated, this philosophy is that "the Customer is King." As the late Sam Walton, the founder of Wal-Mart, once put it: "There is only one boss: the customer." This means that the needs and desires of the firm's actual and potential customers guide the firm's decisions. It follows that once an organization has embraced such a market orientation, it must next go to the second step in the marketing process—the very serious and complicated business of identifying and satisfying customers needs.

IDENTIFYING AND SATISFYING CUSTOMER NEEDS

People don't buy quarter-inch drills; they buy quarter-inch holes.

Ted Levitt

In the factory we make cosmetics; in the drugstore we sell hope.

Charles Revson
Revlon

These two lovely little quotations emphasize just how important it is for the astute marketer to understand just what the consumers' needs are and how consumers go about making decisions. This is Step One of the marketing management process. A useful starting point to cultivate such an understanding is to clearly distinguish between the *features* of a product or service and its *benefits*.

Customer Value and Satisfaction

Features are what an enterprise builds into a product or service, from power steering and satellite radio in cars to energy efficiency and ice machines in refrigerators. They are quite tangible and *objective*.

Benefits, on the other hand, are what customers receive from using the product or service. They are by their very nature inherently *subjective*. That is, they are *perceived* by the customer.

It follows that properly managing the *perceived benefits* of the firm's market offerings is essential to the *value equation*, which may be written as:

$$\text{Value} = \frac{\text{Perceived benefits}}{\text{Price}}$$

From this equation, we can see that a customer will experience value from a product or service when the perceived benefits exceed the price of the product. What is not evident in the equation (but nevertheless crucial) is that the value of the firm's product must exceed that of competitors.

From this equation, the astute marketer also understands that that there are two ways that an organization can increase value. One is by increasing perceived benefits. The other is by lowering price. As we shall see later in this chapter, it is greatly preferable to compete "above the line" on perceived benefits rather than engaging in price competition.

Of course, closely related to the concept of customer value is the idea of *customer satisfaction*—but how is this measured? One common way is to make an implicit comparison between (1) the *expected performance* of a product or service prior to purchase and use and (2) the *perception of actual performance* during and after use. In fact, there are three possibilities.

First, if expectations exceed perceived performance, customers experience *dissatisfaction*. That is, they do not perceive good value. Secondly, if perceptions of performance match expectations, the customer experiences *satisfaction*. They got what they paid for—no more and no less. Thirdly, when perceived performance exceeds expectations, the customer experiences *delight.* Many enterprises try to achieve customer delight by augmenting their products and services to deliver more benefits than the customer anticipates. In this way, marketers not only create value but also will likely *create more value than their competitors.*

The Role of Market Research

We can see from the above discussion that marketers place considerable emphasis on understanding what the consumer wants and needs, how the consumer perceives value, and what feelings of satisfaction, dissatisfaction, or delight the consumer may experience. A major tool used in the actual implementation of these ideas is called *market research* or, alternatively, *market intelligence.*

Market research focuses on the firm's current and potential products and markets; and two big questions of such research include: (1) What is the customer *decision-making unit* and (2) what is the *decision-making process?*

The Customer Decision-Making Unit

The decision-making unit (DMU) is comprised of a set of roles played by various members of the household or organization making a purchase. In an organizational context, the DMU is referred to as the *buying center,* and note that regardless of whether a household or an organization is making the purchase, five key roles are present.

First, an *information gatherer/gatekeeper* seeks out and/or controls the flow of product-related information into the decision process. Secondly, an *influencer* exerts influence, but does not actually make the decision. Thirdly, the *decision maker* is one or more individuals with decision-making authority. Fourthly, the *users* are the individuals who will actually consume the product. Finally, the *purchaser* or *purchasing agent* is the person charged with the responsibility for making the actual procurement.

While all of this sounds a bit dry and technical, actually it can be quite interesting. Consider, for example, a common household purchase like breakfast cereal. A child sees a TV commercial for a new cereal and requests it from his mother. The child has played the role of information gatherer. If the child's request is accompanied by whining, the child also is playing the influencer role.

Now if the mother chooses to add the cereal to the family shopping list, she has assumed the decision maker role. When the child's father dutifully plucks the cereal from the supermarket shelf during his weekly shopping trip, he plays the purchaser role. The next morning at the breakfast table the child assumes the role of the user.

We see, then, that any given individual may play multiple roles in the DMU and multiple people may play a single role. More broadly, understanding the DMU and which members are playing what roles is important in product positioning and promotional strategy—we will talk about this further below. Perhaps most importantly, marketers cannot assume that the purchaser, or even the user, is the decision maker, that is, the one who must be convinced of the product's value.

The Decision-Making Process

The *decision-making process* (DMP) is most often construed as *problem solving* by the consumer. Typically, the DMP is initiated by *problem recognition*. For example, you might have a job interview next week, which leads you to conclude "I need a new suit." Once the problem is recognized, the problem-solving process then proceeds in a series of stages.

First, an *information search* identifies potential solutions in the form of various products or brands. Next, there is an *alternative evaluation* that weighs the advantages and disadvantages of the various options in order to arrive at the best brand. Thirdly, there is the actual *purchase*, which is followed by the *consumption* or *use* of the product.

Note that the resolution of one problem may instigate another problem-solving episode. For example, you may think: "I just bought a great new suit; now I need a shirt, tie, and shoes to go with it." And off you go again.

In the analysis of such problems, the astute marketer will take into account the degree of *consumer involvement* in any given product search. This involvement is determined by the degree to which the consumer considers the decision important and hence is motivated to make an optimal (or near-optimal) choice.

For example, a "high involvement" decision might involve an MBA student buying a new interview suit. In contrast, many consumer purchases like that for chewing gum or toothpaste or paper towels are "low involvement" because they lack significance; such low involvement decision processes are faster and less complex.

It is important for the marketer to have a sense of the degree of typical consumer involvement because this will have an important influence on the marketing strategy adopted.

DEVELOPING THE MARKETING STRATEGY– TARGETING AND MARKET SEGMENTATION

A *marketing strategy* identifies (1) the firm's *target markets*, (2) the firm's product and service *offerings* that it plans to provide to satisfy the target market's needs, and (3) how the firm will build a *sustainable competitive advantage*, defined as an advantage that cannot be easily duplicated by competitors.

For example, Starbucks targets consumer who want to take a break from their daily activities. It offers consumers in its target market an appealing variety of beverages in a relaxing environment. Starbucks defends its position against competitors by building strong customer loyalty and saturating geographic areas with stores.

Selecting the Target Market and Market Segmentation

Selecting a *target market* means first identifying the different types of customers in that market. This is done through a process known as *market segmentation*. The fundamental criteria for evaluating market segments are that: (1) customers in the segment must have similar needs, seek similar benefits, and be satisfied by a similar offering; and (2) those customers' needs must be different from the needs of customers in other segments.

Market segmentation is important because not everyone wants the same restaurant, soft drink, truck, or microprocessor. For example, families traveling on a vacation have different needs than executives on business trips. That is why Marriott offers different types of hotels that appeal to customers in each of these segments, from the Courtyard and Residence Inn to the Ritz Carleton.

Segmenting Consumer and Business Markets

Table 5-1 illustrates the wide variety of approaches for segmenting consumer markets. For example, the HEB supermarket chain segments the market geographically and targets consumers in Texas. Gerber segments its market by family life cycle, targeting families with children under the age of three. And Crest segments the toothpaste market by benefits sought, targeting consumers with a need to prevent tooth decay.

Business markets likewise can be segmented using some of the same variables as consumer markets. For example, Dell segments the market for PCs by customer size. It markets to small businesses and retail consumers through its Internet site called Dell Direct. It also markets to large corporate customers through its sales force.

T A B L E   5-1

Segmenting Consumer Markets

Segmentation Descriptor	Example of Categories
Geographic	
Region	Pacific, Mountain, Central, South, Mid-Atlantic, Northeast
Population	Density rural, suburban, urban
Climate	Cold, warm
Demographics	
Age (years)	Under 6, 6–12, 13–19, 20–29, 30–49, 50–65, over 65
Gender	Male, female
Family life cycle	Single, married with no children, married with youngest child under 6, married with youngest child over 6, married with children no longer living at home, widowed
Family income	Under $19,999; $20,000–29,999; $30,000–49,999; $50,000–74,999; over $75,000
Occupation	Professional, clerical, retired, student, homemaker
Education	Some high school, high school graduate, some college, college graduate, graduate degree
Religion	Catholic, Protestant, Jewish, Islam
Race	Caucasian, African American, Hispanic, Oriental
Nationality	U.S., Japanese, British, French, German, Italian, Chinese
Psychosocial	
Social class	Lower, middle, upper
Lifestyle	Striver, driver, devote, intimate, altruist, fun Seeker, creative
Personality	Aggressive, shy, emotional
Feelings and behaviors	
Attitudes toward offering	Positive, neutral, negative
Benefit sought	Convenience, economy, prestige
Stage in decision process	Unaware, aware, informed, interested, intend to buy, bought previously
Perceived risk	High, medium, low
Innovativeness	Innovator, early adopter, early majority, late majority, laggard
Loyalty	None, some, completely
Usage rate	None, light, medium, heavy
Usage situation	Home, work, vacation, leisure
User status	Nonuser, ex-user, potential user, current user

Three Useful Criteria for Segmenting Markets

As you can see, a market can be segmented in any number of different ways.
The question for the astute marketer is: Which is the best way? In fact, there are
three important criteria for evaluating whether a market segment is a viable
target. These include: (1) actionability, (2) identifiability, and (3) accessibility.

Actionability means that the definition of a segment must clearly indicate what the enterprise should do to satisfy customer needs. For example, the retailer Lane Bryant caters to full-figured women and the different styles and fit they require. It segments the women's apparel market based on one obvious demographic characteristic—physical size.

Identifiability is important because it permits the firm to determine two very important facts: (1) What is the segment's size and (2) With whom should the firm communicate to promote its offering. In this regard, most major marketers begin by segmenting on the basis of age and sex, data that are readily available from the U.S. Census and commercial services. Gillette, for example, can easily ascertain how many men between the ages of 18 and 34 years are in the market for its Mach 3 razor.

The third criterion—*accessibility*—is the ability of the firm to deliver the appropriate products and services to the customers in the segment. For example, customers for Marriott's convention hotels versus resort hotels are accessed in very different ways because they use different sources to collect information about hotel services.

In this regard, research has shown that convention hotel customers are best reached through newspapers such as *USA Today* and The *Wall Street Journal*, while resort hotel customers are best reached through advertisements on TV and in travel and leisure magazines.

As a practical matter, no one approach typically meets all the criteria for useful customer segmentation. For example, segmenting by demographics and geography is ideal for identifying and accessing customers, but these characteristics often are unrelated to customers' needs. Thus, these approaches may not indicate the actions necessary to attract customers in these segments.

On the other hand, knowing what benefits customers are seeking is useful for designing an effective offering. However, this approach can present a problem in identifying which customers are seeking these benefits.

For these reasons, *composite segmentation plans* use multiple variables to identify customers in the target segment. They define the profile of target customers by benefits sought, lifestyles, and demographics.

Targeting and the Broader Competitive Environment

When evaluating target markets and market segments, firms need also to consider both the attractiveness and structure of the market as well as the nature of the firm's resources that can be used to exploit the opportunity.

Market attractiveness is determined by its size, the competition in the market, and environmental factors such as political and legal constraints. Obviously, larger markets offer greater potential for sales and thus are more attractive. But larger markets also attract more competitors.

As for *market structure*, you will learn about the four different forms of market structure in the chapter in this book on managerial economics. These forms are: monopoly, oligopoly, monopolistic competition, and perfect competition. You will also learn in that chapter about how factors like "barriers to entry" and the "bargaining power of suppliers" help determine this structure and the attendant competitive strategies companies may adopt.

We will not delve too deeply into this material now. Suffice it to say that the astute marketer needs to be aware not just of who the customers are and what they want but also who the competitors are and what these competitors are likely to do in any given market setting. That is where a knowledge of market structure can be so very helpful.

For example, in highly competitive markets characterized by numerous sellers, low barriers to entry, slow market growth, and high fixed costs, price wars are likely to erupt, employee raids may occur, advertising and promotion expenses will increase, and profit potential falls. These are obviously not highly attractive markets.

DEVELOPING THE MARKET STRATEGY–BUILDING SUSTAINABLE COMPETITIVE ADVANTAGE

Let us turn now to Step Two of marketing management. This is to *develop the marketing strategy* and thereby create a *sustainable competitive advantage*.

You have already learned quite a bit about building competitive advantage in Chapter Three on management strategy. For example, you learned that the production team of a company can develop "cost advantages" through more efficient and lower cost production techniques. You also learned that an organization can benefit from "transaction advantages" through better supply chain management.

A third major source of competitive advantage is, however, where the marketing team has an opportunity to shine. This is *product differentiation*. By successfully differentiating a product, the marketing team can both increase the demand for that product and also "steepen" the demand curve. This will increase the firm's ability to charge higher prices and earn higher profits.

As to how marketers go about increasing product differentiation, there are at least three ways beyond simple advertising. These include: (1) building customer loyalty, (2) providing outstanding customer service, and (3) developing long-term relationships with channel members.

Building Customer Loyalty

Customer loyalty means more than simply liking one product more than another. It also means that customers will be reluctant to patronize your competitors. Indeed, your most loyal customers will continue to buy your product even if competitors lower prices.

One way to build customer loyalty is to develop a clear, distinctive image for your offering and then consistently reinforce that image through marketing activities. *Positioning* is a very important marketing tool to achieve these goals.

Positioning involves the design and implementation of a marketing program to create an image for the firm and its offering relative to its competitors. Such positioning emphasizes that the image in the customer's mind—not the manager's mind!—is the critical one. Accordingly, marketers must research what the organization's image is and make sure that this image is consistent with what customers in its target markets want. One useful tool used in this process is the *perceptual map*.

Figure 5-2 provides a hypothetical perceptual map of the women's apparel market in Washington, D.C. Such maps are frequently used to represent the customer's image of, and preference for, competing brands in a target market.

In the figure, we see that each of the retailers—from Old Navy and T.J. Maxx to American Eagle and Saks—compete in two dimensions. One dimension represents the amount of customer service—with companies like K-Mart and Target rating very low on the service scale and Nordstrom almost off the chart on the high end.

The second dimension captures style—with retailers like Hot Topics and Wet Seal providing the most contemporary fashions and companies like Sears and J.C. Penney still selling more on the traditional end.

Note that the *ideal points*, which are marked by dots on the map, indicate the characteristics of an ideal retailer for consumers in the different market segments. For example, consumers in Segment 3 prefer a retailer like Marshalls that offers high-fashion merchandise with low service. On the other hand, consumers in Segment 1 want the less expensive and more traditional apparel offered by Wal-Mart and Kmart and are not concerned about service.

Note also that in this particular map, the ideal points are located so that the distance between the retailer's positions, which are marked with "X,"

F I G U R E   5-2

A Hypothetical Perceptual Map of the Women's Apparel Market in Washington, DC

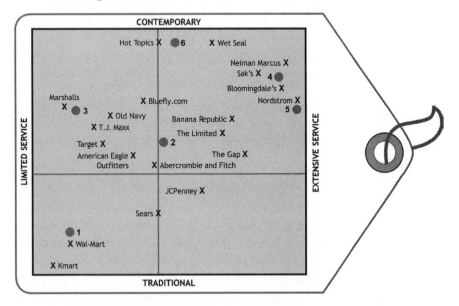

and the ideal points indicate how consumers in the segment evaluate the retailer relative to the ideal. In this approach, *retailers that are closer to an ideal point are evaluated more favorably by the consumers in the segment than retailers located further away.* Thus, consumers in Segment 6 clearly prefer The Gap to Sears because The Gap is closer to their image of their ideal retailer.

The broader point here, of course, is that the images that customers have of a firm's products influence their purchase decisions. Thus, the marketing team develops loyalty by having their products and services viewed as satisfying the needs of customers in any given target. These images in customers' minds are difficult to change and thus are the basis for a sustainable competitive advantage.

Using Customer Service to Build Loyalty

As suggested in the perceptual map above, a second way to build customer loyalty is to offer excellent customer service. This way of business has been the very lifeblood of companies like Nordstrom and Neiman Marcus—featured in the upper right quadrant in the figure above.

Note, however, that offering consistently good service can be quite difficult. This is because customer service is provided by employees, and, as you will learn in a later chapter on *organizational behavior*, humans are less consistent than machines.

Indeed, firms that offer good customer service must instill its importance in their employees over a long period of time so that "excellent service" becomes part of the firm's organizational culture, with culture being a very important concept in organizational behavior. Nonetheless, while it takes considerable time and effort to build a tradition and reputation for customer service, good service can be a valuable strategic asset. Once a firm has earned a service reputation, it can sustain this advantage for a long time because it is hard for a competitor to develop a comparable reputation.

Using Relationships with Channel Members

Still a third way for a marketer to build a sustainable competitive advantage is to build solid relationships with so-called "channel members." By developing strong relationships with marketing intermediaries such as distributors and retailers, manufacturers can develop a sustainable advantage over competitors.

For example, a proactive manufacturer might secure the exclusive services of the best manufacturer's representative in an area, get preferred treatment from respected retailers, or encourage a distributor to promote their products rather than a competitor's products. Snapshot Application 5-1 illustrates how Caterpillar has used its relationships with its channel members to build a competitve advantage in its construction and mining business.

DESIGNING THE MARKETING PROGRAM (THE 4Ps)

Having formulated the marketing strategy, you are now ready to design the *marketing program*. This program consists of a set of decisions regarding the famous "4 Ps" of marketing—*product*, *promotion*, *place*, and *price*. We will now consider each of these variables in the so-called *marketing mix*.

Product Variable Decisions

Product variable decisions run the gamut from the actual design of the product and fine tuning the marketing effort through a product's "life cycle"

S N A P S H O T   A P P L I C A T I O N   5-1

RELATIONSHIPS WITH DEALERS GIVE CATERPILLAR A COMPETITIVE ADVANTAGE

The biggest reason for Caterpillar's success has been our system of distribution and the close customer relationships is fosters ... The backbone of the system is our dealers who sell and service our machines and diesel engines. They have played a pivotal role in helping us build and maintain close relationships with our customers.

Donald Fites
Former Chairman and CEO

Caterpillar is the world's leading manufacturer of construction and mining equipment. The company has long-term partnering relationships with its dealers and involves dealers in its product development and cost reduction programs. As the above quotation indicates, these relationships are in large part responsible for the company's continued leadership in a highly competitive industry.

For example, when a dealer alerted the factory that hoses in a new grader were being installed incorrectly, Caterpillar retrained the assemblers and fixed the machines in the factory. The company also notified other dealers around the world about the problem and what they needed to do to correct it.

The dealer relationships that Caterpillar has built are the result of the following practices:

* *Share the pain as well as the gain*—Caterpillar supports its dealers during economic downturns that dramatically affect the sales of capital equipment. By insuring the viability of its dealers in bad times, Caterpillar benefits from having a strong network in place when the economy turns around.

* *Provide extraordinary support*—Caterpillar provides extensive training for its dealers and systems to help them run their business more efficiently. When a competitor focuses on a dealer's territory, Caterpillar lowers its wholesale prices to help the dealer.

* *Communicate frequently and honestly*—Caterpillar has complete trust in its dealers and thus provides them with real-time access to service information, sales trends and forecasts, customer satisfaction data, and other critical information. Routine contact occurs between Caterpillar employees at all levels and function with dealers.

* *Personalize relationships*—Caterpillar's relationships are based on personal ties. The senior managers at Caterpillar have close relationships with the owners of its dealerships. In many cases, a family-owned dealer has worked with Caterpillar for over 50 years, and Caterpillar has assisted the family in helping with the transitions of management between family generations.

to nurturing brand equity, launching new products as brand or category extensions, and appropriately packaging the product for both functionality and attractiveness.

Product Design and Conjoint Analysis

Consider, for example, how the marketer might work with the production team to come up with the "best product design at the right price." In this effort, a very powerful marketing tool known as *conjoint analysis* can be very useful. In applying this tool, consumers are asked to rank a set of potential products that vary systematically along a number of dimensions.

Table 5-2 depicts a hypothetical conjoint analysis for a new hand lotion. Across the five dimensions, we see that there are fully 108 possible combinations of features ($3 \times 3 \times 3 \times 2 \times 2$). For example, one such combination might be yellow, lemon-scented lotion with aloe priced at 15 cents an ounce, and offered in a plastic container. Another might be a more expensive 20 cents per ounce pink, minty, and lemony lotion in a glass container.

Such conjoint analysis allows a marketer to identify the optimal combination, as perceived by target consumers. As you can see, price is

T A B L E   5-2

A Hypothetical Conjoint Analysis for Hand Lotion

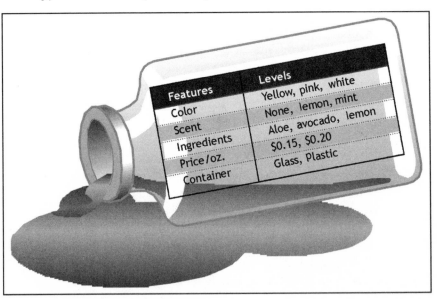

Features	Levels
Color	Yellow, pink, white
Scent	None, lemon, mint
Ingredients	Aloe, avocado, lemon
Price/oz.	$0.15, $0.20
Container	Glass, Plastic

included as one of the dimensions. This allows the marketer to identify the option with the highest perceived value.

Product Life Cycle Analysis

Another way marketers make decisions about products and services involves tuning in to the so-called *product life cycle* (PLC). Indeed, products, just like people, move through a recognizable life cycle, as is illustrated in the stylized PLC in Figure 5-3.

This hypothetical PLC shows how total retail sales vary over time for a hypothetical product, with sales rising steadily in the introduction and growth stages, peaking during the maturity phase, and then going into decline. Of course, actual PLCs vary tremendously on the time dimension. Consider, for example, Ivory Soap versus the "pet rock." Ivory's PLC has lasted well over 100 years, while the pet rock came and went like a comet in 1975.

In thinking about how to use the concept of the PLC in a marketing context, it is important to understand that product life cycles exist at

F I G U R E   5-3

A Stylized Product Life Cycle

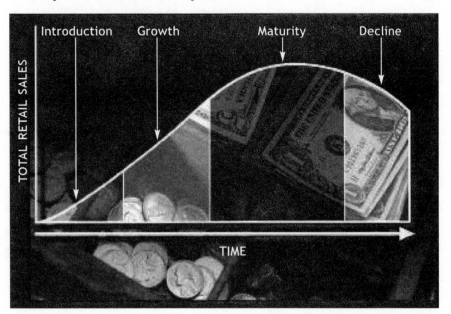

multiple levels. These levels include not just the *product category* of soap or beer or VCRs. They also include the *product form* as well as the *brand*.

Consider, for example, the beer product category. Within this category, several product *forms* exist, including premium, popular, light, imported, and crafted—and each of these categories has its own PLC! For example, premium beer has been in the decline stage while light beer is very much in the growth stage. Moreover, within each product form, different brands are likewise going through their own cycles. For example, Bud Light has been in its growth stage, while Miller Lite has been in decline.

Note here a very important point: Conventional wisdom holds that the product form PLC is largely outside the control of the marketer. That is because it can be driven by technology, for example, MP3 files replacing CDs, which had replaced audio tapes. It can also be driven by changing consumer tastes, such as SUVs and light trucks replacing sedans and minivans. Nonetheless, the astute marketer should be able to exert some control over the *brand* PLC, extending it through judicious product, price, and promotion decisions!

Brand Equity, Brand Extensions, and Category Extensions

Still a third important product variable decision involves the nurturing of so-called *brand equity*. In B-school speak, brand equity is simply the added value a brand name attaches to a product.

For example, Coca-Cola is generally regarded as the world's most valuable brand. In fact, its trademark accounts for an estimated 60 percent of the Coca-Cola Company's market capitalization!

One very important reason to nurture strong brand equity is that it is a tremendous source of leverage for launching new products. This practice is known as *brand extensions*—with approximately 80 percent of such brand extensions being *line extensions*. For example, a "parent" brand like Gatorade introduces a new product like Gatorade Fierce in the same basic category.

As for *category extensions*, these extend the parent brand into other related product categories. For example, Nike moves from athletic shoes to sporting equipment and apparel.

The Broader Point   Strong brand equity of the parent brand heightens the probability that these brand, line, and category extensions will succeed in the marketplace. To see what is "behind the scene" in brand equity, take a few minutes to review Snapshot Application 5-2, which features the legendary retailer L.L. Bean.

L.L. BEAN AND THIS THING CALLED BRAND EQUITY

Leading thinkers about brand equity such as David Aaker and Kevin Keller generally point to multiple factors that contribute to brand equity—the "surplus value" a brand contributes to a product or service. Among these factors are brand awareness and brand associations.

Brand awareness is the degree to which consumers readily recognize and are familiar with the brand name. Ideally, a brand name enjoys "top-of-mind" awareness such that it is the first brand that comes to mind when the consumer thinks about purchasing in the product category. It is difficult to imagine a brand that is seen as possessing a high degree of brand equity without being well known among a broad cross-section of its potential customers. In a sense, strong brand awareness is a *necessary condition* for brand equity.

However, the true essence of brand equity lies in the *brand associations*. These are those things that come to mind when the brand name is mentioned. The salient brand associations can be thought of as the "meaning" of the brand to the consumer. This is most often referred to as the *brand image*.

Consider, for example, cataloger L.L. Bean. Some of the common brand associations of L.L. Bean, which the company reinforces through its advertising and Web site, are:

- *Friendly*—L.L. Bean is comfortable and familiar and very easy to approach.
- *Honest*—L.L. Bean is straightforward and honest. It would never mislead its customers. It provides straightforward, factual information about its products.
- *Expertise*—L.L. Bean's employees are experts about their products and the outdoors. They will do anything they can to help customers choose which product is best for them—or even help them find the best place to camp!
- *Practical*—Building on its Yankee New England roots, L.L. Bean offers products that are functional, with no nonsense features and fair prices.

For the brand image to contribute maximally to brand equity, it needs to be comprised of brand associations that are *strong, unique, and favorable*. That is, consumers must hold strong beliefs about the brand associations that are desirable to the consumer. Ideally, these favorable associations are unique to the brand and thus cannot be co-opted by other brands in the category. In such a way, brand equity becomes a source of an important sustainable competitive advantage.

The Art of Packaging

As a final observation on product variable decisions, we dare not leave out the all-important issue of *packaging*. It not only has to contain and protect the product until the consumer chooses to use it. Packaging also plays a very important in-store communication function via its labeling, shape, functionality, and other package information. And, of course, at its best, clever and innovative packaging can add considerably to the value of the product by facilitating its use—just think about the squeeze ketchup bottles or the pop-up tissue box.

Promotion

Let us turn now to the second "P" in the marketing mix—*promotion*. This consists of five interrelated tools known collectively as the *promotional mix*: advertising, sales promotion, public relations, personal selling, and direct marketing.

Advertising refers to paid media insertions in mass media such as television, radio, newspapers, magazines, the yellow pages, outdoor, and the Internet. Of course, one of the major goals of advertising is to increase brand awareness and brand image.

Sales promotions basically come in two garden varieties. *Consumer promotions* include such tools as coupons, sampling, premiums, rebates, and sweepstakes. In contrast, *trade promotions* encompass everything from sales contests and trade shows to allowances and cooperative advertising.

As for *public relations*, this is the firm's attempt to manage the *publicity* it receives in the media. Unlike advertising, publicity cannot be "bought" or controlled directly. However, neither is it free. Indeed, good publicity often is the result of a concerted effort by the firm in the form of press releases, special events, and the like, to influence the nature of the publicity received by the firm.

Personal selling involves both face-to-face and telephone interactions between a paid representative of the firm and a prospective customer. Such personal selling is truly the "backbone" of the promotional mix, with millions of people and billions of dollars devoted to it annually by firms of all sizes and in all industries.

Finally, *direct marketing* refers to promotional approaches that entail direct contact with prospective customers in their homes or workplace. The three most common forms are *direct mail*, *telemarketing*, and *e-mail*.

Of course, "junk mail," telemarketing, and "spam" are among the most despised forms of promotion. Nevertheless, direct marketing remains a popular promotional mechanism because (1) it is effective, if managed correctly, and (2) its results are easily measured.

Place

The *Place* element of the marketing mix derives its label from the "place" where consumers purchase (and possibly consume) the product or service. The three key concepts related to the Place decision include the *channel of distribution*, *supply chain management*, and *channel value-add*.

Channel and Supply Chain Management

The various business and consumer channels of distribution are illustrated in Figure 5-4. These *indirect channels* relate to the use of the aforementioned *marketing intermediaries* such as distributors, wholesalers, and retailers. On the other hand, when a company like Dell sells directly to end users—for example, via its website—it is referred to as a *direct channel*.

As to which channels are most effective, here is just a bit of what we know. Consumer goods manufacturers most often utilize indirect channels because it is inefficient to deal with millions of individual consumers. Instead, distributors and retailers provide the desired market coverage.

In contrast, business-to-business marketers often interact directly with their customers via the company sales force. In this vein, smaller manufacturers that cannot afford to maintain their own sales force use *manufacturers' representatives*, another form of marketing intermediary.

Note that it is important to clearly distinguish the channel of distribution from the physical flow of goods. Conceptually, the channel facilitates transactions between buyers and sellers, but it does not always entail physical possession or even ownership of the goods.

For example, manufacturers' reps do not take title or possession of the product lines they sell. Instead, once a sale is made, the manufacturer ships the product directly to the buyer—a practice known as *drop-shipping*. Thus, the channel of distribution has a goal of *transaction efficiency*. In contrast, *supply chain management*, which you learned about in the previous chapter, strives to maximize the efficiency of the *physical* flow of product, while delivering desired customer value.

FIGURE   5-4

Indirect Channels of Distribution

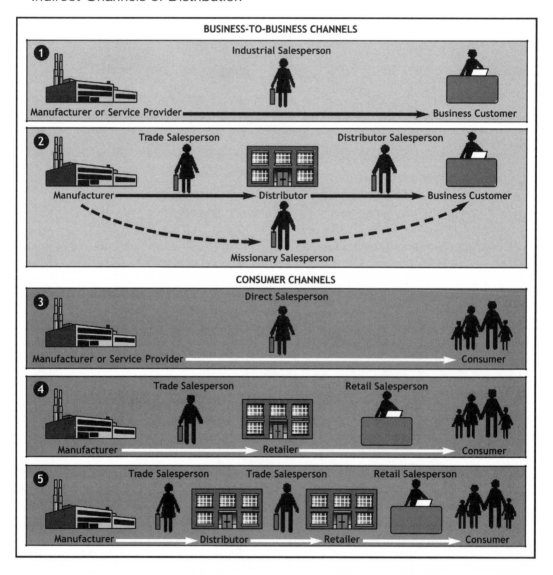

The Creation of Value-Add

The guiding principle for all Place decisions is the creation of *value-add*. The old view of the channel was a "pipeline" metaphor, where the producer dumped product into one end, and the same product dropped out of the other end into the hands of the consumer. The emergent metaphor is that of a *value-add chain*, wherein each channel member adds value to the product in some fashion. Most often, the value-add rests in the services each of the channel members "wrap around" the physical product. In this regard, the channel is seen as creating *time value*, *place value*, and *form value*.

For example, a 24-hour convenience store creates *time value* by being open at any time the consumer desires to make a purchase. Similarly, fast food purveyors create *place value* by having multiple locations on heavily traveled streets. As for *form value*, it is created when a channel member alters the product in some way.

For example, a mountain bike manufacturer might ship unassembled bicycle components to a carefully selected dealer network. The dealers are then responsible for proper assembly of the bikes, thus offering more value to customers who would rather not assemble the bikes themselves.

As a final observation on the Place issue, some retailers attempt to add value by creative management of store *atmospherics*, that is, the ambience of the store. For example, the Rainforest Cafe invites its guests to join a "safari" to their table, Starbucks has turned a simple cup of coffee into an art form, and merchants like Nike Town and Tiffany carefully manage all aspects of the shopping experience to add to the enjoyment of the consumer.

Price

The final element of the marketing mix, *price*, effectively measures what the consumer gives up in exchange for all the benefits received from a product or service. Indeed, the fundamental role of price is to capture the value of the product in the mind of the consumer. In setting prices, the marketer may choose from one or more of five different pricing approaches.

Cost-based pricing approaches such as cost-plus and standard markup pricing focus internally on the firm's cost structure to ensure that the price charged covers all fixed and variable costs of producing and selling the product. In contrast, *profit-based* approaches such as *target pricing* extend the cost-based logic to incorporate a desired dollar amount or percent return on investment.

Note, however, that while these two approaches might be a useful starting point for price deliberations, they nonetheless ignore important market demand and competitive considerations. These are considerations, we are quick to add here, that you have already learned quite a bit about in the chapter in this book on management strategy and will learn more about in the chapter on managerial economics.

Because of such considerations, the third approach of *demand-based pricing* can be very useful. Such pricing begins with either formal or informal market research to assess the nature of the demand for the product. Is demand price-elastic or price-inelastic? And what do consumers perceive a "fair" price for the product to be?

Still a fourth approach involves *competition-based pricing*. Here, the firm "shops the competition" to determine prices of similar products or direct substitutes. Using such an approach, the marketer essentially "works backward" from likely price points determined through research and compares the projected revenue against costs. If the margins are not great enough, then the product may need to be re-engineered to squeeze out some of the costs.

Finally, *value-based pricing* is closely related to demand-based models. The value-based process begins with research to determine the *value-in-use* of the product to the consumer. That value can then be benchmarked against the value-in-use of competing products to arrive at an appropriate price.

Consider, for example, one marketing team's assessment of a new extruded wooden beam composed of scrap lumber and a super-adhesive blended under very high pressure. This team fiercely debated whether to discontinue the project due to high production costs under the implicit assumption that the new product would have to be priced at or below the price of regular lumber.

However, in the beta-site testing of the product, the marketing team learned that the extruded beams were not only much stronger than standard lumber but also more amenable to the large spans required in factories and warehouses. *Because of the higher value of the new product relative to lumber*, as perceived by potential customers, the marketing team was able to set a higher price, making the project viable in terms of projected profitability.

As a final comment on the pricing decision, please understand that typically no one pricing model is used in isolation. Rather, marketers tend to approach the pricing decision from multiple perspectives in order to "triangulate" on the final asking price.

BUILDING AND MANAGING RELATIONSHIPS

Let us turn now to the last step in the marketing management process, that of *building and managing relationships*. Historically, a major marketing goal has been to increase the customer base. In this approach, salespeople continually prospect for new customers, and advertising is designed to make customers aware of the firm's products and services and then buy them.

Today, however, firms are increasingly directing their marketing activities toward another goal altogether. This is the building and maintaining of long-term relationships, not just with their key customers, but also with their channel members.

For example, Procter & Gamble (P&G) now has sales teams located at the headquarters of major customers like Wal-Mart and Kroger. These teams are dedicated to finding ways that P&G can work more effectively with its retailers to increase sales and profits for both parties.

This change in perspective from building the customer base to building and managing relationships is supported by a very important research finding: *It can cost as much as six times more to sell products and services to new customers than existing customers!* Moreover, small increases in customer retention can lead to dramatic increases in profits. That is why firms are beginning to concentrate on providing more value and generating more sales from their best customers rather than continually seeking new ones.

In this new relationship-building paradigm, the goal of marketing programs has shifted from the old yardstick of *market share* to the new metric of *share of wallet*. This is defined as the percent of the customer's purchases in the firm's product or service categories. In fact, this focus on building relationships has important strategic implications.

For example, strong buyer–seller relationships enable firms to achieve differential advantages in the market place by working together to improve the offering to the ultimate customer. The advantages created through these relationships are, in turn, sustainable because the activities engaged in by the firms, as they work together, are hard for competitors to understand and difficult to duplicate.

To end this chapter, we are going to first look briefly at the dynamics of building better business-to-business relationships. Then, we will move to the goal of building better business-to-consumer relationships and a more extended discussion of a very important process called Customer Resource Management or CRM. This is a process that has been greatly aided by the emergence of very powerful software programs made by companies like Siebel Systems, PeopleSoft, and the German giant SAP.

Business-to-Business Markets

Cost reduction throughout the total system can be accomplished when trust replaces skepticism.

Lou Pritchett
Former Procter & Gamble VP

One important key to the development of successful, long-term business-to-business relationships is *trust*. Trust is a belief by one party that the other party will fulfill its obligations in a relationship.

Trust is particularly important in business-to-business markets because when buyers and sellers trust each other, they are more willing to share ideas, clarify goals, identify problems, and develop innovative approaches. This, in turn, means that there is no need for the parties to waste resources constantly monitoring and checking up on each other's actions, because each believes that the other will not take advantage of them.

For these kinds of reasons, trusting suppliers, customers, and employees has been one of the most effective, yet most underutilized, techniques available in managing business-to-business relationships.

Typically, in a business-to-business context, mutual trust evolves when a seller satisfactorily meets its obligations with respect to a minor task, motivating the buyer to trust the seller with a more important activity. For example, the seller might demonstrate his or her dependability by promising and then delivering a small order on time. The buyer then feels more confident in the seller to place a larger order. After a sequence of transactions of increasing importance in which the seller meets its commitments, the buyer eventually feels comfortable sharing some proprietary information about the company's plans for new products that might use the seller's services.

As a successful relationship develops, both parties make *credible commitments* to the relationship, where such credible commitments are tangible investments in the relationship. They involve making investments in the relationship that cannot be easily deployed to other relationships.

For example, a firm may hire or train employees, invest in equipment, and develop computer and communication systems to meet the needs of a specific customer. These investments lock the seller into the relationship and signal the seller's commitment to the relationship with the seller.

Business-to-Consumer Markets and Customer Relations Management (CRM)

In business-to-business markets, relationships are typically managed personally through salespeople. However, in *business-to-consumer markets*, due to the large number of customers serviced by suppliers of consumer products and services, *systems* like CRM play a larger role. Consider the following situation:

> Shari Ast is on her third business trip this month. She takes a cab from Boston Logan airport to the Ritz Carleton, her favorite hotel. As the door man opens the car door for her, he greets her, "Welcome back to the Ritz Carleton, Ms. Ast." When she goes to the registration desk, the receptionist gives her the room key and asks if she would like to have her stay charged to her American Express card. Then she goes to her room and finds just what she prefers—a room with a view of the Boston Commons, a single queen size bed, an extra pillow and blanket, a FAX machine connected to her telephone, and a basket with her favorite fruits and snacks.

Shari's experience is an example of the Ritz Carleton's customer relationship management program. In fact, CRM is both a very powerful business philosophy as well as a very practical set of strategies, programs, and systems that focus on identifying and building loyalty with a firm's most valued customers.

Figure 5-5 provides an overview of the CRM process. We see that it is an iterative process that turns customer data into customer loyalty through four activities: (1) collecting the customer data and building the data warehouse; (2) analyzing the data to target and segment markets; (3) developing the CRM program; and (4) implementing the CRM program.

Let us work our way sequentially through each of these activities in some detail as each, in its own right, is quite interesting, while the total process reveals much about the state of modern marketing management.

Building the Data Warehouse and Targeting

We see in the upper left box of Figure 5-5 that CRM begins with the collection of the customer data and the construction of the database. This *customer data warehouse* typically includes a complete history of the purchases made by the customer, the prices paid, the items bought, and whether or not the

F I G U R E   5-5

The CRM Process

merchandise was purchased in response to a special promotion or marketing activity. It may also include a record of all the interactions that the customer has had with the firm, including inquiries made through telephone calls, information about contacts initiated by the firm such as sending catalogs and direct mail, and even demographic and psychographic data.

In the top right box of the figure, CRM then proceeds with the data analysis and identifying the kind of market segments we discussed earlier—those groups of customers that have similar needs, purchase similar merchandise, and respond in a similar manner to marketing activities.

For example, the Eddie Bauer company discovered that morning shoppers are more price sensitive, and more likely to buy products on sale than evening shoppers, while evening shoppers tended to be in the "professional shopper" segment. Using this information, Eddie Bauer installed electronic window posters in some test stores that allowed different images to be displayed at different times of the day. In the morning, the displays featured lower priced merchandise and items on sale, while, in the evening, the more expensive and fashionable merchandise was displayed.

As to how the marketing team actually goes about developing this kind of information, there are at least two very interesting techniques that are worth flagging. The first is so-called *data mining*. It is used to identify patterns in the data that the analyst is unaware of prior to searching through the data.

For example, an electronic retailer in London discovered that customers who had bought portable DVD players typically commuted to work by train. Using this information, the retailer experienced a 43 percent increase in portable DVD player sales when it redirected most of its communication budget from daytime television commercials to newspapers and billboards along the train tracks.

A second type of analysis is called *market basket analysis*. This focuses on the composition of the basket (or bundle) of products purchased by a household during a single shopping occasion. This analysis is often useful for suggesting where to place products in a store or opportunities for joint promotions.

For example, based on market basket analyses, Wal-Mart changed the traditional location of several items. Bananas were put next to the corn flakes to help sell more cereal as well as in the produce section, and facial tissues were placed in both the traditional paper-goods aisle as well as next to cold medicine.

Developing and Implementing CRM Programs

We see next in the lower right box in Figure 5-5 that the third step in the CRM process is developing marketing programs for the different customer segments. These involve programs aimed at three goals: (1) retaining their best customers, referred to as the "platinum" segment; (2) converting good "gold" and perhaps "iron" customers into platinum; and (3) getting rid of unprofitable "lead" customers.

Figure 5-6 illustrates this implied *customer pyramid*. It ranks customers from the most profitable to the least profitable by the type of metal used in the description above—precious metals like platinum and gold for the best customers and ordinary metals like iron and lead for the least profitable.

As to how the marketing team might go about actually ranking customers to place them in this pyramid, one common approach relies on a technique called *lifetime customer value* (LTV). A customer's LTV is the expected contribution from the customer to the firm's profits over his or her entire relationship with the firm.

Note that an LTV score for each customer can be estimated in the second stage of CRM by using past behaviors to forecast not only future purchases

F I G U R E   5-6

The Customer Pyramid (*Source*: Valerie Zeithami, Roland Rust, and Katherine Lemon, "The Customer Pyramid: Creating and Serving Profitable Customer," *California Management Review 43* (Summer 2001), p. 125. Reprinted by permission.)

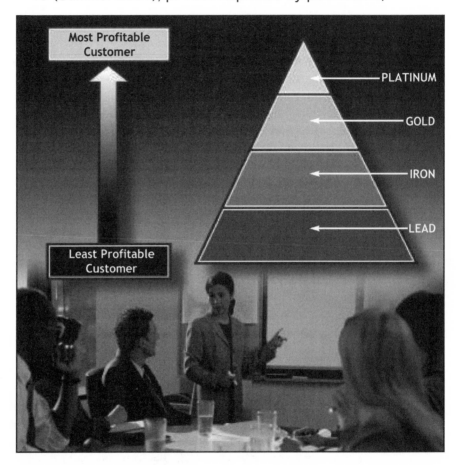

but also the gross margin from these purchases and any costs associated with servicing the customers. In this regard, customer costs include both the cost of advertising and promotion used to acquire the customer and the cost of processing merchandise that the customer has returned.

For example, a customer who purchases $200 worth of groceries from a supermarket every other month would have a lower LTV for the supermarket than a customer who buys $30 on each visit and shops at the store three times a week. Similarly, a customer who only buys apparel from a department store when it is on sale would have a lower LTV than a customer who typically pays full price and buys the same amount of merchandise.

The broader point here is that the set of LTV scores developed in the CRM process can be used to segment customers into the kind of groupings illustrated above in the customer pyramid. In this pyramid, platinum customers typically constitute the top 25 percent of LTVs. These platinum customers are the most loyal, tend not to be overly concerned about price, and place more value on service. They also typically account for over 80 percent of a firm's sales!!

In contrast, the gold customers are more price sensitive. Even though they buy a significant amount of merchandise from the firm, they are not as loyal as platinum customers and probably patronize some of the firm's competitors.

As for the lead customers, *they actually cost the company money.* They often demand a lot of attention, but do not buy much from the firm. For example, real estate agents often encounter people who want to spend their weekends looking at houses but are really not interested in buying one. Catalog retailers similarly have customers who repeatedly buy three or four items and return all but one of them. The cost of processing these two or three returned items is much greater than the profits coming from the one item that the customer kept.

Marketing to the Customer Pyramid

The process of no longer selling to unprofitable customers in the pyramid can be referred to as "getting the lead out." This can be done by: (1) offering less costly approaches for satisfying the needs of "lead" customers, or (2) charging the customers for the services they are abusing.

Consider Fidelity Investments. It averages about 550,000 website visits a day and more than 700,000 daily calls, about three-quarters of which go to automated systems that cost the company less than a $1.00 each. The remaining calls are handled by call center agents, who cost $13 per call.

To get its lead out, Fidelity contacted 25,000 lower-tiered customers who were placing a lot of calls to agents and told them they must use the website or automated calls for simple account and price information. Each name was flagged and routed to a special representative who would direct callers back to automated services—and tell them how to use it. "If all our customers chose to go through live reps, it would be cost-prohibitive," says a Fidelity spokeswoman.

Of course, at the other end of the pyramid, there are many different marketing techniques enterprises use to retain their best platinum customers. One common approach is to offer frequent customer programs like the airlines' frequent flyer programs. Such programs involve a higher level of service, discounts on purchases, or points earned from purchases that can be redeemed for special rewards.

At the same time, the astute marketer will try to convert both iron and gold customers to the platinum category. This can be accomplished by using techniques like *cross-selling* and *add-on selling*.

As an example of cross-selling, consider the sophisticated approach of Fresh Farm, a Norfolk, Virginia, based supermarket chain. It has a "Gold Card" program for its best customers. When Gold Card member Debra Onsager enters the store, she "swipes" her card at a kiosk, and a high-speed printer provides a personalized shopping list with up to 25 deals. The deals offered are based on Debra's purchase history. If Debra's history shows she frequently purchases corn chips but does not buy dip, she will get a deal on bean dip printed on her shopping list to encourage her to try a new product. If she passes up the deal this time in the market, the next time the value of the bean dip coupon will be automatically increased.

As for add-on selling, it involves selling additional new products and services to existing customers, such as a bank encouraging a customer with a checking account to also apply for a home improvement loan from the bank. Oprah Winfrey is a master of such add-on selling. She has capitalized on her daytime TV show popularity to sell and promote a wide number of products to her target audience—women interested in self-improvement. These products range from books, movies, and television specials through her Harpo Productions and a cable TV channel to her widely read magazine called "O".

CONCLUSIONS

In concluding this chapter, we wish to express our hope that we have accomplished at least two goals. First, while we have obviously only just scratched the surface of the field, we hope you now have a very good overview of the Four Steps of Marketing Management. Secondly, we also hope that through the key concepts and numerous examples we have offered that we have sufficiently motivated you to enthusiastically study a subject that is absolutely crucial to the success of any truly modern organization.

CHAPTER 6

Operations and Supply Chain Management—Getting the Stuff Out the Door

Steven Nahmias*

> Call it distribution or logistics or supply chain management ... In industry after industry ... executives have plucked this once dismal discipline off the loading dock and placed it near the top of the corporate agenda. Hard-pressed to knock out competitors on quality or price, companies are trying to gain an edge through their ability to deliver the right stuff in the right amount of time.
>
> Ronald Henkoff

In a world of intense global competition, companies are finding it increasingly difficult to exert any pricing power. As a result, many business executives have discovered that the best way to boost the bottom line is to cut costs through more efficient operations and supply chain management.

However, a funny thing has happened on the road to this more aggressive "operations strategy." Many business executives have discovered that such a strategy not only helps cut costs. It also can improve customer satisfaction and thereby boost demand and revenues as well. Let me show you what I mean with this tale of two discount retailing giants—K-Mart and Wal-Mart. Both of these huge chains were born in the same year, 1986, but their CEOs—one flamboyant, the other shy and shunning publicity—each walked a very different path.

---

*Steven Nahmias is a Professor for the Operations & Management Information Systems Department in the Leavey School of Business at Santa Clara University. He has also served on the faculties of Stanford University, Georgia Institute of Technology, and University of Pittsburgh. This chapter is abstracted from his textbook *Production and Operations Analysis*, Fifth edition, Irwin McGraw-Hill, 2005. More than 100 colleges and universities including Stanford, Berkeley, MIT, and the Harvard School of Business have adopted the text.

On the one hand, K-Mart's Joseph Antonini believed the road to success lay in a sleek marketing campaign populated with celebrity pitchmen. He supplemented this marketing glitz with an aggressive acquisition and diversification campaign.

On the other hand, Wal-Mart's Sam Walton was almost obsessed with operations and supply chain efficiency. He poured tens of millions of dollars into a companywide computer system linking cash registers to headquarters. This enabled him to quickly restock goods selling off Wal-Mart's shelves. He also invested heavily in trucks and distribution centers to enhance his control and thereby cut costs.

For a while, the K-Mart hare ran circles around the Wal-Mart tortoise. Within just a few years, K-Mart became a household name whereas Wal-Mart was virtually unknown outside rural pockets of the Deep South. Even more to the point, by 1987, K-Mart's sales were almost *twice* that of Wal-Mart.

Eventually, however, Sam Walton's operations and supply chain management strategies overcame Antonini's marketing pizzazz. By the 1990s, while the blue-lit aisles of K-Mart began to fill with distribution horror stories, Wal-Mart's incredibly sophisticated distribution inventory and scanner systems meant that customers *never* encountered depleted shelves or price-check delays. Perhaps not surprisingly, by 1994, Wal-Mart's annual sales almost tripled that of K-Mart—and the rest is, as they say, history.

The point of this story is not that marketing does not matter. Of course, it does. Rather, it is that a comprehensive operations strategy can also be an effective marketing tool. And it is well worth noting here, that this is exactly the *same* lesson that American auto manufacturers had to learn in the hardest of ways.

Consider that in the 1950s and 1960s, the Big Three U.S. automakers—GM, Ford, and Chrysler—had a virtually monopoly on most of the world's auto production. However, like Joe Antonini, the business executives at the helms of these Big Three behemoths chose to put their resources *not* into better-engineered cars and lowering costs but rather into slick marketing campaigns and annual cosmetic styling changes. Meanwhile, the executives at Japanese companies like Honda and Toyota were investing in the latest automotive technology and sophisticated logistics systems like one of the ones we will be talking about in this chapter—the vaunted "Just In Time." Again, as they say, the rest is history.

So just what does an aggressive operations strategy really entail? Figures 6-1 and 6-2 lay out the sprawling territory as they provide an

F I G U R E   6-1

The Big Questions and Key Concepts of Operations Management, Part I

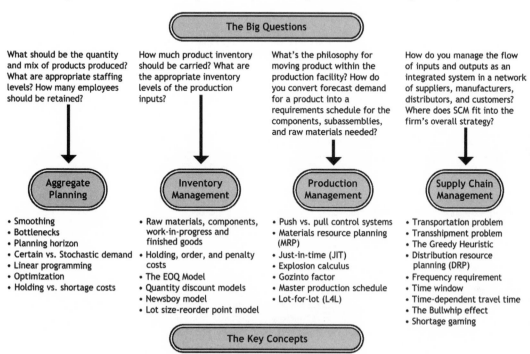

The Big Questions

| What should be the quantity and mix of products produced? What are appropriate staffing levels? How many employees should be retained? | How much product inventory should be carried? What are the appropriate inventory levels of the production inputs? | What's the philosophy for moving product within the production facility? How do you convert forecast demand for a product into a requirements schedule for the components, subassemblies, and raw materials needed? | How do you manage the flow of inputs and outputs as an integrated system in a network of suppliers, manufacturers, distributors, and customers? Where does SCM fit into the firm's overall strategy? |

Aggregate Planning

- Smoothing
- Bottlenecks
- Planning horizon
- Certain vs. Stochastic demand
- Linear programming
- Optimization
- Holding vs. shortage costs

Inventory Management

- Raw materials, components, work-in-progress and finished goods
- Holding, order, and penalty costs
- The EOQ Model
- Quantity discount models
- Newsboy model
- Lot size-reorder point model

Production Management

- Push vs. pull control systems
- Materials resource planning (MRP)
- Just-in-time (JIT)
- Explosion calculus
- Gozinto factor
- Master production schedule
- Lot-for-lot (L4L)

Supply Chain Management

- Transportation problem
- Transshipment problem
- The Greedy Heuristic
- Distribution resource planning (DRP)
- Frequency requirement
- Time window
- Time-dependent travel time
- The Bullwhip effect
- Shortage gaming

The Key Concepts

overview of the big questions and key concepts of the field of operations management. *Please study these figures very carefully before diving into the rest of this chapter.*

From these figures, you will see that the *big questions* of operations management span eight decision areas that run the gamut from aggregate planning and the management of inventories, production, and the broader supply chain to the scheduling of operations and projects, the layout and locating of facilities, and the assurance of both quality and reliability. By the same token, the *key concepts* range from mathematical tools like optimization and linear programming and engineering concepts like "bottlenecks" and the "explosion calculus" to a virtual alphabet soup of operations models, from EOQ and JIT to MRP and PERT.

What we are going to do now is work our way sequentially through these big decisions and key concepts. As we do this, please know that if you

F I G U R E   6-2

The Big Decisions and Key Concepts of Operations Management, Part II

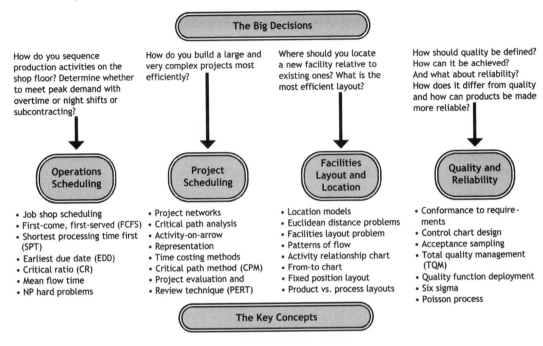

were to actually slog through the operations trenches in a business school, you would be required to do quite a bit of heavy mathematical lifting. But here, in this chapter, what I will really be asking you to do is to focus more globally on both the intuition and logic that underpin each of these decisions and concepts.[1]

AGGREGATE PLANNING

As we go through life, we make both micro and macro decisions. Micro decisions might be what to eat for breakfast, what route to take to work, what

---

1. Note that missing from Figures 6-1 and 6-2 is a very important ingredient of effective operations management, namely, *forecasting*. This has been discussed in Chapter 4 and will be discussed further in your statistics chapter.

auto service to use, or which movie to rent. Macro decisions are the kind that change the course of our lives: where we will live, which job we will take, and who we will marry.

Business executives must also make both micro and macro decisions every day. For example, in the operations planning context, one macro level decision is determining what should be the quantity and mix of the products actually produced. Another such macro decision concerns the size and appropriate staffing levels of the workforce.

Such macro planning necessarily begins with the forecasts of sales. Historically, this type of macro planning in operations is known as *aggregate planning* because the goal is to determine workforce and production levels for the entire firm (or some large subset of the firm such as a division or a factory). The following are three of the most important issues that aggregate planning models must address:

- *Smoothing* refers to the costs and disruptions that arise as a result of changing production and workforce levels from planning period to planning period.

- *Bottlenecks* occur during periods of peak demand when the company's resources are strained. A good aggregate plan takes peak demand forecasts into account early enough to mitigate these effects.

- *The planning horizon* is the number of periods into the future that the aggregate plan covers. One must choose the planning horizon carefully. If too short, sudden changes in demand cannot be anticipated. If too long, demand forecasts become unreliable.

As an equally important fourth aggregate planning issue, there is also the *treatment of demand*. This issue here is whether you will know the level of demand for an input or a product with *certainty* and treat it accordingly or whether you will recognize and treat such a demand as uncertain or, as they say in the probability business, "*stochastic*"?

A variety of aggregate planning models in operations management deal with these issues, and each of these models share one thing in common. They are all based on some form of *optimization*.

As you will learn more about in the statistics chapter in this book, optimization requires an objective, which in business is almost always either minimizing cost or maximizing profit; and the purpose of aggregate planning is to minimize at least four different kinds of costs. The aforementioned *smoothing costs* arise when you have to change either your production or workforce levels as demand or inventory needs change, while *holding costs* can be measured by the so-called *opportunity costs* of any funds you have invested in excess inventory.

But note that if you are caught short of inventory, you can experience another type of cost known as *shortage costs*. These are the costs associated with back-ordered or lost demand. So one of the most important tasks of aggregate planning is to balance holding costs against shortage costs; that is, optimize.

Now please note this important practical contradiction. Aggregate planning models can be a valuable aid in planning production and manpower levels for a company precisely because they provide a means of absorbing demand fluctuations by smoothing workforce and production levels. However, despite these advantages, aggregate planning does not hold an important place in the planning of the production activities of most companies!

There are a number of reasons for this. One is the difficulty of properly defining an aggregate unit of production to analyze. Another reason is that it is often difficult to obtain accurate cost and demand information. But perhaps most importantly, aggregate planning models *rarely reflect the political and operational realities of the environment within which the company is operating*.

For example, most aggregate planning models assume that workforce levels can be changed easily. However, this is probably not very realistic for many companies.

To understand why, it is useful to comment briefly on the history of aggregate planning modeling. It got its start with a seminal work published in 1960 called *Planning Production, Inventories and Workforce*. This book was written by four professors at Carnegie Tech (later to become Carnegie Mellon University), and as part of the research for that book, Professors Holt, Modigliani, Muth, and Simon developed an aggregate planning model for Pittsburgh Paints that would be easy to implement, as it was based on a linear decision rule.

Note, however, that the Pittsburgh Paints executive team chose *not* to implement the professors' recommendations. Why? Because the model required the company to make continual changes in the size of the workforce. But this was a traditional company that placed a very high value on maintaining a stable workforce.

INVENTORY MANAGEMENT

Let us turn now to our second set of big questions, those having to do with inventory management. These questions include: How much product inventory should be carried? What are the appropriate inventory levels of the production inputs?

In approaching these questions, please first note that the investment in inventories among the countries in the global economy is truly staggering—on the order of $1.5 trillion in the United States alone. The pie chart in Figure 6-3 gives the breakdown of these inventories by U.S. economic sector; the kinds of inventory models I will review in this section are most applicable to the manufacturing, wholesale, and retail sectors, which comprise about 80 percent of the total. Seen from this point of view, inventory control can have a *huge* impact on the efficiency of any economy.

To really get a handle on the inventory problem, we first have to identify the four different types of inventories that companies may have to carry. By recognizing the different types of inventories, we will come to understand that not all inventories serve the same function and therefore different types of inventory levels must be modeled differently.

For starters, in a manufacturing plant, there are the *raw materials* required for production or processing. There also may be *components* such as subassemblies that will later be included in a final product.

A third type of inventory is *work-in-process* (WIP). These are inventories that in the plant are waiting to be processed. Finally, there are the all-important *finished goods*—the produced products waiting to be shipped out.

Now one of the core ideas of efficient operations is to minimize the costs associated with inventories. And to look at a company that has taken this idea to a highly profitable extreme, we need look no farther than Dell, Inc.

Dell, Inc.'s Hyperefficient Inventory Management

In 1985, I decided to purchase a personal computer for home use. At the time, a basic IBM XT sold for around $5,000 (think of the computing power you can purchase today for that!). This was a bit much for my tight budget, so I took a chance on a mail-order computer from a small start-up in Texas called PCs Limited.

For $795, I got a basic box with an 8088 processor (running at two speeds), and two floppy drives. After adding a video card, a monitor, and a

F I G U R E   6-3

The Inventory Big Picture

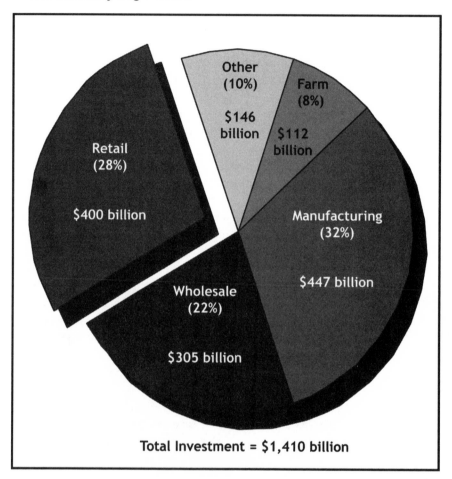

Total Investment = $1,410 billion

hard drive, my total cost was under $2,000 for a machine that ran faster than an IBM, had a larger hard drive, and better video capabilities. It worked flawlessly for years. PCs Limited later became Dell. While Dell's phenomenal success is the result of many factors, a key one is their hyperefficient management of inventories.

To understand why, it is useful to start with the nature of the personal computer marketplace. The central processor is really the computer, and its power determines the power of the PC. In the PC marketplace, Intel has been a leader in designing every new generation of processor chip, and each new generation of microprocessors that Intel has led the market with renders the old technology obsolete. Because these new chips come out every year or so, computers and computer components have a relatively short life span. Moreover, as new chips are being developed at an ever-increasing pace, the obsolescence problem for PCs is becoming even more critical.

So what is Dell's solution to being stuck with any obsolete PC inventory? It is both simple and elegant: *Don't keep any product inventory!* How does Dell do this? It only builds PCs on a made-to-order basis.

Note, however, that Dell still must store components. Although Dell cannot guarantee all components are used, the company's marketing strategy is designed to move as much of the component inventory as possible. In this regard, Dell focuses only on the latest technology, and both systems and components are priced to sell quickly. Furthermore, because of their high volume they can demand quantity discounts from suppliers.

Perhaps the best part of this business model is that Dell targets high-end users who demand the latest technology and are willing to pay for it. This means Dell's profit margins are higher in this market segment, and this, together with its efficient inventory and supply chain management, have helped account for Dell's exceptional stock price performance in an industry where margins are very slim.

Now, there is an obvious question that arises in the wake of Dell's success: Why are companies around the globe holding quite literally *trillions* of dollars of inventories? This is where the inventory story gets really interesting because there are some very rational motivations for holding inventory.

Why Companies Hold Inventories

For starters, there are *economies of scale* that make it is less costly to order or produce in large batches than in small batches. This means that your firm's fixed costs can be amortized over a larger number of units.

Secondly, there are a variety of *uncertainties*. These include demand uncertainty, lead time uncertainty, and supply uncertainty. Each of these types of uncertainty create incentives for holding inventory.

Thirdly, there is simple *speculation*. The idea here is that you may want to hold more inventories of, say a raw material like copper or palladium, because you believe the prices of these materials are going to rise.

Fourthly, at any one time, your company may also be holding *transportation inventories*. These are simply the pipeline inventories that are in transit from one location to another.

Finally, you may also want to hold *smoothing* inventories to quite literally smooth out an irregular demand pattern.

Now, in the optimization problem that determines the optimal level of inventories, there are a number of major costs that must be considered in the modeling effort. On the one hand, and as an argument *against* holding inventories, there are *holding costs* that range from the opportunity cost of lost investment revenue and physical storage costs to higher insurance premiums, breakage and pilferage, and obsolescence.

On the other hand, and as an argument for holding more inventories, there are *order costs*. These generally consist of two components: a fixed component and a variable component. The fixed component typically involves the setting up for a production run. The variable component is a unit cost paid for each unit ordered or produced.

In the same vein, there are also *penalty costs* that are incurred when demand exceeds supply. In such cases, excess demand may be backordered (to be filled at a later time)—thus creating a lot of costly paperwork. Alternatively, the demand may be lost completely—along with the profits you may have earned from fulfilling that demand. Either way—backorders or lost demand—your company also risks losing customer goodwill.

So how do business executives determine the optimal level of inventories to hold? One type of inventory model used is based on the assumption that demand is known with certainty. The other type of model assumes demand is not known and that it is assumed to be a random variable, where (as you will learn more in your statistics chapter) a random variable is a quantity whose value is not known with certainty, but whose range of outcomes and probabilities of those outcomes are known. Let us look briefly now at each type of model.

The Basic EOQ Model–Modeling Under Demand Certainty

In this regard, I must tell you that there are quite literally thousands of mathematical models that have been proposed for controlling the flow of inventories. But the good news here is that virtually all are related in some way to the granddaddy of all inventory control models, the *EOQ model*.

EOQ stands for "economic order quantity," and the model was first derived by Ford Harris, a young engineer with the Westinghouse Corporation in Pittsburgh, Pennsylvania, back in the early 1900s. This simple model treats the basic trade-off between the fixed or set-up costs of ordering and the variable cost of holding the inventories. Here is the basic math: If h represents the holding cost per unit time and K the fixed cost of set-up, then the formula for the order quantity, Q, that minimizes costs per unit time is

$$Q = \sqrt{2K\lambda/h}$$

where λ is the rate of demand.

Now here is a handy little tip for you nonmath types. Even if this formula appears a bit daunting, your intuition should still allow you to see that the amount of inventories your firm is going to want to hold are going to go down as holding costs, h, rise in the expression and as the set-up costs, K, fall.

And please note, that even though the EOQ formula is optimal only under very restrictive assumptions, it is nonetheless very robust for several reasons: (1) It is a very accurate approximation for the optimal order quantity when demand is uncertain; and (2) deviations from the optimal Q generally result in only modest cost errors. For example, a 25 percent error in Q results in an average annual holding and set-up cost error of only 2.5 percent.

Modeling Inventory Management Under Uncertainty

Despite the robustness of this result, it is still important to look at inventory models that, in fact, do allow for uncertainty. Such uncertainties range from the lack of availability of raw materials to the unpredictability of demand. To tune into the idea of uncertainty and what it can mean for operations, consider what it was like going to the airport before the terrible terrorist attack of 9/11.

Before 9/11, many of us would arrive no more than 30 or 40 minutes before the scheduled departure time of our flight. Now, we might arrive two or three hours earlier. We do so because increased airport security has not only increased the average time required, it has also increased the uncertainty of this time. To compensate for this increased uncertainty, we arrive far in advance of our scheduled departure time to provide a

SNAPSHOT   APPLICATION   6-1

USING INVENTORY MODELS TO MANAGE THE SEED-CORN SUPPLY CHAIN AT SYNGENTA

Each year, farmers plant tens of thousands of acres of corn worldwide to meet the demands of a growing population. Minnesota-based Syngenta Seeds is one of eight firms that account for 73 percent of the $2.3 billion U.S. seed-corn market.

Syngenta obtains this seed-corn by growing its own corn and harvesting the seeds. But each season, Syngenta faces its own problem of how much corn to grow.

This inventory problem is complicated by several factors. One is that there are hundreds of different seed hybrids. Some hybrids do better in warmer, more humid climates, while others do better in cooler dryer climates. The color, texture, and sugar content of the corn produced by different hybrids vary as well. Even more problematic, farmers will not re-use a hybrid that yielded disappointing results. For all these reasons, annual demand is hard to predict.

In addition to facing uncertain demand, seed-corn producers also face uncertain yields. Their seed-corn plantings are subject to the same set of risks faced by all farmers: frost, drought, and heat spells.

In sum, Syngenta faces both uncertain demand and supply. But it also faces an additional problem because it plants seed-corn in both Northern and Southern hemispheres. Since the hemispheric seasons run counter to each other, the plantings are done at different times of the year.

In particular, the seed-corn is planted in the spring season in each hemisphere, so that the South American planting occurs about six months after the North American planting. This gives the company a second chance to increase production levels in South America to make up for shortfalls in North America, or decrease production levels in South America when there are surpluses in North America.

A team of researchers from the University of Iowa in collaboration with a Syngenta executive tackled the problem of planning the size of the seed-corn planting. Using discrete approximations of the demand and yield distributions, they were able to formulate the planning problem as a linear program that could be solved on a firmwide scale. A retrospective analysis showed that the company could have saved upwards of $5 million using the model. In addition, the analysts were able to identify a systematic bias in the forecasts for seed generated by the firm that resulted in consistent over-production. This mathematical inventory model is now used to help guide the firm on its planting decisions each year.

buffer. This same principle applies when managing inventories under uncertainty.

Now please note here that the key difference between deterministic versus uncertain or "stochastic" inventory control is that in the uncertainty case, one builds in buffers against the uncertainty. As a simple example, consider the news vendor that must decide on how many newspapers to purchase each morning. Suppose that she has kept careful track of her sales over the past year and notes that daily sales vary considerably, but average 100 papers a day. This might lead one to assume the logical choice is to purchase 100 newspapers every morning. Following this approach, she would overstock and understock about equally often.

But please also note this! If the penalty for running out of papers exceeds the penalty for unsold papers, she would be better off buying *more* than 100 papers every morning. For example, if the penalty for running out is twice as high as the penalty for overstock, one can prove that the optimal policy would be to buy enough papers so that she would only run out in one out of three of the days, and have excess stock in two out of three of the days.

The broader point is that sophisticated inventory control models that take into account uncertainty form the basis for many commercial systems in the real world. These models go by a variety of names that include the *newsboy model*, *quantity discount model*, and *lot size–reorder point model*. Snapshot Application 6-1 provides just one example of successful implementation of a very sophisticated inventory control model. After you read it, we will move on to the next set of big decisions involving production management.

PRODUCTION MANAGEMENT

What should be your philosophy for moving a product within the production facility? How do you convert forecast demand for a product into a requirements schedule for the components, subassemblies, and raw materials needed? These are two big questions of production management.

In fact, there are two fundamentally different philosophies business executives can adopt for managing the flow of goods in the factory—*push* vs. *pull*. A *push control system* such as *Materials Requirements Planning* (MRP) is one in which production planning is done for all levels in advance. Once production is completed at one level, units are literally pushed to the next level. In contrast, a *pull system* such as *Just In Time* (JIT) is one in which items are moved from one level to the next only when requested.

Note that both push and pull systems are quite different from the traditional inventory control models discussed in the previous section, as those methods are rarely appropriate in a factory context. Let us talk first about MRP.

The Push of Materials Requirements Planning (MRP)

Materials Requirements Planning is based on forecasts for the final products or "end items" over a specified planning horizon. Using MRP, executives and managers can determine production quantities not just for the end items, but for all the other components and subassemblies at each level of the system.

To understand this idea, consider Figure 6-4. It illustrates a typical product structure diagram on the top, and an example of how such a diagram might look for the production of a specific good on the bottom—in this case trumpets. Sandwiched between these two diagrams are pictures of the trumpet and its subassemblies.

In the top figure, we see the various components of the "end item" trumpet. In the bottom figure, we also see in the "child level" of the product structure diagram that the factory has to first put together both slide assemblies and valves. These assemblies and valves then go into the "parent level" valve casing assembly and that, together with the parent level bell assembly, go into the final end item of trumpet production. This is a three-level MRP system.

Now the application of MRP to this problem relies on a key concept called the *explosion calculus* and a part of that concept called the *gozinto factor*. The MRP explosion calculus is a set of rules for converting a master production schedule (MPS) into a build schedule for all the components comprising the end product—where the MPS is a production plan for the end item or final product by period. As part of that calculus, the gozinto factor tells us how many of part A are required for part B.

Note that the master production schedule is derived from the forecasts of product demand after these forecasts are adjusted for customer returns and any inventory on hand. At each stage in this process, the MRP modeler computes the production amounts required at each level of the production process by performing two basic operations: (1) offsetting the time when

F I G U R E   6-4

Product Structure for the Harmon Trumpet

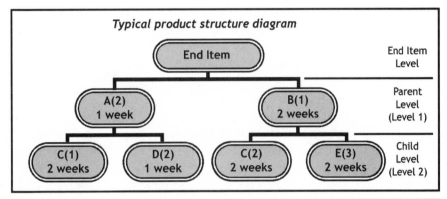

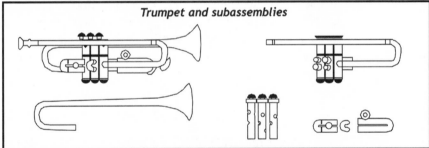

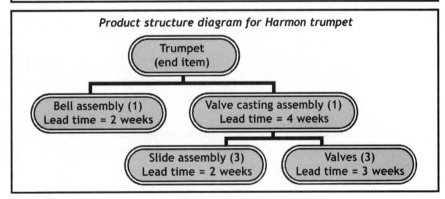

production begins by the lead time at the current level; and (2) multiplying the higher level requirement by the gozinto factor.

As it turns out, the simplest production schedule at each level is called *lot-for-lot* (L4L). It produces the number of units required each period. However, if one knows the holding and set-up costs for production, it is possible to construct a more cost-efficient lot-sizing plan.

Of course, MRP as a production management planning system has both advantages *and* disadvantages. Its main advantage is that it incorporates forecasts of future demand into the production planning function. However, some of the disadvantages include: (1) forecast uncertainty is ignored; (2) capacity constraints are largely ignored; (3) the choice of the planning horizon can have a significant effect on the recommended lot sizes; (4) lead times are assumed fixed, but they really should depend on the lot sizes; (5) MRP ignores the losses due to defectives or machine downtime; (6) data integrity can be a serious problem; and (7) in systems where components are used in multiple products, it is necessary to peg each order to a specific higher level item. Because of these disadvantages, many corporations prefer pull control systems such as Just-In-Time.

The Pull of Just-In-Time (JIT)

The Just-In-Time (JIT) philosophy grew out of the *Kanban* system developed by Toyota. What made Kanban so successful at Toyota was that it reduced changeover times for different automobile models from several hours to several minutes!

Kanban is the Japanese word for the posting board used to keep track of the flow of manufactured items. The Kanban system controls the flow of goods in the plant by using a variety of different kinds of cards, each of which is attached to a palette of goods. Production cannot commence until production ordering Kanbans are available. This guarantees that production at one level will not begin unless there is demand at the next level. This prevents work-in-process inventories building up between work centers when a problem arises anywhere in the system.

In fact, with pull systems such as JIT, the fundamental goal is to reduce work-in-process to a bare minimum. To do so, items are only moved when requested by the next higher level in the production process.

Just-in-time has several advantages and several disadvantages when compared with MRP as a production planning system. Advantages include: (1) JIT reduces work-in-process inventories, thus decreasing inventory costs and waste; (2) it is easy to quickly identify quality problems before large inventories of defective parts build up; and (3) when coordinated with a JIT purchasing program, JIT assures the smooth flow of materials throughout the entire production process.

Still, JIT is not for every corporation because MRP has several of its own advantages relative to JIT. For starters, MRP has the ability to react to changes in demand, since demand forecasts are an integral part of the system (as opposed to JIT which does no look-ahead planning). Also, MRP allows for lot sizing at the various levels of the system, thus affording the opportunity to reduce set-ups and set-up costs. Finally, MRP plans production levels at all levels of the firm for several periods into the future, thus affording the firm the opportunity to look ahead to better schedule shifts and adjust workforce levels in the face of changing demand.

SUPPLY CHAIN MANAGEMENT

Supply chain management (SCM) has been getting the attention of more company CEOs and boards of directors simply because it provides an opportunity to trim costs and beat the competition. Improving relationships with vendors, outsourcing of manufacturing and/or logistics, transitioning the manufacturing function overseas, and opening up new channels of distribution are just a few of the ways firms are using SCM to gain a competitive edge.

The actual term "supply chain management" dates back to the late 1980s, and both software and consulting firms specializing in SCM solutions are now commonplace. These companies have grown at a remarkable rate and include giants like SAP and Oracle.

Although the term supply chain management is relatively new, the problems addressed by SCM clearly are not. In fact, nearly all of the material presented in this chapter in some way involves SCM, and SCM broadly interpreted is much the same as operations management.

What makes SCM unique enough to look at separately is that it looks at the problem of managing the flow of goods as an *integrated system*. As the Director of the Stanford Supply Chain Forum has put it: "Supply chain management deals with the management of materials, information, and financial flows in a network consisting of suppliers, manufacturers, distributors, and customers." Although simple, this definition captures the essential elements of what supply chain management is all about. Figure 6-5 illustrates the supply chain umbrella.

From Figure 6-5, we see that the supply chain umbrella covers issues of supply such as vendor management and inbound logistics, operations problems such as production scheduling and capacity planning, and distribution issues such as customer service and outbound logistics. Implicit in this figure is the question as to where the supply chain fits into the overall business strategy.

From a marketing perspective, examples of strategic positioning include whether to be a low-cost provider such as Hyundai or a high-quality provider like Mercedes-Benz. However, the design of the supply chain also reflects a firm's strategic positioning.

In the supply chain, the primary strategic trade-off is between cost and response time. Managers, for example, must choose between rapid and more costly air transport and the slower and cheaper boat or truck delivery. In a similar vein, managers must ask whether deliveries will be more reliable if the product is moved using the firm's internal system or a third party.

F I G U R E   6-5

The Supply Chain Umbrella

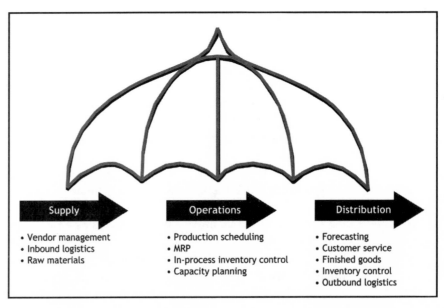

In this regard, *third-party logistics* is becoming more and more important for the same reason that third-party manufacturing has become so widespread—sometimes it is just much more efficient to subcontract activities of the firm out.

So how do executives and managers actually go about the business of conducting SCM analysis? What models do they use? Here is just a small sampling.

The Transportation and Transshipment Problems

The *transportation problem* is illustrated in Figure 6-6 for the Pear Disk Drive company. Pear's problem involves the application of a mathematical model

F I G U R E   6-6

Pear Disk Drive's Transportation Problem

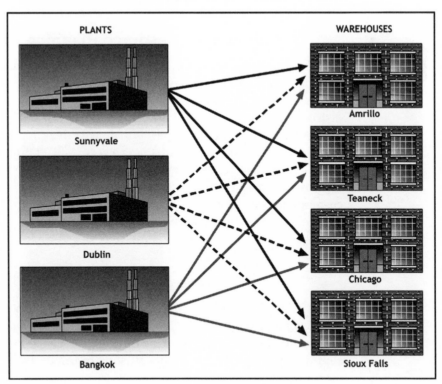

for optimally scheduling the flow of goods from production facilities to distribution centers.

In the figure, we see that Pear has three different manufacturing plants spread out around the world and four different warehouses spread around the country. Given the production levels of each of the plants and the different transportation costs, the goal of the model is to find the optimal flow paths and the amounts to be shipped on those paths to minimize the total cost of all shipments. Such a problem can be solved in operations management using techniques such as *linear programming* and key concepts such as the *greedy heuristic*.

Note that the transportation problem is a special type of network where all nodes are either supply nodes called sources (for example, Pear's factories) or demand nodes called sinks (for example, Pear's warehouses). However, the technique of linear programming can also be used to solve more complex network distribution problems such as the *transshipment problem*. In this case, one or more of the nodes in the network are transshipment points rather than supply or demand points.

Distribution Resource Planning (DRP)

Distribution resource planning or DRP is another important supply chain management tool. It applies the logic of materials resource planning developed for manufacturing systems to the problem of managing distribution.

A related distribution issue has to do with determining delivery routes in supply chains. As it turns out, this is a very difficult problem indeed. This is because it must deal with everything from how often visits to customers must occur (the *frequency requirement*) and the requirement that visits to customer locations be made at specific times (the *time window*) to scheduling around rush-hour congestion in large urban areas (*time-dependent travel time*).

The Bullwhip Effect

Let us end this section on SCM by addressing one of the most interesting phenomena of supply chains, the *bullwhip effect*. Because of this effect, the variance of orders seems to increase dramatically as one moves up the supply chain, and this can create all sorts of problems, particularly at the production level.

To understand this effect, consider the problem that was facing executives at Procter & Gamble, who were studying replenishment patterns for one of their best-selling products: Pampers disposable diapers. They were surprised to see that the orders placed by distributors had much more variation than sales at retail stores. Furthermore, as one moved up the supply chain, orders to the factory had even greater variance. This was all quite puzzling because demand for diapers is pretty steady at the consumer level.

Procter & Gamble wound up coining the term the "bullwhip effect" for this phenomenon, and there are a number of reasons as to why it occurs. One of the most important of these reasons is *shortage gaming*.

You may recall from the chapter on macroeconomics how Cisco Systems ignored a coming recession and got caught with large amounts of inventory. One of the reasons was likely the bullwhip effect from shortage gaming. At the height of the economic boom, Cisco's routers were in short supply and customers were placed on allocation. When Cisco's customers found that they could not get all the units they requested, they simply inflated orders. The result is that Cisco was faced with "phantom demand," which it met with overproduction, and wound up holding the inventory bag.

OPERATIONS SCHEDULING

Let us turn now to the two big question of operations scheduling. How do you sequence production activities on the shop floor? How do you determine whether to meet peak demand with overtime or night shifts or subcontracting? These are questions that can be resolved by looking at the particular issue of *job shop scheduling*.

Job Shop Scheduling

Job shop scheduling is often referred to as *sequence scheduling*, and it is the most common scheduling problem in the factory. A job shop is a set of machines and workers to operate the machines. Jobs may arrive all at once or randomly throughout the day.

For example, consider an automotive repair facility. On any given day, one cannot predict in advance exactly what kinds of repairs will come to the shop. Different jobs require different equipment and possibly different personnel. A senior mechanic would be assigned to a complex job, such as a

SNAPSHOT   APPLICATION   6-2

MILLIONS SAVED WITH SCHEDULING SYSTEM FOR FRACTIONAL AIRCRAFT OPERATORS

Celebrities, corporate executives, and sports professionals all use private planes for travel, but for most, it does not make economic sense to purchase their own planes. An attractive alternative is fractional ownership. It provides owners with the flexibility to fly to over 5,000 destinations (as opposed to about 500 for the commercial airlines). Other advantages include privacy, personalized service, fewer delays, and the ability to conduct business on the plane.

The concept of a fractional aircraft program is similar to that of a time-share condominium, except that the aircraft owners are guaranteed access at any time with as little as four hours notice. The fees are based on the number of flight hours the owner will require: one-eighth share owners are allotted 100 hours of annual flying time, one-quarter owners 200 hours, and so on. The entire system is coordinated by an FMC (fractional management company). Clearly, the problem of scheduling the planes and crews can become quite complex.

When scheduling planes and crews, the FMC must determine schedules that (1) meet customer requests on time, (2) satisfy maintenance and crew restrictions, and (3) allow for specific aircraft trip assignments and requests. The profitability of the FMC will depend upon how efficiently they perform these tasks.

A group of consultants attacked this problem and developed a scheduling system known as ScheduleMiser that drives a larger planning system known as Flight Ops. The inputs to this system are trip requests, aircraft availability, and aircraft restrictions over a specified planning horizon. Note that even though owners are guaranteed service with only four hours notice, the vast majority of trips are booked at least three days or more in advance. This gives the FMC a reliable profile of demand over a two-to-three day planning horizon.

ScheduleMiser is based on a mixed-integer mathematical formulation of the problem. The objective function consists of five terms delineating the various costs in the system. Several sets of constraints are included to ensure that demands are filled, crews are properly scheduled, and planes are not overbooked. This system was adopted and implemented by Raytheon Travel Air in November of 2000 (now Flight Options) for scheduling their fleet of over 100 aircraft. Raytheon reported a saving of over $4.4 million in the first year of implementation of this system.

transmission replacement, while a junior mechanic would be assigned to routine maintenance.

Suppose, now, that all customers bring their cars into the shop first thing in the morning. The shop foreman must determine the sequence to schedule the jobs to make the most efficient use of both the people and machines available. Some of the relevant characteristics of the sequencing problem therefore include the pattern of arrivals, the number and variety of machines, and the number and types of workers.

So how does one go about the business of solving the job shop scheduling problem? There are at least four possible rules to choose from.

FCFS stands for *First-Come, First-Served*. With this rule, you simply schedule jobs in the order they arrive to the shop. In contrast, SPT stands for *Shortest Processing Time first*. You schedule the next job with the shortest processing time. Alternatively, there is *EDD*—the *Earliest Due Date*. Here, you schedule the jobs that have the earliest due date first. Finally, there is the more complicated *Critical Ratio scheduling* (CR). This type of scheduling is more complicated because you must first calculate the critical ratio by subtracting the current time from the due date and then dividing by the processing time. Once you have done this, you schedule the job with the smallest CR value next.

So how do you go about evaluating the desirability of each of these rules? Well, one common criterion is *mean flow time*.

The *flow time* of any job is the amount of time that elapses from the point that the job arrives in the shop to the point that the job is completed. The *mean flow time* is just the average of all the flow times for all the jobs. An important result is that SPT scheduling minimizes the mean flow time. Another result of interest is that if the objective is to minimize the maximum lateness, then the jobs should be scheduled by EDD.

Snapshot Application 6-2 is just one example of how effective operations scheduling can streamline costs. After you read it, we will move on to project scheduling.

PROJECT SCHEDULING

How do you build large and very complex projects most efficiently? This is the big question of project scheduling, where projects are simply a collection of activities that often must be done in a specific order. As Figure 6-7 illustrates for the development of a small commercial software project, projects may be represented graphically as a network.

F I G U R E   6-7

A Project Scheduling Network Example

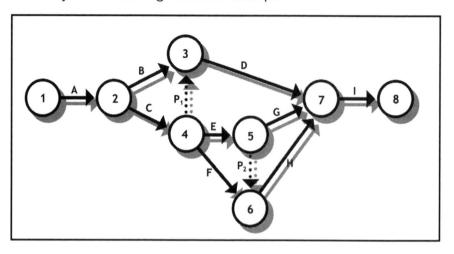

In this case, the figure presents an *activity-on-arrow* representation. Note that each of the letters in the figure represent a task that must be completed. The project starts with the letter A, which, in this case, is a market survey in order to determine exactly what the potential clientele will require and what features of the software are likely to be most attractive. Once this stage is completed, the actual development of the software program can begin.

The power of this kind of analysis is that it allows the project scheduler to find the *critical path* of the project and ensure that it is finished in the least possible time. It does so by helping to answer these three questions:

1. What is the minimum time required to complete the project?

2. What are the starting and ending times for each of the activities?

And perhaps most importantly:

3. Which activities can be delayed without delaying the project?

The Critical Path Method

In this regard, the length of the *critical path* gives the earliest completion time of the project. Activities not along the critical path have slack time—that is, they can be delayed without necessarily delaying the project.

Note that simple algorithms for finding the critical path are readily available to operations managers. They are also embedded into commercial project management packages, such as Microsoft Project.

To see in more detail how this *critical path method* might work, consider a typical construction project. Each additional day that elapses results in higher costs. These costs include direct labor costs for the personnel involved in the project, costs associated with equipment and material usage, and overhead costs.

Let us suppose now that you have the option of decreasing the time of selected activities, but also at some cost. As the times required for activities along the critical path are decreased, the expediting costs *increase*, but the costs proportional to the project time *decrease*. Hence, there is some optimal time for the project that balances these two competing costs. The problem of cost-optimizing the time of a project can be solved manually or via the aforementioned linear programming.

Now here is a twist: In some projects, such as construction projects, the time required to do specific tasks can be predicted accurately in advance. However, this is generally not the case with research projects. Indeed, when undertaking the design of a new piece of software or a new product, it is often difficult, if not impossible, to predict activity times accurately in advance.

In such cases, a more reasonable assumption is that activity times are *random variables*. That is where the alternative method of project scheduling known as the *Project Evaluation and Review Technique* or PERT comes in. This is an approach that was developed by the Navy to assist with planning the Polaris submarine project in 1958.

FACILITIES LAYOUT AND LOCATION

Where should you locate new facilities, particularly relative to existing ones? What is the most efficient layout for your new facilities? These are big questions not just for business entities but also for the military, nonprofit institutions, and government.

The Locational Decision

Where to locate a new facility is a complex and strategically important problem. Hospitals need to be close to high-density population centers. Airports need to be near large cities—but not too near to cause noise pollution. And so on.

In a more global context, new factories are often located outside the United States to take advantage of the lower labor costs overseas. However, these savings often come at a high price. Political instability, unfavorable exchange rates, infrastructure deficiencies, and long lead times are just a few of the problems that can arise from locating facilities abroad. Often such decisions are more strategic than tactical, and require careful weighing of the advantages and disadvantages at the level of top management.

Note, however, that in cases where the primary objective is simply to locate a facility closest to its customer base, the quantitative methods of operations management can be very useful. In these cases, one must first specify how distance will be measured.

For example, *straight-line distance* (also known as Euclidean distance) measures the shortest distance between two points. However, straight-line distance is not always the most appropriate measure.

To see this, consider the problem of locating a firehouse. In this calculus, one must take into account the layout of streets. Thus, using *rectilinear distance* as measured by only horizontal and vertical movements would make more sense than using straight-line distance.

Another consideration is that not all customers are of equal size. For example, a bakery would make much larger deliveries to a supermarket or warehouse store than to a Seven Eleven. Here one would use a *weighted distance criterion*.

The point? There are a number of quantitative techniques that operations managers use to make locational decisions. Now we shall see that the same is true for design and layout issues.

Design and Layout

The objectives of a plant layout study might include just some of the following: (1) to minimize the investment required in new equipment and the time required for production; (2) to utilize existing space most efficiently; (3) to provide for worker convenience, safety, and comfort; and (4) to minimize the materials handling costs.

A key concept in determining a suitable layout is that of *patterns of flow.* Figure 6-8 illustrates six horizontal flow patterns.

The simplest pattern is the straight line flow, as might be encountered on an assembly line. Its main disadvantage is that separate docks and personnel are required for receiving and shipping goods—while the

FIGURE   6-8

Six Horizontal Flow Patterns

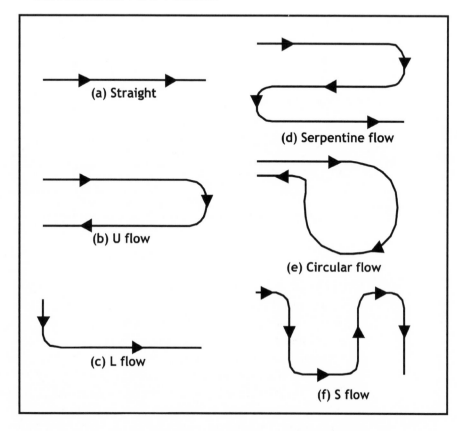

U-shape flow has the advantage over the straight line of allowing shipping and receiving to be at the same location.

Another design layout issue is whether to locate operations near each other. For example, in a hospital, the emergency room *must* be near the hospital entrance, and the maternity ward should be close to the area where premature babies are cared for. Figure 6-9 represents two possible graphical techniques for analyzing and representing the relative desirability of locating two facilities near each other.

The chart on the top for a fast food restaurant is the *activity relationship chart* or "rel chart" for short. It is a graphical means of representing the desirability of locating pairs of operations near each other through a

F I G U R E   6-9

Activity Relationship and From–To Charts

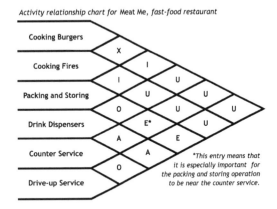

Activity relationship chart for Meat Me, fast-food restaurant

Cooking Burgers
Cooking Fires
Packing and Storing
Drink Dispensers
Counter Service
Drive-up Service

X I I U U O U U E* U A E A O

*This entry means that it is especially important for the packing and storing operation to be near the counter service.

From-to chart showing distances between six department centers (measured in feet)

To From	Saws	Milling	Punch Press	Drills	Lathes	Sanders
Saws		18	40	30	65	24
Milling	18		38	75	16	30
Punch Press	40	38		22	38	12
Drills	30	75	22		50	46
Lathes	65	16	38	50		60
Sanders	24	30	12	46	60	

"closeness" rating. In this case, the letter A stands for "absolutely necessary." At the other end of the alphabet, the letter X stands for "undesirable," while E stands for "especially important" and U for unimportant.

The chart on the bottom for a machine shop is a *from–to chart*. This particular chart gives the distances between activities. It can be used to compute costs associated with various layouts.

More broadly, in a factory setting, the appropriate type of layout depends on the manufacturing environment and the characteristics of the product. A *fixed position layout* is appropriate when building large items such as planes or ships that are difficult and costly to move. Workstations are located around the object, which remains stationary. More typical is the *product layout* where machines or workstations are organized around the sequence of operations required to produce the product. Product layouts are most typical for mass production.

As we will now see in Snapshot Application 6-3, some companies are experimenting with highly innovative approaches to layouts of office buildings.

PLANNING OPERATIONS FOR QUALITY AND RELIABILITY

While we all have a sense of what *quality* means, the term is, in fact, quite ambiguous. Is a Rolls Royce a higher quality automobile than a Toyota

S N A P S H O T   A P P L I C A T I O N   6 - 3

SUN MICROSYSTEMS PIONEERS NEW FLEX OFFICE SYSTEM

Sun Microsystems, based in Santa Clara, California, was founded in 1982, and in two decades has grown into a worldwide supplier of hardware and software products with sales exceeding $10 billion a year. One problem faced by Sun, and other Silicon Valley based firms, is the aforementioned high cost of real estate. Residential housing costs, for example, are now higher in parts of the Bay Area than anyplace else in the United States, including the historically more expensive markets of New York, Boston, and Honolulu. While the stock market crash of 2000 has dampened the commercial real estate market somewhat, these costs are still quite high when compared to virtually any other metropolitan area.

To help to combat these costs, Sun embarked on an innovative program of flexible office assignments for its employees. The traditional business model, followed by virtually every company in the world, is that each employee is assigned a personal office. But a key question rarely asked in business is this: What is the actual usage of these offices?

The answer will depend, of course, on the industry and job function of the individual. But according to Crawford Beveridge, Sun's chief human resources officer, 30 to 35 percent of typical company employees are not in their offices at any given time of the day. Why is this so?

The reasons vary, but include classes, conferences, customer visits, sick days, vacations, off-site meetings, and telecommuting. This means that *fully one-third of most companies' real estate is not being utilized*. Moreover, in Sun's particular case, this number is likely to be even larger, as many employees are permitted to work at home to avoid long commute times.

To improve space utilization, Sun developed an innovative program whereby most employees are *not* assigned a unique office. Those employees are part of the so-called iWork system, and they are able to reserve an office for a specified time at one of several locations in advance.

To make all this work, they obviously have to carry any needed personal effects with them. But what really makes this system work is a card that employees can plug into any Sun workstation, and immediately have access to all their files.

Sun's goal in the iWork program is to have 1.8 employees for each office and dramatically reduce their overhead costs for real estate. How well is the program working? First Beveridge estimates that Sun has been able to retain 680 employees it would have lost by giving these employees telecommuting options. Secondly, he estimates that Sun is currently saving about $50 million annually in real estate costs and estimates that when iWork is fully implemented it will save the firm $140 million annually.

Camry? If the answer is yes, based on what criteria? The Toyota costs a fraction of the Rolls price. Yet when it comes to breaking down, the Toyota is probably more reliable.

So how do we define quality? Phillip Crosby has provided a workable definition within the context of *"conformance to requirements."* He argues that "those who want to talk about quality of life must talk about that life in specific terms, such as desirable income, health, pollution control, political programs, and other items that can be measured."

The idea, then, is that conformance to requirements, or conformance to specifications seems to make the most sense as a definition of quality in the operations management context. That is because such requirements and specifications can be measured and quantified. And if they can be quantified, they can be improved. Still and all, this definition falls short of capturing all of the aspects of what we mean by quality and how the customer perceives it.

Monitoring Quality

As for how we monitor quality in a manufacturing context, there are a number of statistical methods available to operations managers. One such method is the *statistical control chart*, which provides a means of monitoring a process, and the related key concept of *acceptance sampling*.

Acceptance sampling occurs after a lot of items are actually produced. Such acceptance sampling can be performed either by the manufacturer or by the consumer. In most cases, 100 percent inspection of items is impractical, impossible, or too costly. For these reasons, a more common approach is to sample a subset of the lot, and choose to accept or reject the lot based on the results of the sampling. The most common sampling plans are (1) *single sampling*, (2) *double sampling*, and (3) *sequential sampling*.

Total Quality Management (TQM) and the Quality Movement

As the quality movement began to take hold in the United States and other parts of the world, it gave birth to an important new business term you have no doubt heard about—*total quality management* (TQM). Briefly, this is the complete commitment of all parts of the firm to the quality mission.

An important part of TQM is listening to the customer. This process includes customer surveys and so-called "focus groups" to find out what customers want. It also includes distilling this consumer information, prioritizing customer needs, and linking those needs to the design of the product. For example, one means of accomplishing the last item is a technique called *quality function deployment* (QFD).

More broadly, several agencies worldwide promote quality in their respective countries through formal recognition. This process was started in Japan with the Deming Prize, which was established and funded by quality guru W. Edwards Deming. In the United States, outstanding quality is recognized with the Baldridge Prize, a prize established in 1987. It is named after the late Senator Malcom Baldridge, and this prize is actually awarded by the U.S. President.

Still another important development in the realm of quality is ISO 9000. ISO stands for International Standards Organization, and certification requires firms to clearly document their policies and procedures. While the certification process can be costly in both time and money, it is often required to do business in many countries.

Snapshot Application 6-4 highlights another key concept associated with the management of quality and reliability—that of *six sigma*. A six sigma quality standard translates into very, very small defect rates of 3.4 parts per million or less. After you finish reading this Snapshot Application about the value of six sigma programs, we will finish up this chapter with a brief discussion of reliability.

Reliability

When we think of Japan's economic success, it is the automobile industry that many of us think of. But why have companies like Toyota and Honda been so successful at grabbing market share from the likes of GM and Ford? Perceived product quality is probably the key reason that so many Americans choose to buy Japanese cars. But what *dimension* of quality is the most important? The most likely answer to that question—strongly suggested by annual consumer surveys—is the *reliability* of Japanese cars.

Reliability, as a field, separated from the mainstream of statistical quality control in the 1950s with the postwar growth of the aerospace and electronics industries in the United States. The Department of Defense, in particular, took a keen interest in reliability studies when it became all too painfully apparent that there was a serious problem with military components and systems. In fact, one study found that in 1950, only one-third of the Navy's electronic devices were working properly.

S N A P S H O T   A P P L I C A T I O N   6–4

NAVISTAR SCORES WITH SIX SIGMA QUALITY PROGRAM

Navistar International is a major U.S. manufacturer of trucks, buses, and engines and has several plants around the world. In 1985 Navistar's worldwide workforce numbered over 110,000. Due to a crippling UAW strike and a recession, the company had to severely trim the workforce to survive. Today it numbers around 20,000. To combat cost and quality problems it was experiencing at the time, Navistar decided to launch a Six sigma quality program in the mid-1990s.

Six sigma programs have their own culture. Specially trained employees are dubbed black belts after one month's training, and master black belts after additional training. The black belts are assigned specific projects, and have the power to go directly to top management with proposed solutions. Of course, for such an approach to work, not only the employees, but also the management, must be firmly committed to the program.

While Six sigma programs rarely achieve the low defect rates they seek, the goal is clear: do what needs to be done in the organization to effect a fundamental change in both management's and labor's attitudes about quality. Note, however, that quality programs do not come free. For starters, Navistar had to pay a consulting company more than $6 million to implement its program.

Does everyone believe in the value of Six sigma programs? Evidently not. For example, Charles Holland, president of a consulting company based in Knoxville that specializes in statistical quality control methods, dubs the Six sigma program as a "silver bullet" sold at "outrageous prices."

If this is true, what motivated Navistar to plunk down $6 million for this program? According to John Horne, the company's chief executive in 1995, the company needed an antidote to the slide it was experiencing: "We didn't have a strategy; most companies don't." The strategy that Horne adopted was to go after the company's problems at the plant level. The main target of the Six sigma program was the massive and deeply troubled 4,000 square foot plant in Springfield, Ohio.

The effort has been credited with $1 million savings in the first year, and greater savings in subsequent years. The total savings in this one plant alone has been projected at $26 million—well above the $6 million cost of the program.

So what is the difference between statistical quality control and reliability? Statistical quality control is concerned with monitoring processes to ensure that a manufactured product conforms to certain specifications. The random variables of interest are numbers of defects and the degree of conformance variation.

In contrast, reliability considers the performance of a product over time. The random variables of interest in this dimension concern the amount of elapsed time between failures. In fact, three of the most significant disasters of recent times—the nuclear disasters at Three Mile Island and Chernobyl and the dramatic loss of the Challenger space shuttle—were the result of reliability failures.

As for how one goes about the business of modeling reliability, there are a number of important tools available to operations managers. These include *maintenance models, age replacement strategies, reliability functions,* and the *Poisson process,* just to name a few.

The bigger picture here, however, is that solid reliability studies allow business executives and managers to establish the most efficient preventive maintenance and planned replacement programs. They also allow executives to analyze and profitably market a wide variety of warranty programs. And these are just a few more ways that a careful study and mastery of operations management can contribute to the bottom line.

CHAPTER 7

Financial Accounting— "Doing the Numbers" for Investors, Regulators and Other External Users

Leslie K. Breitner*

From Lord Wellington to H.M. Office of the Exchequer

Gentlemen:

Whilst marching from Portugal to positions which command the approach to Madrid and the French forces, my officers have been diligently complying with your requests, which have been sent by H.M. ship from London to Lisbon and thence by dispatch rider to your headquarters.

We have enumerated our saddles, bridles, tents, and tent poles, and all manner of sundry items for which His Majesty's Government holds me accountable... Each and every farthing has been accounted for, with two regrettable exceptions for which I bear your indulgence.

Unfortunately, the sum of one shilling and ninepence remains unaccounted for in one infantry battalion's petty cash, and there has been a hideous confusion as to the number of jars of raspberry jam issued to one cavalry regiment during a sandstorm in Western Spain. This reprehensible carelessness may be related to the pressure of the circumstances, since we are at war with France, a fact which may come as a bit of a surprise to you gentlemen in Whitehall.

This brings me to my present purpose, which is to request elucidation of my instructions from His Majesty's Government, so as I may better understand why I am dragging an army over these barren plains. I construe that perforce it

---

*Leslie K. Breitner is a Senior Lecturer at the Daniel J. Evans School of Public Affairs at the University of Washington and a former faculty member at Harvard's John F. Kennedy School of Government. She is the co-author of *Essentials of Accounting*, 8th edition, and *Core Concepts in Accounting*, 8th edition, Prentice Hall.

must be one of two alternative duties, as given below. I shall pursue either one with the best of my ability, but I cannot do both.

1. To train an army of uniformed British clerks in Spain for the benefit of the accountants and copy-boys in London. Or perchance,
2. To see to it that the forces of Napoleon are driven out of Spain.

Your obedient servant,
Wellington[1]

INTRODUCTION

Too often business executives think of accounting in the manner described by Wellington—as a superfluous activity designed to satisfy bean counters, bureaucrats, or regulators at the expense of focusing on broader goals. However, as we will learn in the next two chapters, accounting is an extremely useful and important language.

In this chapter on financial accounting, we will discover how investors, analysts, lenders, customers, vendors, and other interested parties *external* to the organization can use the tools and concepts of accounting to further their goals. In the next chapter on managerial accounting, we will likewise see how business executives can use accounting information *internally* to achieve both tactical and strategic advantage.

What is the core distinction between financial and managerial accounting? *Financial accounting* is concerned with the preparation and use of three overall financial statements that regulatory authorities require of most organizations. These are the *balance sheet*, *income statement*, and *statement of cash flows*.

In contrast, *managerial accounting* focuses on the costs of products and services and how executives can use those costs for budgeting, cost analysis for profit planning, management control of resources and the cost structure of the firm, and so-called performance reporting for managerial and employee accountability.

To begin our exploration of *financial* accounting, please take a few minutes to review carefully the set of big questions and key concepts that are illustrated in Figure 7–1.

---

1. Message from Sir Arthur Wellesley, Earl of Wellington, to the British Foreign Office in London, written in Spain, August 1812.

F I G U R E   7-1

The Big Decisions and Key Concepts of Financial Accounting

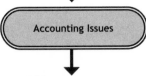

The Big Questions

What are the key financial statements required by law? Are these statements of more interest to external users of accounting data like investors or creditors or internal users like executives and managers?

Are the numbers presented in the financial statements accurate and truthful? Is the company engaging in aggressive accounting practices? Is the data based on "hard numbers" or estimates? Are the earnings of high or low quality?

How do you tell the financial story of an organization from reading its financial statements? How do you determine whether the organization is profitable, can meet its obligations, has the right amount of debt, is investing in assets that add value, and can sustain itself in the future?

The Key Financial Statements

Accounting Issues

Financial Statement Analysis

- The Balance Sheet
  - A Permanent Account
  - Assets = Liabilities + Owners' Equity
  - Double-entry System
  - Current vs. Non-current Assets
- The Income Statement
  - A Temporary Account
  - Net Income = Revenue - Expenses
- The Statement of Cash Flows
  - Operating Activities
  - Investing Activities
  - Financing Activities

- Truthfulness
- Accuracy
  - "Hard Numbers" vs. Estimation
- Aggressive Accounting
- Quality of Earnings
- Notes to the Financial Statements

- Ratio Analysis
- Trend Analysis
- Financial Statement Analysis
  - Profitability Analysis
  - The Dupont Model
  - Liquidity Analysis
  - Financial Structure and Leverage Analysis
  - Asset Management
  - Sustainability
    - Auditor's Opinion Letter
    - Going Concern Opinion
  - Other Critical Success Factors

The Key Concepts

The first set of big questions concerns the construction of the *balance sheet*, the *income statement*, and the *statement of cash flows* and why these statements are of far more use to *external users* of accounting data like investors and lenders than *internal users* like managers and executives.

The second set of big questions focuses on the truthfulness and accuracy of the accounting data reported, and focuses on such issues as the use of *aggressive accounting practices* and the effect on so-called *quality of earnings*. These are issues that were at the heart of the great accounting scandals involving companies like Enron, Global Crossing, Tyco, and Adelphia.

The third set of big questions frames the core of this chapter—*financial statement analysis* and its key concepts, ranging from *ratio* and *trend analysis* to *profitability analysis*, *liquidity*, and *leverage*. In this part of the chapter, you will begin to learn one of the most valuable skills taught in business school: how to tell the financial story of an organization by reading its financial statements.

THE KEY FINANCIAL STATEMENTS

Let us look now at the three key financial statements—the balance sheet, the income statement, and the statement of cash flows.

The Balance Sheet

The *balance sheet* provides a "snapshot" of a company's financial position at a given point in time. Table 7-1 provides a simplified balance sheet for the fictional future technology company Sisco Systems. Take a few minutes to look it over before we proceed. In particular, please note its two-column structure, with assets in the left column and both liabilities and equity in the right column.

This fundamental accounting equation drives the balance sheet:

$$\text{Assets} = \text{Liabilities} + \text{Equity}$$

Total assets equal the total of *liabilities* plus shareholder *equity*. This is the *dual-aspect concept*, and the balance sheet must always maintain this equality. This means that every accounting transaction affects at least two items and preserves the basic equation. That is why accounting is a *double-entry system*. This means that if one side of the balance sheet is increased, either the other side must be increased too, or the first side must contain an offsetting decrease.

What kinds of assets might a company like Sisco have? There are current assets such as cash in the bank, *accounts receivable*, the money owed to the firm by buyers, *inventories* being held in the warehouse for sale, and any *marketable securities* such as stocks or bonds held by the firm.

The assets of a company also include *noncurrent assets*, ranging from property, plant, and equipment like factories, office buildings, and furniture to the *intangible assets* contained in such things as patented technologies and

T A B L E   7-1

A Simplified Balance Sheet of Sisco Systems

Sisco Systems Balance Sheets (As of 31 December 2002 and 2003)		2007		2008
Assets				
Current assets:				
Cash and cash equivalents		$6,000		$11,000
Marketable securities		70,000		74,300
Accounts receivable, net		32,000		31,000
Inventories		13,000		14,700
Total current assets		**$121,000**		**$131,000**
Property, plant and equipment	100,000			115,000
Accumulated depreciation	(30,000)	70,000	(35,000)	80,000
Goodwill		3,000		4,000
Intangible assets		7,000		8,500
Total Assets		**$201,000**		**$223,500**
Liabilities and stockholders' equity				
Current liabilities:				
Accounts payable		$3,000		$6,300
Accrued compensation/wages payable		2,000		2,400
Accrued income taxes		5,000		6,800
Current portion of long-term debt		10,000		10,000
Total current liabilities		**$20,000**		**$25,500**
Long-term debt		81,000		71,000
Total liabilities		**$101,000**		**$96,500**
Stockholders' equity:				
Common stock and paid-in capital		60,000		71,000
Retained earnings		40,000		56,000
Total stockholders' equity		**$100,000**		**$127,000**
Total liabilities and stockholders' equity		**$201,000**		**$223,500**

the *goodwill* and brand equity that a company builds up through its marketing efforts.

On the liability side of the equation, and by similar construction, the *current liabilities* of a company include the money it owes to its vendors and banks in the form of *accounts payable* and *bank loans payable*, as well as things like its *accrued tax liabilities*—the sales and income and other taxes it owes the government. Current liabilities are only those due in the next accounting period.

As for the *noncurrent liabilities* and *equity,* these reflect the *sources of funds* used to acquire such assets. As you will learn in the chapter on corporate finance, the two primary sources of funds for a company are *debt* and *equity,* where debt is money borrowed at a specified interest rate and equity comes about by the selling of stock shares to investors. These equity holders or shareholders are, in effect, the owners of the firm. As for *retained earnings*, these result from the entity's profitable operations over time and are not to be confused with cash!

Taking a big picture view of the balance sheet, ratios like the *debt-to-equity ratio* and *current ratio* are two of the most important in both accounting and finance because they are important measures of a company's *risk* and *liquidity.* Why is this so?

By law, creditors and lenders have a much stronger claim on the company's assets than shareholders should troubles arise within a company. In particular, creditors and lenders can sue if the amounts due them are not paid, and they are first in line (behind only the IRS) when it comes to recovering money from the firm. In contrast, equity investors have only a *residual claim*—meaning that they can only get back their money *after* the creditors have been paid. That is why, as we have just indicated, equity is generally more risky than debt.

One final point about the balance sheet—we note that it is a set of *permanent accounts.* That is, the balance at the end of one accounting period is quite literally the balance at the start of the next one. This means that the balance sheet accounts never revert to zero simply because it is the end of the accounting period. This, in turn, means that you cannot really know how things have changed from the last accounting period to the current one just by looking at the balance sheet.

Because the balance sheet lacks such detail, you also do not know what operating activities might have given rise to those changes. Indeed, even if you had two balance sheets, one for the end of each of two accounting periods, you would still be in the dark without a summary of the operating activities. That is where the *income statement* comes in. It is in the income statement that investors and other external users of the data can find the necessary detail to evaluate performance. This is because the income statement summarizes the operating activities, albeit without regard to the associated flows of cash, for an accounting period.

The Income Statement

The income statement provides a summary of a company's earnings for a period of time. It is important because net income is the primary determinant of an organization's cash flows and therefore the value of its stock. Note, however, that there is an important caveat about this statement. It is true only if both revenues are collected in cash and expenses are paid out in *cash*! The key equation to remember for the income statement is:

$$\text{Net income} = \text{Sales revenues} - \text{Expenses}$$

Table 7-2 provides a simplified income statement for the aforementioned Sisco. Again, take a minute or two to look at it carefully to parse its structure and familiarize yourself with some of the terms.

In thinking about the income statement, it is useful to think about it as a set of *temporary accounts* that begin at the start of the accounting period and revert to zero at the end of the period. Accordingly, the income statement summarizes only the activities of one accounting period, that is, the activities that take place between two balance sheets. These accounts are in the form of *revenues*, which provide the sources of resources, and the *expenses*, which document the consumption of firm resources.

Note, however, that although we can get information about the operating activities of the firm in the form of revenues and expenses from the

T A B L E   7-2

A Simplified Income Statement for Sisco Systems

Sisco Systems Income Statement (For the Year Ended 31 December 2008)	
Revenue	**$56,000**
Operating expenses	
Cost of sales	10,000
Research and development	6,000
Depreciation and amortization	5,000
Sales and marketing	8,000
General and administrative	3,000
Total operating expenses	$32,000
Operating income	**$24,000**
Provision for income taxes	8,000
Net income	**$16,000**

income statement, we still cannot determine anything about the actual flows of cash into or out of the organization! That is where the third major financial statement comes in, the *statement of cash flows*.

The Statement of Cash Flows

> If there's great net income, you should see it in the cash flow … If there's a disconnect there, then there's an issue.
>
> Gregory Glidden

As with the income statement, the statement of cash flows is a summary for a period of time. Table 7-3 provides a simplified version of the statement of cash flows of Sisco Systems. This statement documents the "sources and uses" of cash during the accounting period. Because the statement of cash

T A B L E   7-3

A Simplified Statement of Cash Flows for Sisco Systems

Sisco Systems Statement of Cash Flows (For the Year 2008)	
Cash flow from operating activities	
Net income	$16,000
Depreciation, amortization and other noncash items	5,000
Marketable securities	(4,300)
Accounts receivable	1,000
Inventories	(1,700)
Accounts payable	3,300
Accrued compensation	400
Income taxes	1,800
Net cash flow from operations	**$21,500**
Cash flow from financing activitites	
Common stock issued	$11,000
Repayment of long-term debt	(10,000)
Net cash flow from financing activities	**$1,000**
Cash flow from investing activities	
Additions to property, plant and equipment	$(15,000)
Change in goodwill	(1,000)
Change in intangible assets	(1,500)
Net cash flow from investing activities	**$(17,500)**
Net change in cash and cash equivalents	**$5,000**

flows is used to explain the change in the cash account from one balance sheet to the next—where did cash come from and where it go?—it is essentially a summary of the changes in every balance sheet account except cash. This link to the other financial statements makes it a very valuable statement! Its construction, however, is the least intuitive of the financial statements.

Note that the statement of cash flow has three sections. The *cash flow from operating activities* represents the sources of cash for an organization generated by its own operating activities. The *cash flow from investing activities* includes the acquisition of new fixed assets and the proceeds of selling fixed assets. Finally, the *cash flow from financing activities* includes the funds obtained from long-term borrowing, repayment of the loans, and obtaining funds from the issuance of additional stock.

Different sources of cash flow can paint very different pictures of a company's fortunes. If, for instance, cash flow increases because of increased sales, that is a very good sign for potential investors. However, a cash flow increase that results from the sale of valuable assets may indicate that the company is in trouble and needs cash to pay some of its bills and interest payments on its debt. The statement of cash flows helps investors and other external users of an organization's data sort all of this out.

Perhaps because it is the most complex of the three statements to understand, many MBA accounting courses do not give the statement of cash flows enough attention. That is unfortunate because in periods of growth or financial crisis, the external users of a company's financial statements may pay far more attention to the statement of cash flows than to the income statement—as you will see shortly with an example about Global Crossing.

ACCOUNTING ISSUES

> Nothing will save an investor from management that simply lies to auditors and shareholders.
>
> Jim Gallagher

How can the three major financial statements be used to answer important questions posed by investors, creditors, and other external users of the data. To set the stage for this discussion of *financial statement analysis*, let us first draw an important distinction between *accounting issues* and *financial management issues*. This distinction is drawn in Figure 7-2 by David W. Young. Take a few minutes to look at it carefully before moving on.

FIGURE 7-2

Accounting versus Financial Management Issues

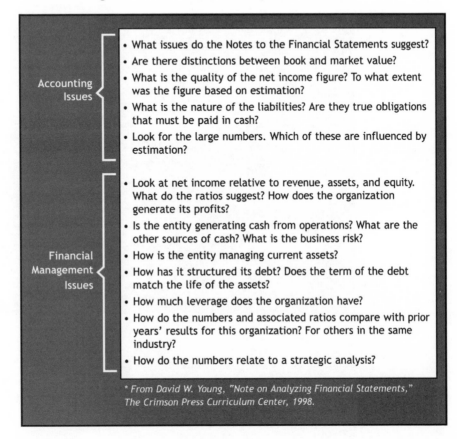

Accounting Issues

- What issues do the Notes to the Financial Statements suggest?
- Are there distinctions between book and market value?
- What is the quality of the net income figure? To what extent was the figure based on estimation?
- What is the nature of the liabilities? Are they true obligations that must be paid in cash?
- Look for the large numbers. Which of these are influenced by estimation?

Financial Management Issues

- Look at net income relative to revenue, assets, and equity. What do the ratios suggest? How does the organization generate its profits?
- Is the entity generating cash from operations? What are the other sources of cash? What is the business risk?
- How is the entity managing current assets?
- How has it structured its debt? Does the term of the debt match the life of the assets?
- How much leverage does the organization have?
- How do the numbers and associated ratios compare with prior years' results for this organization? For others in the same industry?
- How do the numbers relate to a strategic analysis?

* From David W. Young, "Note on Analyzing Financial Statements," The Crimson Press Curriculum Center, 1998.

Accuracy and Truthfulness

As you might glean from the table, *accounting issues* have to do with the accuracy and truthfulness of the accounting data as they appear on the financial statements. To use financial statement data in a subsequent analysis, a user must have faith in them. It is not just that an organization may actually provide false numbers or hide data. While that certainly has happened with companies as well known as Enron, HealthSouth, Qwest Communications, and WorldCom, this falsifying or hiding of data tends to

F I G U R E   7-3

Seven Financial Shenanigans

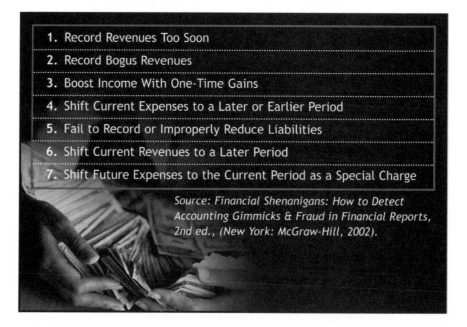

1. Record Revenues Too Soon
2. Record Bogus Revenues
3. Boost Income With One-Time Gains
4. Shift Current Expenses to a Later or Earlier Period
5. Fail to Record or Improperly Reduce Liabilities
6. Shift Current Revenues to a Later Period
7. Shift Future Expenses to the Current Period as a Special Charge

Source: Financial Shenanigans: How to Detect Accounting Gimmicks & Fraud in Financial Reports, 2nd ed., (New York: McGraw-Hill, 2002).

be far more the exception than the rule.[2] A more likely scenario arises when companies try to simply bend, rather than break, accounting rules or otherwise engage in *aggressive accounting*. Take a look at Figure 7-3. It lists "Seven Financial Shenanigans" for which every investor should be on the lookout.

The Quality of Earnings

A more subtle and potentially equally important issue has to do with whether the numbers reported are based on "hard numbers" or, alternatively, *estimates*. In particular, it is important to look carefully at any

---

2. In an ironic twist of the accounting scandals, all of these companies are either pursuing or considering pursuing filing for federal tax refunds or credits for payments made on the billions of false earnings they claimed. "Tax Refunds Follow False Data," *Associated Press*, Marcy Gordon, May 3, 2003.

large numbers in a report and ask the question: "Which of these may have been influenced by estimation?" In addition, it is important to examine the nature of the liabilities and whether they are to be settled by an outflow of cash or by providing a product or service owed to a customer.

More generally, it is useful to examine the data to determine the so-called *quality of earnings*, which has been defined as "increased earnings due to increased sales and cost controls, as compared to artificial profits created by inflation of inventory or other asset prices."[3]

Accounting Irregularities

As a final caveat, it is important to look at the *Notes to the Financial Statements* for any red flags or clues to irregularities. The devil may be in the details, as illustrated in this news excerpt about the Canadian telecom giant BCE:

> Consider, for example, BCE's fourth-quarter results. Depending on which column of figures you prefer, the company had either a profit of $321 million or a loss of $326 million.
>
> "That's a hell of a spread," says [Russ] Healey [president of Strategic Analysis Co.]. The difference, BCE explains in detailed notes to its financial statements, has to do with one-time charges for restructuring (cutting staff) and goodwill expenses (which reflects the reduced value of certain acquisitions).[4]

FINANCIAL STATEMENT ANALYSIS

Let us turn now to perhaps the most important use of financial accounting data: *financial statement analysis*. Table 7-4 provides a summary of various *financial management issues* along with some of the more important *ratios* that may be extracted from the financial statements and used in analysis.

The major financial management issues may be grouped into the categories seen in column 1. They include: (1) *profitability*, (2) *liquidity*, (3) *financial structure and leverage*, (4) *asset management*, and (5) *sustainability*.

---

3. Campbell R. Harvey's *Hypertextual Finance Glossary*.
4. "A Giant Stumbles," *Toronto Star*, Dana Flavelle, March 30, 2002. Like many of the telecoms, BCE went on an acquisition binge during the height of the stock market boom in 2000. It bought two media companies for close to $10 billion. When the value of these acquisitions plunged, the company had to write the loss off.

T A B L E   7-4

A Summary of Financial Management Issues and Some Key Ratios

Analytical Issue	Key Questions	Applicable Ratios	Ratio Calculations	2008
Profitability analysis	What rate of return has been earned on the owners' equity or assets?	Return on Investment (ROI)	$\dfrac{\text{Net Income Before Interest and Taxes}}{\text{Average Total Assets}}$	11.3%
		Return on Shareholder Equity (ROE)	$\dfrac{\text{Net Income}}{\text{Average Total Stockholders' Equity}}$	14.1%
	How expensive is a company's stock relative to other companies?	Price/Earnings	$\dfrac{\text{Current Market Price Per Share}}{\text{Earnings Per Share}}$	
	What has been the dividend track record?	Dividend Yield	$\dfrac{\text{Annual Dividend Per Share}}{\text{CurrentMarketPricePerShare}}$	
Liquidity analysis	Does the organization have enough cash to meet its current obligations?	Working Capital	$\dfrac{\text{Current Assets}}{\text{Current Liabilities}}$	105,500
	Is it managing its accounts receivable well?	Current Ratio	$\dfrac{\text{Current Assets}}{\text{Current Liabilities}}$	5.14
		Acid-test or Quick Ratio	$\dfrac{(\text{Cash}+\text{Accounts Receivables})}{\text{Current Liabilities}}$	4.56
Financial structure and leverage analysis	Has the organization taken on too much – or too little! – debt?	Debt Ratio	$\dfrac{\text{Total Liabilities}}{(\text{Total Liabilities}+\text{Owners' Equity})}$	43.2%
		Debt-to-Equity	$\dfrac{\text{Total Liabilities}}{\text{Total Owners' Equity}}$	76.0%
Asset management	Are the organization's assets being managed efficiently?	Inventory Turnovers	$\dfrac{\text{Cost of Goods Sold}}{\text{Average Inventories}}$	0.72
	Is there too much or too little inventory?	Total Asset Turnover	$\dfrac{\text{Net Sales}}{\text{Average Total Assets}}$	0.26
Sustainability	Is the business doing enough business to sustain itself?	Auditor's Opinion Letter	Not Applicable	

A complete analysis of financial management issues should also include a review of the organization's *critical success factors*—what the organization must do well to remain successful. The analysis should also consider what crucial aspects of future performance may not be indicated on the current, historically based financial statements.

Ratio and Trend Analysis

Note in the table that for most of these financial management issues, there are one or more ratios that are used as short-hand measures for the relevant analysis. Such *ratio analysis* can be used to evaluate current operations, to study the efficiency and risks of operations, and to compare a company's current performance to its past performance, the performance of other companies within its industry, and the broader market. Ratio analysis is also useful as a means of standardizing financial information for such comparisons. One caveat, however, is that all too often, financial analysts rely far too heavily on ratios alone. This can be a very dangerous habit because ratios tell only part of the story of any organization.

That said, the three major types of ratios that can be extracted from financial statements, as presented in Table 7-4, include: (1) *financial ratios* such as those measuring liquidity and leverage, (2) *operating ratios* such as those measuring activity or turnover and profitability, and (3) *valuation ratios*, which assess a stock price relative to assets or earnings. Typically, the analyst will view these ratios over time to quite literally "chart" an organization's performance. This is called *trend analysis.*

The three major financial statements can be used to generate ratios applicable to each of the major financial management issues.

Profitability Analysis

Obviously, the *profitability* of a company is of paramount importance both to investors and creditors. As you will learn in the chapter on corporate finance, without profits—or the expectation of profits—there can be no dividends paid out or any stock price appreciation and therefore no earned return on investment. Nor may there be adequate funds to pay bondholders, vendors, or other creditors.

The income statement is most useful in determining profitability. Put simply, if revenues are greater than the expenses of an accounting period, a profit is the result. But please also note that an organization can have a profit yet still have *negative* retained earnings if accumulated losses over time are greater than the profits.

Note further that a profit (or surplus), even in nonprofit and public sector organizations, is necessary to help replace assets as they wear out, to finance cash needs associated with growth (including expansion and diversification of fixed assets), and to protect the organization from annual or seasonal fluctuations in revenues and economic uncertainties.[5] From this perspective, the notion that nonprofit or public sector organizations should "break even" is simply unwise.

Two important ratios commonly used to gauge firms are *return on assets* (ROA) and *return on shareholder equity* (ROE). Several other important ratios for profitability analysis include the *price/earnings ratio* and the *dividend yield*. Note also that that while many of the data to calculate these ratios may be found in the financial statements, some of the data, such as the stock price in the "P/E ratio" and dividend yield ratio, must come from external sources.

Besides these bread and butter profitability measures, you will also learn about a very powerful and practical tool called the *Dupont Model*. This is an expansion of the ROA calculation that brings other factors into the estimation of profitability: *asset turnover* (which we will discuss further below), *profit margin*, and the relationship between ROA and leverage. The top management of many corporations considers the utilization of assets to be just as important to overall performance as generating profit from sales.

Liquidity Analysis

Liquidity—or available cash—is critical for a company to be viable. Even though a business may be profitable, if its revenues are not turned into cash in a timely manner, it will lack "liquidity" and there will be a problem paying the bills! So, the timely collection of accounts receivable, the minimization of bad debts, and the timing of accounts payable and other short-term obligations are all important.

The balance sheet and the statement of cash flows together will help ascertain a company's liquidity or lack thereof. The balance sheet provides a glimpse of the relationship between current assets, especially those that can be easily converted to cash, and current liabilities, the obligations of the organization due and payable in the coming year. The statement of cash

5. David W. Young, "Nonprofits Need Surplus Too," *Harvard Business Review*, 1982.

flows helps identify the sources and uses of cash through the analysis of other working capital accounts.

As illustrated in Table 7-4 above, at least three ratios are commonly used to gauge liquidity. *Working capital* is simply an organization's current assets minus its current liabilities, where as we noted earlier, current assets consist of a firm's cash and other short-term assets such as accounts receivable and inventories that are likely to be converted to cash. Note, however, that working capital, in and of itself, is not particularly useful unless it can be related to something else. That is why the working capital equation is typically transformed into the *current ratio*, which is simply current assets divided by current liabilities. Intuitively, if this ratio is too close to 1, it should be clear that an organization's current liabilities may threaten to overwhelm its ability to pay them.

In general, the rule of thumb is that an organization must have a current ratio of at least 2 and an *acid-test* or *quick ratio* (cash plus marketable securities plus accounts receivables divided by current liabilities) of at least 1 in order to have sufficient liquidity. The acid-test ratio is a more conservative measure of liquidity than the current ratio because it excludes inventories from the calculation. This exclusion effectively assumes a "worst case scenario" in which the organization cannot sell any more of its product inventory.

Once again, do not rely too much on such ratios and rules of thumb. For example, what happens with the acid-test ratio if the accounts receivables are not "real?" We know they should be written off, but they are not always! And what if the current liabilities in the current ratio are not due and payable in cash, but rather in services to be performed? My own view is that liquidity is really determined by the ability to pay liabilities as they come due. This ability differs from organization to organization and is better reflected by the relationship between leverage and business risk (certainty of cash flows) rather than by standard ratios.

Financial Structure and Leverage Analysis

A third financial management issue, closely related to the issue of liquidity, is the over-arching issue of the *financial structure* of the organization—how much of its assets are accounted for by shareholder equity versus debt—and the *leverage* that structure imparts.

Investors, lenders, and other external users of the financial statements often worry whether a company has taken on too much debt. Borrowed funds require regular interest payments, which can become burdensome if sales decrease. More subtly, it is also possible for a company not to have assumed enough debt! Debt capital is typically cheaper than equity capital—more about that too in the finance chapter—so a company that relies too much on equity capital is not acquiring funds in the most cost-efficient manner.

When considering these issues, there are a whole series of *leverage ratios* that are germane. Two of the most common are the *debt ratio* (also called the *leverage ratio*) and the aforementioned *debt-to-equity ratio*. These compare the amount of total liabilities to some other relevant part of the income statement or the balance sheet. In general, the greater the debt in relation to any one of these measures, the higher the company's risk and the greater the concerns over its long-term solvency.

Asset Management

In a world of increasing global competition where price margins have been squeezed and revenues in times of recession have been stagnant or falling, the executive teams of corporations around the world have turned to efficient *asset management* as a way of boosting the bottom line. The basic idea behind the concept of asset management—evident in the Dupont Model we discussed earlier—is that if you can reduce the amount of inventory or accounts receivable needed to support a given level of sales, your company can generate more cash for shareholders. This will, in turn, lead to a higher stock price, everything else being equal.

This asset management concept is embodied in several of the key ratios that are used to evaluate *asset activity* or *turnover*. From the formulas introduced in Table 7-4, we see that the *inventory turnover* ratio is found by dividing sales by inventory, while the *total asset turnover ratio* is sales divided by total assets.

To understand just how important asset management can be in generating cash flow and earnings, one need look no farther than a comparison between Dell Computer and its leading rival Hewlett Packard (HP). Both companies are in an industry in which price competition is fierce. However, Dell consistently outperforms Hewlett Packard in profitability. Many analysts attribute this success to Dell's superior business model, in which it sells its products exclusively through direct sales to consumers rather than through retail outlets. This keeps Dell's overhead low relative to HP.

However, as you have already learned in the chapter on operations management, a big part of Dell's success story is its commitment to rapid turnover of inventory. In fact, Dell's business model enables it to achieve a much higher inventory turnover rate compared to HP and the rest of the computer industry. This allows Dell to dedicate fewer assets to support a dollar of sales. This increases the amount of cash left over for shareholders, which is one of the big reasons why Dell trades at a price-to-earnings ratio substantially above other players in the industry.

Sustainability

Is the business doing enough business to sustain itself into the future? This is obviously an important question for both investors and lenders. The answer may not necessarily be found in any one of the three major financial statements and the often confusing thicket of financial ratios. Rather, one of the keys to determining sustainability may be found in another key document known as the *auditor's opinion letter*. As part of the auditing process, companies hire auditors to attest to the financial data prepared by management. These auditors are external to the organization and supposed to be independent.[6] In writing their opinion letters, the auditors are required to indicate if the organization has adhered to *generally accepted accounting principles* (GAAP) in its presentation of the financial statements. If the financial data indicate a lack of sustainability, the auditors must acknowledge this. It is important to read the auditor's opinion for hints about any trouble with the data that might be included in the statements. The most serious of these is the *going concern opinion*, within which the auditors can state that they do not feel the organization is sustainable through the next accounting period. Such a *substantial doubt opinion* will have huge ramifications for the company's stock price and ability to borrow money. This Associated Press news excerpt illustrates just how serious the impact can be:

> Drkoop.com may be terminal. The health information Web site started by former Surgeon General C. Everett Koop is losing so much money that its auditors say there is "substantial doubt" that it can stay in business. Release of the auditors' letter by PricewaterhouseCoopers in drkoop.com's annual report last week halved the value of Drkoop.com shares, which closed Friday at $3.69 each, down $4.31 on the week. Last July, shortly after its initial public offering, the stock sold for more than $36.

---

6. Regrettably, this is not always the case. One of the problems that led to the Enron scandal was the lack of independence of the firm's auditor, Arthur Anderson.

In fact, the auditor got it exactly right as the company went bankrupt soon thereafter.

Other Critical Success Factors

Financial statements certainly do not tell us everything we want to know about an organization. A complete analysis must take into account various *critical success factors*. Which revenues and expenses are likely to recur? That is, which earnings are sustainable into the future? Economic indicators, other industry indicators, and organizational information that may not be contained in the financial statements must also be examined. That is where macroeconomics, managerial economics, finance, and organizational behavior can come into play.

The point is that the financial statements do not tell the whole story. They report only past events. They do not report market values. They are based on judgments and estimates. Nevertheless, they provide extremely important information.

In the next chapter, you will discover how those executives and managers *internal* to the organization are able to use accounting data in strategic planning, budgeting, and operational control. Note, however, that even though financial and managerial accounting are often treated as separate disciplines—and treated in many business schools as separate courses—they are highly interrelated.

CHAPTER 8

Managerial Accounting— "Doing the Numbers" for Decision Making and Control*

INTRODUCTION

> The earlier you get the information, the easier it is to fix a problem.
>
> Richard Kelson
> CFO, Alcoa

Accounting often gets a bad rap as a boring world of green eyeshades and bean counters, but it is an absolutely essential discipline for any organization. No modern corporation is going to grow and prosper without a solid accounting team assisting virtually every other unit and discipline within the organization.

The corporate finance team will need the company's internal accounting system to determine such things as the company's optimal level of debt and cost of capital. The firm's managerial economists and marketing specialists need solid cost data to set prices and volume targets. The operations management unit cannot produce and deliver products from multiple factories, transit centers, and retail outlets around the world without a proper allocation of costs among the various pieces of the production and distribution pie. And the organizational behavior and human resource management teams cannot hire or fire efficiently unless the managerial accountants have put into place a solid system of "responsibility accounting" that can measure performance and hold employees accountable.

---

*This chapter was developed from an extensive review of the major managerial accounting textbooks on the market. It depends heavily on the textbook *Managerial Accounting*, 10th edition, by Ray H. Garrison and Eric W. Noreen. It also features material from *Accounting for Decision Making and Control*, 4th edition, by Jerold L. Zimmerman and *Accounting*, 6th edition, by David H. Marshall, Wayne W. McManus, and Daniel Viele. (All books are published by McGraw Hill/Irwin.)

As you will learn in this chapter, the use of accounting methods, information, and language to analyze and drive almost every aspect of an enterprise is known as *managerial accounting*. Contrary to its public image, it not only comprises a crucial set of organizational skills, it is also quite fascinating.

Figure 8-1 illustrates the big questions and key concepts of managerial accounting. Note that the third circle from the left containing "Different Costs for Different Purposes" is larger than the rest. This is quite intentional, as this particular subject will occupy much of the chapter. Please take a few minutes to review the figure before we begin to analyze each of its components.

THE PURPOSES AND APPLICATIONS OF INTERNAL ACCOUNTING SYSTEMS

Every organization must have an *internal accounting system*, which has at least two main purposes: *decision making* and *control*. The first purpose is to provide the executive team and the broader managerial corps with the right information and knowledge to properly plan and make decisions. The second is to create a system of *performance measurement* and *responsibility accounting* that will help motivate and monitor people in the organization. Any internal accounting system that fulfills these two purposes will be useful in at least five different ways.

First, it will provide the information necessary to identify the most profitable products and services of the organization. Secondly, it will help formulate pricing and marketing strategies that will achieve the targeted volume levels. Thirdly, it identifies any production inefficiencies to ensure that the organization's products are produced at minimum cost. Fourthly, it will enable reward systems that provide the proper incentives for employees at all levels to maximize the value of the firm. Finally, it will enable managerial and cost accountants to work hand-in-hand with financial accountants to provide all appropriate data.

THE ROLE OF BUDGETING IN THE STRATEGIC AND PROFIT PLANNING PROCESS

A budget is a detailed plan for acquiring and using financial and other resources over a specified time period. It represents a plan for the future expressed in formal quantitative terms... The use of budgets to control a firm's activities is known as *budgetary control*.

Ray Garrison and Eric Noreen

FIGURE 8-1

The Big Questions and Key Concepts of Managerial Accounting

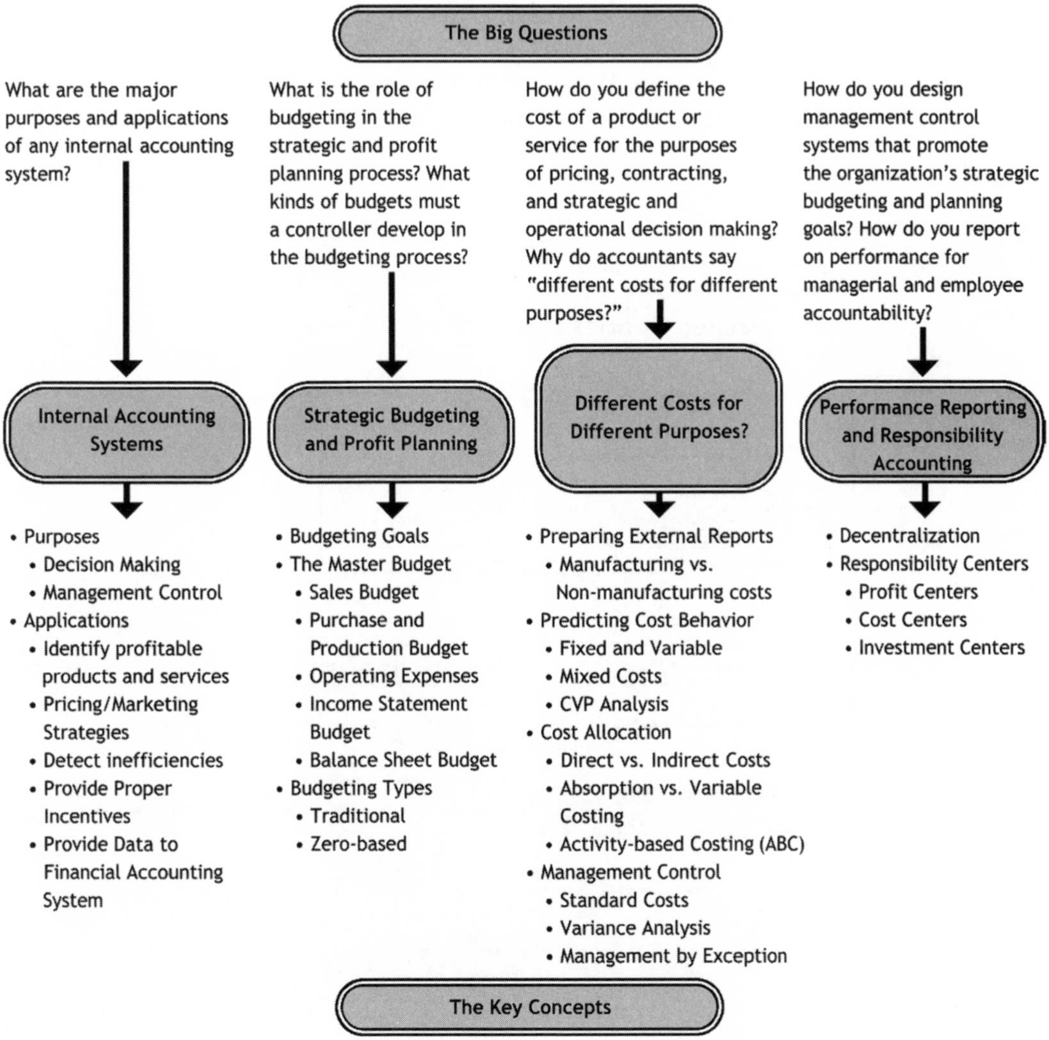

The Big Questions

What are the major purposes and applications of any internal accounting system?

What is the role of budgeting in the strategic and profit planning process? What kinds of budgets must a controller develop in the budgeting process?

How do you define the cost of a product or service for the purposes of pricing, contracting, and strategic and operational decision making? Why do accountants say "different costs for different purposes?"

How do you design management control systems that promote the organization's strategic budgeting and planning goals? How do you report on performance for managerial and employee accountability?

Internal Accounting Systems

Strategic Budgeting and Profit Planning

Different Costs for Different Purposes?

Performance Reporting and Responsibility Accounting

- Purposes
  - Decision Making
  - Management Control
- Applications
  - Identify profitable products and services
  - Pricing/Marketing Strategies
  - Detect inefficiencies
  - Provide Proper Incentives
  - Provide Data to Financial Accounting System

- Budgeting Goals
- The Master Budget
  - Sales Budget
  - Purchase and Production Budget
  - Operating Expenses
  - Income Statement Budget
  - Balance Sheet Budget
- Budgeting Types
  - Traditional
  - Zero-based

- Preparing External Reports
  - Manufacturing vs. Non-manufacturing costs
- Predicting Cost Behavior
  - Fixed and Variable
  - Mixed Costs
  - CVP Analysis
- Cost Allocation
  - Direct vs. Indirect Costs
  - Absorption vs. Variable Costing
  - Activity-based Costing (ABC)
- Management Control
  - Standard Costs
  - Variance Analysis
  - Management by Exception

- Decentralization
- Responsibility Centers
  - Profit Centers
  - Cost Centers
  - Investment Centers

The Key Concepts

On the front lines of strategy implementation, there may be nothing more important in an organization than the development of the *master budget* (or *operating budget*) and the various *detailed budgets* that go into its makeup. Such budgeting is a big part of the job of any company's team of accountants.

At the helm of this effort typically is the company *controller*[1]—the chief accounting officer of the corporation.

The purpose of the master budget is to summarize a company's plans with respect to *all* its major activities—from sales and production to distribution and financing—as represented by the set of *detailed budgets* that go into its makeup. These detailed budgets, and the broader sequence of budgetary activity, are illustrated in Figure 8-2.

F I G U R E   8-2

The Master Budget and Budget Process

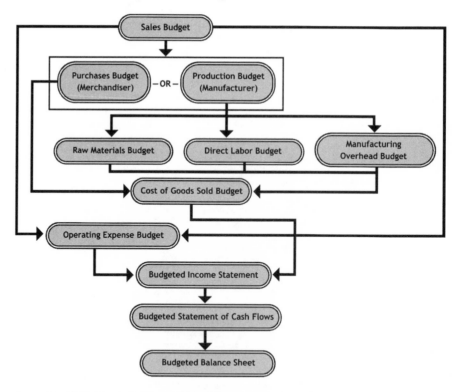

Source: David H. Marshall, Wayne W. McManus, & Daniel F. Viele. *Accounting*, 6th edition, McGraw Hill/Irwin.

---

1. Sometimes the term *comptroller* is used, which is the Old English spelling.

You can see from the figure that the master budget is driven first and foremost by the *sales budget*, which is also called the *revenue budget* or the *forecast*. Once the forecast of sales is made, this provides the basis for the *purchases budget*, if the firm is in a *merchandizing industry* or, alternatively, the *production budget*, if the firm is a manufacturer. In either case, both the purchases and production budgets lead to a *cost-of-goods-sold budget*, with the production budget taking an intermediary stop at *raw materials, labor*, and *overhead budgets*.

Finally, in the tie-in back to the financial statements you learned about in the last chapter, the result is a prospective *budgeted income statement, budgeted statement of cash flows*, and *budgeted balance sheet*.

Why does the controller go through the considerable time and trouble of constructing a master budget? The document is, in fact, one of the most versatile regularly produced within any company. It helps the executive team meet at least six important goals—all of which dovetail nicely with the purposes of internal accounting systems noted earlier:

1. Planning for the future
2. Allocating resources across the firm's various units and products
3. Identifying any potential bottlenecks in the manufacturing, purchasing, distribution, or service delivery processes
4. Coordinating sales and production as well as other activities among the various business units and divisions
5. Establishing benchmarks for performance reviews
6. Communicating the goals of the executive team to the rest of the company

There are at least two broad philosophies of how the controller and the various business units approach this budgeting task. In *traditional budgeting*, the starting point for the budgeting process is last year's numbers. However, an alternative approach, known as *zero-based budgeting*, starts each year from scratch. The benefit of zero-based budgeting is that it forces the executive team to constantly take a fresh look at all of its costs. However, this approach is also much more time-consuming and costly than traditional budgeting, so it is not universally embraced.

Let us turn now to the next set of big questions posed in Figure 8-1 above. These questions relate to perhaps the most important theme in managerial accounting known as *different costs for different purposes*.

DIFFERENT COSTS FOR DIFFERENT PURPOSES

> Do you need a variable cost, do you need a fully burdened cost, do you need overhead applied, are you just talking about discretionary cost? The cost that [you] really need depends on the decision [you] are making.
>
> A Caterpillar Inc. Executive

The idea behind the "different costs for different purposes" accountant's mantra is that costs can be measured in a number of ways. Depending on what the decision making or management control goal is, one method might be preferred to another. This very powerful idea is illustrated in Figure 8-3 and provides the organizational structure for this section. Please take a few minutes to study this figure very carefully before reading on as it provides an excellent big picture overview of this important idea.

From the figure, we see there are at least four different costs that managerial accountants typically track for a variety of purposes.[2] The first is used primarily in the *preparation of external reports* and distinguishes between *manufacturing costs* and *nonmanufacturing costs*. The second deals with the task of *predicting cost behavior* and focuses on the difference between *fixed, variable,* and so-called *mixed costs*. The third focuses on *cost allocation* and addresses the thorny issue of distributing *direct costs* and *indirect costs* over activities such as production. The fourth set of *standard costs* is used for the purpose of *management control* and *responsibility accounting*. Such standard cost analysis is particularly useful to executive teams seeking to structure employee incentives so that everyone within the organization pulls towards the same goals.

As we work our way through each of these four different costs and purposes, you should come to fully understand how powerful an effect the discipline of managerial accounting can have on the management of an organization.

---

2. There are two other "costs for decision making" that are useful to know. A *sunk cost* is a cost that has already been incurred and cannot be avoided no matter what a managerial decision is. Accordingly, they are irrelevant in analyses. In contrast, *opportunity costs are* relevant. They are the income opportunities foregone from the best available use of the resource when you use a resource for something else.

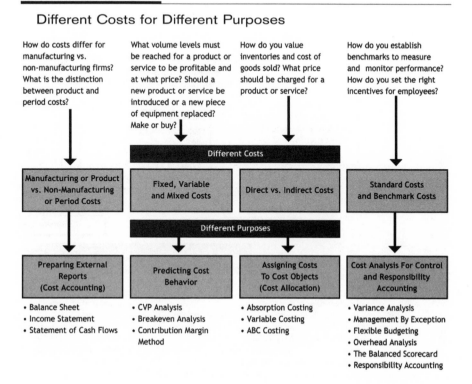

FIGURE   8-3

Different Costs for Different Purposes

Preparing External Reports: Manufacturing versus Nonmanufacturing Costs

Let us begin by looking at how an analysis of *manufacturing costs* versus *nonmanufacturing costs* helps prepare the kind of external financial reports you learned about in the previous chapter. Figure 8-4 provides a summary.

The figure shows how manufacturing costs or so-called *product costs* are carved up into labor, raw materials, and overhead costs. It also shows how *nonmanufacturing* or so-called *period costs* consist of both marketing and selling costs as well as administrative costs. Because these kinds of costs are primarily used in financial accounting, we are not going to spend much time on them but simply move on to more interesting analytical pastures.

F I G U R E   8-4

Manufacturing versus Nonmanufacturing Costs for External Reporting

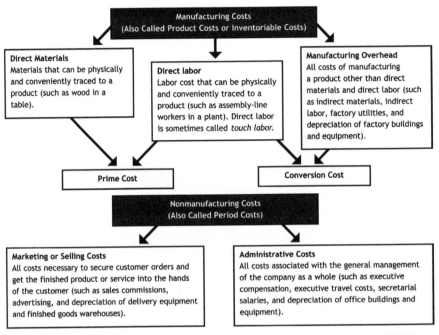

Source: Ray H. Garrison & Eric W. Noreen, *Managerial Accounting*, 10th edition, McGraw Hill/Irwin.

Predicting Cost Behavior: Fixed, Variable, and Mixed Costs

The second set—*fixed costs, variable costs*, and *mixed costs*—enables the prediction of cost behavior. This is one of the most important tasks of the managerial accountant because it helps the organization determine what volume levels of products or services must be reached for the products or services to be profitable. Note that in the analysis of cost behavior, the word *volume* is the key. That is, when we classify costs by their behavior, what we are really doing is looking at how a particular cost changes with respect to the volume driving it. Figure 8-5 illustrates the four major types of cost behavior—both fixed and variable and two types of mixed costs—*semi-variable* and the *step-function*.

F I G U R E   8-5

Four Major Types of Costs

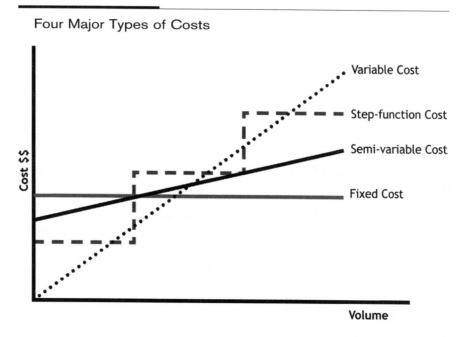

As we see in the figure, a fixed cost will not change as volume changes. The example most often used to illustrate this concept is the cost of rent. For a factory, this remains unchanged no matter what is the volume or capacity utilization. Hence the fixed cost line is perfectly horizontal; that is, it does not change with output.

At the other end of the cost spectrum, a variable cost responds in a linear manner with changes in volume, while at no volume, there are no variable costs. That is, every time another unit is produced in a manufacturing company, there is an additional variable cost associated with things like raw materials and labor.

Between these extremes, there are semi-variable costs. These have a fixed component at no volume, and then a variable component that responds to changes in volume. For example, a utility bill usually represents a semi-variable cost. There is a base cost to have service and then a charge for each unit used. Accordingly, the semi-variable cost line slopes upward, but it also intercepts the vertical axis at a value above zero.

Finally, step-function costs are fixed for shorter ranges than fixed costs. With each change in volume, they move to the next fixed level. Supervisory labor often falls into the step-function cost category.

Note that a firm's *cost structure* describes the pattern of these four types of costs, and for different kinds of industries, these patterns can vary widely. Capital-intensive firms like the airlines, utilities, and industrial metal producers have very high fixed costs, while labor-intensive service industries such as insurance, financial services, and retail businesses have very high variable costs. As to why all of this matters, at least one answer can be found in the discussion of one of the most useful tools of cost behavior analysis—cost-volume-profit analysis, CVP for short.

Cost-Volume-Profit (CVP) Analysis

Cost-volume-profit (CVP) analysis uses the cost behavior patterns we have described above to interpret and forecast changes in operating income that might result from changes in revenue, cost, or the volume of activity. One especially important application of CVP analysis is to determine the *break-even point* for a company or one of its units or products.

The key to the CVP concept is that as revenue increases as a result of selling more products or services, variable expenses will increase proportionally. However, and this is the important point, fixed costs will not increase because they are not a function of the level of volume and revenue-generating activity.

Because CVP analysis emphasizes the behavior pattern of variable costs and the impact that changes in volume may have on costs and profits, it is useful both for planning and for evaluating the actual results achieved. As an illustration, consider Snapshot Application 8-1, paying particular attention to the key concept of *contribution margin*. The contribution margin shows the funds that a given activity will contribute to an organization to cover not only fixed costs but also add to operating income. Note that for an activity to break even, its contribution margin must at least equal its fixed costs.

Cost Allocation: Direct versus Indirect Costs

The distinction between direct costs and indirect costs is made for the purpose of *cost allocation* and, more specifically, to determine the *full cost* of a particular product, service, or function.

There are numerous applications for such cost allocation, not least of which is properly valuing inventories and the cost of goods sold, and setting prices. This is important because many firms ignore full costs and unwittingly sell some of their products at too low a price and at a loss. In these cases, the company is effectively "cross-subsidizing" the losing product with profits from other products. Such companies will not remain in business for long.

When *cost accounting* uncovers such instances of cross-subsidization, one prudent managerial decision may be to increase the product's price if market conditions allow. Note that the task of price-setting is an excellent example of the synergy between the lessons of managerial economics with respect to supply and demand issues and the lessons of managerial accounting with respect to the accuracy of the data underlying the analysis.

In this particular case, if the price cannot be raised because the market is highly competitive, the executive team can discontinue the subsidized product. But such a decision cannot be made if the executive team cannot access information on the product's true cost.

Determining full costs is sometimes difficult because indirect costs such as those associated with rent, insurance, utilities, and other *overhead* can be hard to pin down. (Typically, direct costs such as labor and raw material are easier to determine.) The managerial accountant's task, then, is to properly allocate or attach indirect costs to the various products and services to determine what the full cost of production is so that prices can be set (again, subject to market conditions) to cover all costs. It is important that executives and managers focus on determining the activities that actually drive the costs.

To illustrate, consider two different products manufactured by one firm. Both are produced in the same physical plant. However, one product uses much less of the plant floor and considerably less of the plant's overall electricity needs. In such a case, you certainly would not want to divide the rent equally between the two products for cost purposes.

Absorption versus Variable Costing

When allocating costs, the managerial accountant team can typically choose between several competing methods of costing—each with its own virtues and vices. One method is called *absorption costing* or, alternatively, the *full cost method*. A second is called *variable costing, direct costing,* or *marginal costing* and omits the fixed overhead component.

SHOULD XEROX PLACE COIN-OPERATED MACHINES AND CVP ANALYSIS?

Suppose the executive team within the walk-up copy division of Xerox Corp. is considering a proposal to place coin-operated photocopying machines in public areas such as libraries, bookshops, and supermarkets. Customers will pay 5 cents per copy while the outlet providing the space will receive one-half cent per copy for a net revenue per copy of 4.5 cents.

On the cost side, Xerox will provide the outlet with the machine, service, paper, and toner. Machine costs may be treated as *fixed* because Xerox will charge its walk-up division a flat monthly fee of $185 per month for each machine. Service costs may be calculated by noting that for every 30,000 copies, there will be an average cost of $90 per service call. Paper and toner together will cost one-half cent per copy. With this data, we can lay out the variable cost per copy as follows:

Paper and toner	$0.005
Store owner	$0.005
Service ($90/30,000)	$0.003
Variable costs	$0.013

Now, the *contribution margin*, simply the *difference* between the price and variable costs per copy, may be calculated as follows:

Price	$0.050 per copy
Less variable costs	$0.013 per copy
Contribution margin	$0.037

Given the contribution margin and monthly fixed costs of $185 per machine, the number of copies each machine must sell monthly to recover costs is the ratio of fixed costs to the contribution margin. This quantity of copies is called the *break-even point* and is calculated as:

$$\text{Break-even point} = \frac{\text{Fixed costs}}{\text{Contribution margin}}$$

$$= \frac{\$185}{\$0.037} = 5,000 \text{ copies}$$

Thus, using CVP analysis, we discover that if the copier makes 5,000 copies each month, it will produce enough net revenue after variable costs to cover the fixed costs and break even. More broadly, this example illustrates how classifying costs into fixed and variable components provide a simple decision rule as to where to place the copiers. If a store is expected to produce fewer than 5,000 copies per month, a copier should not be located there. The break-even volume thus provides a useful management tool for where to place machines.

Objective	Performance Indicators	Targets
Financial Perspective:		
Efficient use of assets	Return on assets	17% per year
Grow underwriting	Premium growth	4% per year
Innovation and Learning Perspective:		
Employee training	Percent of employee hours spent in training	5% per year
Employee retention	Percent employee turnover	6% per year
Internal Business Process Perspective:		
Reduce error rates	Percent of time employees spend correcting errors	2% per year
Automate customer inquiries	Grow percent of customers logging on company website	18% per year
Customer Perspective:		
Grow market share	Increase number of under-35 insurance buyers	3% per year
Customer satisfaction	Percent of customers saying they are "very satisfied" on customer surveys	80%
Fast response to loss claims	Days to process loss claims	95% of all claims processed within three days

Source: Jerold L. Zimmerman, *Accounting for Decision Making and Control*, 4th edition, McGraw Hill.

With absorption costing, the cost of a unit of a product consists not only of the direct labor and materials and variable costs of production, but also includes an allocated share of the fixed overhead. In contrast, variable costing only considers those costs of production that vary with output such as materials, labor, and the variable portion of overhead. Thus, it contains absolutely no fixed overhead costs. The application of each method can yield dramatically different costs per unit and significantly affect managerial decisions. The slavish application of absorption costing, for instance, can lead to some rather perverse outcomes, as illustrated in Snapshot Application 8-2.

The broader point of this snapshot application is that absorption costing can obscure the true contribution of profitability of a product or customer. This problem can be particularly acute in industries such as manufacturing, metals, and autos, which are highly capital intensive and therefore have high fixed overhead. The problem can also be exacerbated by recessionary drops in the business cycle and attendant reductions in capacity utilization.

Although variable costing makes it much easier to estimate the true profitability of products or customers, many accountants prefer absorption costing because their overriding concern is to match costs to revenues. Managers, on the other hand, are looking for insights that will inform better decision making at the margins—whether to offer a new product, cancel an existing one, and so on. In that regard, however, variable costing may not be the best alternative either, especially in industries where product costs are heavily influenced along the value chain by expenditures on everything from R&D, design, and marketing to distribution and customer service costs.

S N A P S H O T   A P P L I C A T I O N   8 - 2

ABSORPTION COSTING AND PERVERSE INCENTIVES AT NORTH AMERICAN NISSAN

An automobile manufacturing company must choose between absorption costing and variable costing. If it chooses absorption costing, its executive team will seek to run the company's plants at the highest capacity possible. With the high fixed costs of these plants, the profit per unit car sold will rise significantly as the company increases its capacity utilization. By running its factories at full capacity just to "make a profit," however, the company might wind up dumping a glut of cars onto the market. As a result, the company will be forced to lower its prices, and if the price drop is greater than the unit decrease in costs from running the plant at higher capacity, profits will actually fall. This is precisely what happened to the Nissan's North America division and the likely culprit was an over-reliance on absorption costing.

Source: Ray H. Garrison and Eric W. Noreen, *Managerial Accounting*, 10th edition, McGraw Hill/Irwin, 2003.

Activity-Based Costing (ABC)

Because of the drawbacks of traditional absorption costing and as an alternative to simple variable costing, more sophisticated methods have been developed to include fixed overhead costs. One such method is *activity-based costing* (ABC).

In contrast with traditional absorption cost accounting, in which predetermined overhead rates are computed by dividing budgeted overhead costs by some measure of budgeted activity such as labor hours, ABC charges a product only for the capacity it uses. In a manufacturing context, for example, the ABC process attempts to identify the so-called *cost drivers* that consume resources on the factory floor, such as machine setups, materials handling, or quality inspections. Rather than using a single cost driver as do some of the traditional cost accounting systems, ABC looks at a variety of cost drivers and allocates overhead costs based on as many of them as are necessary to get the information desired. This is illustrated in Snapshot Application 8-3.

S N A P S H O T   A P P L I C A T I O N   8-3

ABC RESCUES DIAMOND COURIER

Claudia Post got fired from her job as a bicycle courier in Philadelphia so she started her own! Within 17 months, Diamond Courier's revenues exceeded $1 million, and that is when Claudia decided to go for the gold. She quickly diversified into truck deliveries, airfreight services, a parts-distribution service, and even a legal service that served subpoenas and prepared court filings. Within three years of opening her doors, her annual sales were over $3 million, and she employed over 100 people. The only problem was that her company was losing money!

Using an activity-based cost analysis of her basic bike delivery service, she found that the average cost of a delivery was almost ten dollars but she was charging less than five. Even more interesting, the bike delivery portion of the business, which Claudia figured was the very core of Diamond's business, generated just 10 percent of total sales and barely covered its own direct-labor and insurance costs. So what did Claudia do? She dumped the bike delivery portion of the business along with the airfreight and parts-distribution businesses, which were also money-losing, and turned the company around.

Source: Susan Greco, "Are We Making Money Yet?" Inc., July 1996.

Without question, ABC accounting provides a much more accurate picture of product costs than traditional costing methods, but it has a downside: ABC takes time and resources to implement and to maintain and the pay-off may not always justify the expense. This problem is compounded by a certain resistance to ABC in the accounting ranks of many companies, bolstered by the fact that the ABC type of analysis cannot be used externally and is not required by generally accepted accounting principles (GAAPs).

Cost Analysis for Control: Standard Costs

With the fourth set of different costs—*standard costs*—we more squarely address the primary areas of concern in *management control*:

- The determination of costs to achieve the firm's strategic, tactical, and functional goals
- The identification and acquisition of resources
- The management of costs—a key source of earnings
- The focus on performance to obtain results
- The concentration on accountability

The *standard cost–management by exception* method has a very long tradition in managerial accounting. The idea behind standard costing is to set some kind of standard statistical "norm" or *benchmark* for measuring performance and then focus on the major statistical deviations or *variances* from the norm.

In their textbook, Garrison and Noreen point out that manufacturing, service, food, and not-for-profit organizations all make use of standards to some extent. For example, auto service centers like Firestone and Sears often set specific labor time standards for installing a carburetor or doing a valve job and then measure actual performance against the standards. By the same token, fast food outlets such as McDonald's have exacting standards for the quantity of meat in Big Macs, hospitals have standards for food and laundry, and so on.

When significant variances from the benchmarks are identified, the executive team can then focus on these variations as they typically signal some type of production or service inefficiency. This is called *management by exception*, which posits that the appropriate focus of the executive team and managerial corps should only be on those parts of the organization where the strategic, tactical, or functional plans are not working smoothly. It follows from this observation that time and effort should not be wasted on areas where things are going well. Because the standard cost–management by exception approach is so widely practiced, it is worth spending a bit more time here looking into the actual details.

Setting Standard Costs and Management by Exception

Generally, managerial accountants use two kinds of standards. *Quantity standards* specify how much of an input should be used to make a product or provide the service. *Cost* or *price standards* specify how much should be paid for each unit of the input. When actual quantities or costs depart significantly from the standards, this should be a red flag to managers and warn them to investigate the discrepancy. The standards are separate because, again as Garrison and Noreen have pointed out, "...different managers are usually responsible for buying and for using inputs and these two activities occur at different points in time. It is important, therefore, that we cleanly separate discrepancies due to deviations from price standards from those due to deviations from quantity standards."

The observable differences between standard prices and actual prices and standard quantities and actual quantities are known in the accounting and statistical trades as *variances* and the process of computing and interpreting variances is called *variance analysis*. This is a form of standard cost analysis that relies on one of the key concepts you will learn about in the chapter on quantitative methods and statistics—the *standard deviation*.

Variance Analysis

Figure 8-6 illustrates a typical *statistical control chart* used in variance analysis. In the chart, you can see a solid line in the middle of the figure that represents the standard cost line, where data points have no variation from the standard cost mean. The dashed line above the mean represents one standard deviation in the favorable direction. The dashed line below the mean represents one standard deviation in the unfavorable direction.

But which of the data points dispersed throughout the statistical control chart should the executive team focus upon? The answer to that question lies in a typical rule of thumb used in variance analysis and management by exception: *Focus only on those data points that exceed one standard deviation in the unfavorable direction.*

Using this rule of thumb, the point of greatest interest in the graph would be Point A. Note, however, that the executive team might also want to

F I G U R E   8-6

A Typical Statistical Control Chart and Variance Analysis

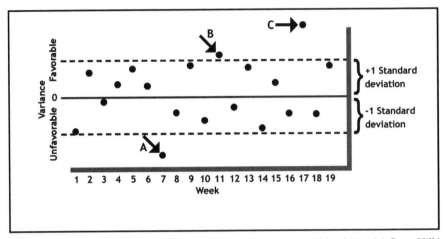

Source: Ray H. Garrison & Eric W. Noreen, *Managerial Accounting*, 10th edition, McGraw Hill/Irwin.

look at what went so very right with Points B and C to see if any lessons can be gleaned with a broader application.

Advantage and Disadvantages of the Standard Cost Approach

The standard cost approach has several advantages. The standards are usually simple to calculate and appear reasonable to employees. Standard costing also greatly simplifies book-keeping because instead of tracking unique actual costs for each and every job, standard costs can be substituted. There are some important problems worth flagging, however.

For one thing, the method typically assumes that labor costs are variable, but in some cases, labor that is committed contractually represents more of a fixed cost. In such a case, a focus on labor efficiency might lead to an inefficient buildup of inventories.

Similarly, a favorable variance might not always be favorable. For example, from a strict cost perspective, decreasing the amount of hamburger meat used in a McDonald's Big Mac might be considered a favorable variance. However, it could easily be unfavorable if it resulted in dissatisfied customers and lost revenue that dwarfed the cost savings.

Because of such problems, standard cost–variance analysis-management by exception is not considered a panacea of performance reporting in many corporations.

The Balanced Scorecard

An additional technique important in managerial accounting is the *balanced scorecard* approach. The balanced scorecard concept was developed by Robert Kaplan and David Norton, popularized in several *Harvard Business Review* articles and has been adopted by large companies like Allstate Insurance, AT&T, Citicorp, and Mobil.

A balanced scorecard comprises an integrated system of performance measures that are derived from, and support, the company's strategy. Different companies need different balanced scorecards because they have different strategies and identify for themselves different key measures. As Professor Jerold Zimmerman points out, "Some companies, such as Dell ... and McDonald's chose *operational excellence*. Others chose *customer intimacy* (Home Depot) or *product leadership* (Intel and Sony)."

Of course, the broader point, which is illustrated in Figure 8-7, is that the most successful companies will excel in one chosen dimension that is

F I G U R E   8-7

The Four Perspectives of the Balanced Scorecard

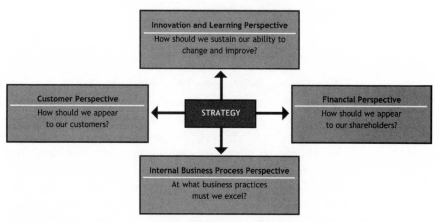

Source: Jerold L. Zimmerman, *Accounting for Decision Making and Control*, 4th edition, McGraw Hill.

consistent with their strategic focus, but will also maintain high standards on the other dimensions—that is the "balanced" part of the scorecard.

Moving clockwise in the figure, we see that an executive team that implements a balanced scorecard approach will look at its management control system from at least four different perspectives: (1) an innovation and learning perspective, (2) a financial perspective, (3) an internal business process perspective, and (4) a customer perspective.

DECENTRALIZATION AND RESPONSIBILITY ACCOUNTING

The last set of big questions and key concepts in our original Figure 8-1 addresses the topics of performance reporting and responsibility accounting. Perhaps the most important question is: How do you design management control systems that will promote the organization's strategic budgeting and profit planning goals, particularly in growing organizations that have become highly decentralized? The answer lies at least partly in the use of so-called *responsibility centers* that can hold individual business units, executives, managers, and/or employees accountable.

The ensuing discussion is merely an extension of many of the themes we raised in our analyses of different costs for different purposes. After all, one of the major purposes of managerial accounting tools like "standard costs" and "management by exception" is the measuring and monitoring of performance and the use of those results to achieve greater managerial and employee accountability.

Decentralization and Responsibility Accounting

As Garrison and Noreen have succinctly put it, "Someone must be held responsible for each cost or else no one will be responsible, and the cost will inevitably grow out of control." In smaller companies and start-ups the responsibility is relatively concentrated in a few, perhaps even one person. As companies grow and mature, however, this must give way to a more decentralized structure. As will be presented in the chapter on organizational behavior, this can take many forms—company structures can be organized around functions, divisions, matrices, or networks.

Regardless of which form of decentralization an executive team chooses, more and more decisions, by definition, will be made at layers of the organization that are further and further from the top. Such decentralization can pose significant problems if the performance of these decentralized "actors" in the business drama cannot be adequately measured and monitored. Increasingly complex performance management systems are necessary to accomplish this, and their development has been further spurred by two factors: the demand for accountability brought about by recent accounting scandals and growing concern over the cost side of the profit-generating equation.

One such system, known as *responsibility accounting*, posits that executives, managers, and employees should only be held responsible for what that they can actually control. This necessitates a view of the enterprise that segments it into responsibility centers.

Responsibility Centers

A responsibility center can be an area, function, unit, or other delineation of the enterprise for which a locus of control can be determined. The three major types are *cost centers*, *profit centers*, and *investment centers*.

In a *cost center*, managers will have control over cost but not over revenue or investment funds. Typical cost centers include service departments such as accounting, finance, general administration, legal, personnel, and so on. In such cost centers, standard cost variances such as we have already discussed are often used to evaluate the performance.

A *profit center* is any business segment in which a manager has control over both cost *and* revenue. Typically, a profit center's performance is judged on the level of net income, which, as you learned in the last chapter, is simply the difference between the revenues and expenses. Alternatively, perform-ance may be judged by comparing actual profits to those profits *targeted* in the master budget.

An *investment center* is a segment of an organization whose manager has control over costs and revenue, and investments and operating assets. Garrison and Noreen offer the example of a vice president of the truck division of General Motors who might have a good deal of discretion over investments in the division such as funding research for more fuel-efficient sport utility vehicles.

No single system will work well in every organization or even for every part of a single organization. Rather, each of the three different systems has appropriate applications depending upon the department, business unit, process, or product being evaluated. This point is illustrated in Figure 8-8,

Cost, Profit, and Investment Centers in a Typical Organization

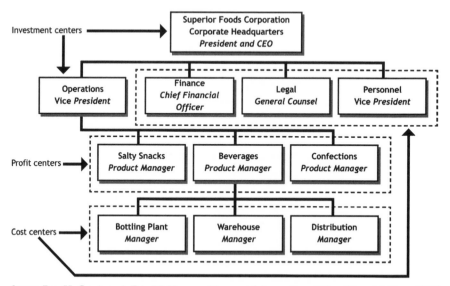

Source: Ray H. Garrison & Eric W. Noreen, *Managerial Accounting*, 10th edition, McGraw Hill/ Irwin.

which provides an example of how segments of a foods business might be classified as investment, profit, and cost centers.

Because responsibility accounting requires that managers be evaluated on only those factors they can control, a key objective is to identify what revenues and/or costs are directly traceable to a specific level of managerial responsibility and control by which managers. That type of detail on the structure of responsibility centers is an integral part of most managerial accounting courses.

CONCLUDING THOUGHTS

As Leslie Breitner, the author of the previous chapter, has observed, prior to the 1990s, the accounting profession paid little attention to the managerial accounting side of the trade. However, beginning in the 1990s, it became increasingly clear that, in a world of increasing global competition and reduced pricing power, many corporations would ultimately succeed or fail on their ability to manage and control costs. That realization brought the following tenets to the forefront of accounting research and practice:

- Costs derived for financial accounting purposes may be inappropriate for managerial decision making.
- Arbitrary means of cost allocation will not lead to optimal decision making and enhanced performance.
- The use of costs for one decision may represent an inappropriate use of costs for other decisions. Cost data must fit the question being asked! Hence, "different costs for different purposes."

This chapter has been devoted to the many useful tools and concepts that allow executives to translate the above tenets into action. Ultimately, that is what a mastery of managerial accounting—in concert with the disciplines of managerial economics, finance, marketing, organizational behavior, and strategy—is all about.

Corporate Finance—
The Big Questions and
Key Concepts

Stephen A. Ross, Randolph W. Westerfield, and Jeffrey Jaffe[*]

INTRODUCTION

Every Chief Financial Officer of every company in the world understands this immutable truth: It is impossible to grow and prosper without new capital investment. It is by undertaking such capital investment that a firm can generate new positive cash flows and thereby add value to the firm.

In fact, such capital investment and the complex "capital budgeting," "capital financing," and "cash management" decisions that underlie it can take many forms. Should your company build a new factory—or perhaps modernize an old one? Should your company buy that expensive new piece of heavy machinery or computer hardware—or simply lease it? Should your company acquire a key rival—or perhaps a key supplier?

The analytical problem underlying such capital investments is this: While investment in new productive capital costs money upfront, the investment will also generate a flow of cash over time that should more than pay for that investment. But how exactly do you value certain up-front costs against typically much more speculative future cash flows to ensure a truly profitable return? How long should you wait to realize that return? What kinds of risks might your company face that might turn what looks to be a

---

[*]Stephen A. Ross is the Franco Modigliani Professor of Financial Economics at the Sloan School of Management, Massachusetts Institute of Technology. Randolph W. Westerfield is the Dean of the Marshall School of Business at the University of Southern California. Jeffrey F. Jaffe is an Associate Professor of Finance at the Wharton School of Business at the University of Pennsylvania. This chapter is adapted from the authors' textbook *Corporate Finance*, 6th edition, Irwin-McGraw Hill.

sure winner into a big loser. How should you evaluate and price those risks? And how should all of these investments be financed—with stocks or bonds or some other credit source?

These are precisely the kinds of questions that MBA students learn to answer in their corporate finance classes. Figure 9-1 organizes these questions within the context of the big questions and key concepts of corporate finance.

LONG-TERM CAPITAL BUDGETING

Profit-maximizing corporate executives undertake capital investment to create value for shareholders. Shareholders benefit from the creation of such value in the form of a higher "total return" that consists both of dividend

---

F I G U R E   9-1

The Big Questions and Key Concepts of Corporate Finance

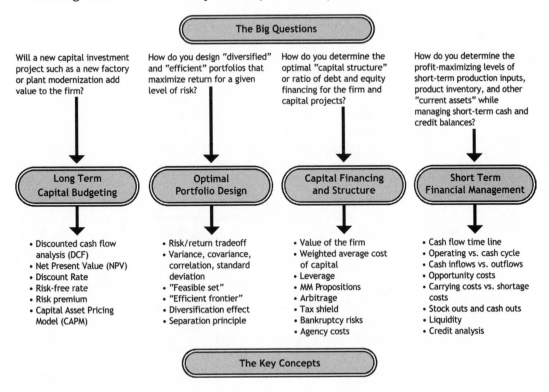

The Big Questions

| Will a new capital investment project such as a new factory or plant modernization add value to the firm? | How do you design "diversified" and "efficient" portfolios that maximize return for a given level of risk? | How do you determine the optimal "capital structure" or ratio of debt and equity financing for the firm and capital projects? | How do you determine the profit-maximizing levels of short-term production inputs, product inventory, and other "current assets" while managing short-term cash and credit balances? |

| Long Term Capital Budgeting | Optimal Portfolio Design | Capital Financing and Structure | Short Term Financial Management |

| • Discounted cash flow analysis (DCF)
 • Net Present Value (NPV)
 • Discount Rate
 • Risk-free rate
 • Risk premium
 • Capital Asset Pricing Model (CAPM) | • Risk/return tradeoff
 • Variance, covariance, correlation, standard deviation
 • "Feasible set"
 • "Efficient frontier"
 • Diversification effect
 • Separation principle | • Value of the firm
 • Weighted average cost of capital
 • Leverage
 • MM Propositions
 • Arbitrage
 • Tax shield
 • Bankruptcy risks
 • Agency costs | • Cash flow time line
 • Operating vs. cash cycle
 • Cash inflows vs. outflows
 • Opportunity costs
 • Carrying costs vs. shortage costs
 • Stock outs and cash outs
 • Liquidity
 • Credit analysis |

The Key Concepts

income and capital gains. That is why the first big question of corporate finance explores the conditions under which a new capital investment like a factory or plant modernization will add value to the firm.

To create the most value for shareholders, executives must have a way of evaluating any such proposed projects and determine their value contribution. Typically, executives must weigh the up-front costs of a capital investment against the longer run stream of cash flow benefits. This necessitates the use of a *discounted cash flow* (DCF) method that takes into account both the *time value of money* and the *risk* of the project.

Net Present Value and Discounted Cash Flow

The basic time value of money principle is that a dollar today is worth more than a dollar tomorrow. That is because if you have a dollar today, you can put it to work in a bank earning interest and have more than a dollar tomorrow.

The basic risk principle is that a *certain* dollar to an investor has more value than a speculative or *uncertain* dollar. In the context of capital budgeting, while the costs of any given project are typically incurred with certainty, the stream of cash flow benefits can only be forecast. For a variety of reasons, the *actual* cash flow stream may not meet *projections*.

Accordingly, corporate executives must account not just for *time* but for *risk* as well. The tool most commonly used to do so is that of *net present value* (NPV). The calculation of NPV is a way of distilling a stream of risky cash flow dollars over time into a single number expressed in today's dollars. Figure 9-2 provides a summary of the capital budgeting decision both in plain English and within the context of the net present value formula.

From the figure, we see that the value of a project to the firm in today's dollars equals the up-front costs of the project (a negative number) plus the stream of cash flow benefits over time period *t* appropriately adjusted or "discounted" for time and risk. We shall soon show you how to apply this formula to an actual project. For now, please simply note that in using the NPV formula, the corporate executive's decision rule is simple: *Capital budgeting projects with a negative NPV will never be considered. Capital projects with a positive NPV are candidates for capital investment but may be subject to further tests or budget constraints.* (See Snapshot Application 9-1 for a variety of ways in which companies may create positive NPV.)

The critical determinant of a project's viability is the size of the *discount rate* used to adjust cash flows for time and risk. The discount rate—one of the most important concepts in finance—may be thought of as having two

F I G U R E   9-2

The Capital Budgeting Decision and NPV Formula

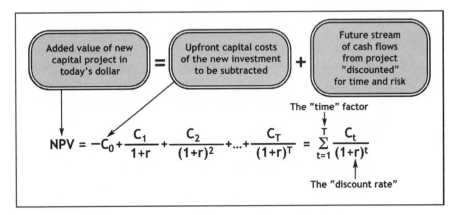

S N A P S H O T   A P P L I C A T I O N   9-1

HOW FIRMS CREATE POSITIVE NPV

Type of action	Examples
Introduce new product	Apple Corp. introduction of the first personal computer in 1976
Develop core technology	Honda's mastery of small-motor technology to efficiently produce automobiles, motorcycles, and lawn mowers
Create barrier to entry	Qualcomm patents on proprietary technology in CDMA wireless communication
Introduce variations on existing products	Chrysler's introduction of the minivan
Create product differentiation	Coca-Cola's use of advertising: "It's the real thing"
Utilize organizational innovation	Motorola's use of "Japanese management practice," including "just in time" inventory procurement, consensus decision making, and performance-based incentive systems
Exploit new technology	Yahoo! Inc.'s use of banner advertisements on the Web and the digital distribution of new services.

components. The first is the "risk-free" return that your company could earn by investing its cash in a totally safe bank savings account, a money market account, or short-term government bond. To that risk-free return we must add a "risk premium"—the additional amount of return a corporation must offer to compensate investors for the risk involved in the project.

As an unbreakable rule, *the higher the discount rate, the smaller will be the NPV of any given project and the less desirable it will be*. To understand why this is so and how the discount rate may be determined, corporate finance students typically work through a four-stage process.

The Time Value of Money in a One-Period Framework

Suppose (fictional) landowner Dudley Trump is trying to sell a nice piece of lakefront property in Alaska (replete with moose) and just yesterday he was offered $10,000 for the property. However, just before he was about to call the buyer and accept the offer, another prospective buyer offered him a lot more—$11,424 to be exact. The catch, however, is that the second buyer will not pay Dudley for a year—although we hasten to add here that the payment will be absolutely certain so there is no risk of default.

Dudley does not have a clue as to how to evaluate these two offers so he gives his financial advisor and MBA graduate Grace Goodheart a call. Grace quickly points out that if Dudley takes the first offer of the ten grand, he can invest it in the bank at an insured and therefore certain rate of 12 percent. That means at the end of the year or "period" in this one-period example, Dudley would have $11,200, which is simply the $10,000 times the 12 percent interest rate. Because this is less than the $11,424 offered by the second buyer, Grace urges Dudley to take the second offer.

That is pretty sound thinking, but let us look just a little deeper into exactly what Grace has done in terms of applying a critical MBA concept. Specifically, she has used the concept of *future value* or *compound value*, which is the value of a sum after investing over one or more periods. In this example, the future or compound value of $10,000 is $11,200.

Now, let us flip Grace's analysis over and look at it from the perspective of something called the *present value* of a future sum. This can be determined by answering this kind of question: How much money must Dudley put in the bank today in order to have $11,424 next year? In fact, we can use some easy algebra to write this question as follows:

$$PV \times 1.12 = \$11{,}424 \quad \text{or rewriting} \quad PV = \frac{\$11{,}424}{1.12} = \$10{,}200$$

Writing this formula more generally, we have:

$$PV = \frac{C_1}{(1+r)}$$

where C_1 is the cash received at the end of the one period and r is the appropriate interest rate or *discount rate*.

Now what this *present value analysis* tells us in our example is that a future payment of $11,424 from the second buyer next year has a present value of $10,200 this year. Because this is more than the $10,000 offer of the first buyer, this analysis informs Dudley that he is better off taking the second offer—at least if the interest rate or "discount rate" is 12 percent.

Next, we will consider a more realistic example to refine the concept of present value into the more readily applicable tool of *net present value* or NPV.

Net Present Value Without Risk

Consider the case of Rolem Dice, a financial analyst at real estate firm Kaufman & Broad who has found a piece of land selling for $85,000—that is the up-front capital cost. Rolem is also absolutely certain that the property can be sold next year for $91,000—that is the future payment. This proposed transaction is illustrated in a typical corporate finance tool—the *cash flow schematic* in Figure 9-3.

From the figure, you can see that the deal nets a certain profit of $6,000, so this seems like a good investment. But is it? Let us answer that question by assuming a risk-free discount rate of 10 percent—that is the current rate of interest offered at the bank. Using the PV formula, the present value of the future sales price of $91,000 calculates to be:

$$\text{Present value} = \frac{\$91,000}{1.10} = \$82,727.27$$

With this information, apply the NPV formula as follows:

$$-\$2,273 = -\$85,000 \quad + \quad \frac{\$91,000}{1.10}$$

(Cost of land today)   (Present value of next year's sales price)

Because the net present value is negative, Rolem Dice will recommend *not* purchasing the land. Note also from this example that the formula for NPV can be written as:

$$NPV = -\text{Cost} + PV$$

F I G U R E   9-3

Cash Flows for Roland's Land Deal

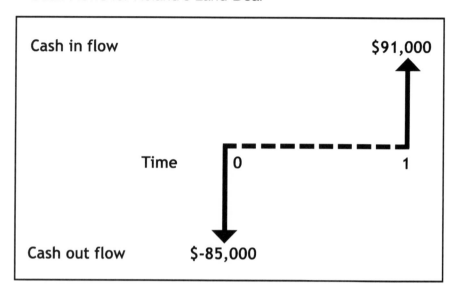

Compare this much-simplified version to the NPV formula in Figure 9-2. The comparison may help you hone your intuitive grasp of this key concept.

Net Present Value in a Multiperiod Framework With Risk

Now let us generalize the NPV approach to a "multiperiod" framework. As we do so, we can also illustrate how uncertainty over the actual receipt of the expected cash flow and a higher assumed discount rate changes the NPV calculation.

Assume, then, that the Super Tech Semiconductor Company is considering the construction of a new fabrication plant at an up-front cost of $100 million dollars. Based on market projections, the executive team expects the plant to generate a cash flow of $10 million in the first year, $20 million in the second year, $30 million in the third year, $40 million for the fourth year, and $50 million for the last year. For a $100 million upfront, Super Tech will collect a whopping $150 million within five years. That *must* be a great investment. Right?

Of course, if we dig just a bit deeper, the analysis becomes much more vexing. For starters, Super Tech faces a time value of money problem because a good part of the projected cash flows come in the "out years" of the project—years three through five. This pales, however, in comparison to the risk of its new fabrication plant gambit.

Indeed, the semiconductor industry is highly cyclical. That means that in bad economic times, the cash flow might be substantially less. Moreover, the semiconductor industry is notorious for overbuilding fabrication capacity and depressing prices with oversupply so that even in good times, the company may fall short of its cash flow projections.

To illustrate NPV in a multiperiod frame accounting for risk, first calculate the NPV for the project using the formula from Figure 9-2 under the very restrictive assumption that the project entails zero risk. Again assuming a risk-free rate of 10 percent, here is the NPV in a case where we have five periods of time:

$$\text{NPV} = -(\$100) + \frac{\$10}{(1+0.05)} + \frac{\$20}{(1+0.05)^2} + \frac{\$30}{(1+0.05)^3}$$

$$+ \frac{\$40}{(1+0.05)^4} + \frac{\$50}{(1+0.05)^5} = \$25.66$$

Since this NPV is positive under the assumptions given, Super Tech should build the plant—and will add a little more than $25 million in value to the firm by doing so.

But now look at how this calculation might change if risk enters the picture. As a first pass, to account for risk, we can simply *assume* a higher discount rate— let us say 15 percent. We assume such a higher rate because, as we noted earlier, an investor in a risky project is going to demand a "risk premium" over and above the risk-free rate he or she could earn in a bank or short-term Treasury note. In this case, the risk-free rate is 10 percent, the risk premium is 5 percent, the assumed discount rate is therefore 15 percent and the NPV is:

$$\text{NPV} = -(\$100) + \frac{\$10}{(1+0.15)} + \frac{\$20}{(1+0.15)^2} + \frac{\$30}{(1+0.15)^3}$$

$$+ \frac{\$40}{(1+0.15)^4} + \frac{\$50}{(1+0.15)^5} = -\$8.73$$

You can immediately see that in this case, Super Tech would *not* undertake the project—*it loses almost $9 million in value to the firm.* This again underscores the importance of the choice of the appropriate discount rate in valuing a project.

In fact, choosing the appropriate risk-adjusted discount rate is one of the most difficult tasks facing business executives. In our example thus far, we took the easy way out—we simply guessed what it might be. But rather than 15 percent, it might really be 20 percent or 25 percent or even 30 percent. So how do corporate executives actually calculate the true discount rate? The most common way is to use one of the most important and powerful tools of finance—the *"capital asset pricing model"* or CAPM.

The CAPM–The Investor's Perspective

To truly understand the CAPM, we must come at the capital budgeting problem from an entirely different perspective—not the corporate executive's point of view, but the investor's. It is with this change in perspective that the subject of corporate finance becomes considerably more interesting—not just to corporate executives trying to build a profitable company, but also to investment bankers, portfolio managers, and financial planners trying to make money in the stock and bond markets.

The precise question we are going to pose now is whether the company's proposed investment is going to increase or decrease the company's stock price. Put simply, if investors believe the project will *add* value to the firm by generating a positive NPV, the company's stock price should rise, holding all other things constant. But if investors believe the project will *subtract* value from the firm, the stock price should fall. Why?

One of the most important tenets of corporate finance is that, at any point in time, *a company's stock price reflects an expectation of a future stream of earnings*. It follows that if some news about a proposed capital project becomes available to market participants that changes expectations, the stock price must change. Snapshot Application 9-2 illustrates this dynamic using a real world example involving AT&T. After you review this snapshot application, we will turn to the nuts and bolts of the capital asset pricing model (CAPM).

The CAPM Equation

Figure 9-4 depicts the equation for the CAPM. We will now explore each of its elements and underlying concepts. On the left-hand side of the equation, we have the expected return on a security. In fact, this is the discount rate for equity capital that we are seeking to estimate. What the model says is that this expected return may be calculated by adding the risk-free rate to the difference between the expected return on the broad market and the risk-free rate times the *beta* of the security.

S N A P S H O T   A P P L I C A T I O N   9-2

THE STOCK MARKET VALUES AN AT&T CAPITAL INVESTMENT

One of AT&T's numerous attempts to penetrate the computer-manufacturing industry helps illustrate how the stock market values such capital investments. On December 6, 1990, the telecommunications giant made a $90 per share or $6.12 billion cash offer for all of NCR Corporation's common stock. Within five days, the value of AT&T's stock dropped roughly $1 billion. Five months later, when these firms finally agreed to a deal, AT&T's stock dropped again.

Why did the stock market reaction suggest that the NCR acquisition was a negative NPV investment for AT&T? It is a very good question because AT&T's executive team thought just the opposite. This executive team was apparently convinced that the telecommunications and computer industries were becoming one industry. The thinking was that since telephone switches are big computers, success in computers must mean success in telephones.

The stock market apparently saw it a different way. Making computers is essentially a manufacturing business and telephone communications service business. The core competency of making computers that NCR possessed—efficient manufacturing—is therefore quite different from that of providing telecommunications service support and software for business.

Of course, even if AT&T had acquired NCR for the "right" reasons, it is possible that it paid too much. The negative stock market reaction suggests that AT&T shareholders believed that NCR was worth less than its cost to AT&T.

From this example, we see that the stock market does indeed react to corporate news by reassessing stock prices. This suggests that *the stock market can actually be quite useful to corporate executives in helping them to evaluate the desirability of proposed capital investments*. This is a very important point often ignored by short-sighted executives.

The even broader point is that it is ultimately the stock market that determines the cost of equity capital for a publicly traded company by the manner in which it evaluates the shares of that company. The market does so by processing information in such a way as to yield a very solid answer to that enduring question: How risky is a particular company and what should be its discount rate for its new capital projects?

The Realized Return

We know what the *risk-free rate* is. It is the rate you can earn in a short-term Treasury note with certainty. What we do not yet know is how risk is defined

---

F I G U R E   9-4

The Capital Asset Pricing Model (CAPM)

$$\overline{R} \quad = \quad R_F \quad + \quad \beta \quad \times \quad (\overline{R}_M - R_F)$$

| Expected return on a security | = | Risk-free rate | + | Beta of the security | × | Difference between expected return on market and risk-free rate |

by the difference between a security's *expected return* and its *realized return*. For the holding of a stock, the *realized return* in any given year consists of two components: (1) the dividend income generated by the stock and (2) the *capital gain* or *capital loss* one might incur while holding the stock.

To illustrate this, suppose at the beginning of the year, you purchased 100 shares of stock in the Defensive Staple Company for $37 a share. This fictional pharmaceutical company produces a number of popular over-the-counter medicines—from aspirin to antacids. Over the course of the year that you held the stock, the company paid you a dividend of $1.85 per share, for a total of $185 on your 100 shares. Moreover, at the end of the year, suppose you sold—or could have sold—the stock for $40.33. That nets you a capital gain of $333 [100($40.33 − $37.00)].

To find the realized return on your investment, you can first calculate the dividend yield. This is simply the dividend income divided by the purchase price, or 5 percent. Then, you calculate the percentage capital gain, which is simply the capital gain divided by the purchase price, or 9 percent. Thus, the total realized return is 14 percent.

The Expected Return and Risk-Free Rate

The *expected return* of a security is just that. It is what investors believe that the realized rate of return will be at the end of the relevant period, typically a year. Of course, the expected return of a security can differ significantly from the realized return and that is the very essence of risk.

As can be seen in Figure 9-4 above, this expected return includes the risk-free rate of return, which appears as the first term on the right side of the equation. However, it also includes a *risk premium* embodied in the second set of terms.

Systematic and Unsystematic or Diversifiable Risk

The unanticipated part of the return—that portion resulting from surprises—is the true risk of any investment. After all, if we got what we had expected, there would be no risk and no uncertainty. There are important differences, however, among various sources of risk, and it is useful to divide such risk into two components: *systematic risk* and the remainder, which is called alternatively *diversifiable, idiosyncratic*, or *unsystematic risk*.

A systematic risk is any risk that affects a large number of assets, each to a greater or lesser degree. Uncertainty about general economic conditions, such as GNP, interest rates, or inflation is an example of systematic risk because these types of conditions affect nearly all stocks to some degree. For example, an unanticipated or surprise increase in inflation affects wages and the costs of the supplies that companies buy. It also affects the value of the assets that companies own, and the prices at which companies sell their products.

In this macroeconomic context, systematic risk may be thought of as the risk associated with investing in the broad financial markets, for example, buying an index fund for the S&P 500. The nature of such risk is primarily cyclical. As the business cycle moves upward in an expansionary mode, the returns to the market tend to be considerably higher than the returns earned during downturns in the business cycle. Invariably, the years of negative returns occur during economic recessions or, in the case of the late 1920s and early 1930s, the Great Depression.

In contrast, unsystematic risk represents the unanticipated part of a company's return resulting from surprises unrelated to the overall market return. It is a risk that specifically affects a single asset or a small group of assets. For example, the announcement of a small oil strike by a company may very well affect the company alone or a few other companies. However, such a small strike is unlikely to have any effect on world oil markets. Similarly, a biotech firm may face the risk of failed clinical trials for a new drug, a manufacturing firm may have one of its patents successfully challenged in court, and all firms face the risk of losing market share and profits from competition from other firms in their industry.

To stress that such information is unsystematic and affects only specific companies, it is, as we have already noted, sometimes called idiosyncratic risk. Note that the distinction between systematic and unsystematic risk is never as exact as we make it out to be. Even the most narrow and peculiar bit of news about a company ripples through an economy. By subdividing risk into its two component parts, however, we are able to make two very important points: (1) unsystematic risk can be diversified away in a portfolio; and (2) the remaining systematic risk can be measured by the *beta* using the *capital asset pricing model.*

The Beta

If the stock price of a company rises faster than the broad market in good times and falls faster than the broad market in bad times, that company is said to be riskier than an investment in the broad market. These companies will have a beta greater than one. Betas above one represent high systematic risk, reflecting greater "volatility" than the market. Such a description might fit companies in highly cyclical sectors like technology.

Alternatively, if the stock price of a company rises more slowly than the broad market in good times and falls more slowly in bad times, that company is less risky than an investment in the broad market and will have a beta *less* than one, representing low systematic risk. Such a description might fit companies in noncyclical "defensive" sectors like food, drugs, and beverages.

To illustrate, suppose that financial analysts believe that there are four likely states of the economy: depression, recession, normal expansion, and boom. In that context, we are considering buying the stock of two different companies—the now familiar Super Tech and Defensive Staple. As Super Tech operates in the highly cyclical semiconductor industry, its returns are expected to follow the economy closely. On the other hand, because Defensive Staple provides products that people need in good times and bad, its returns are expected to be much more noncyclical. In the four scenarios simulated by the financial analysts, the expected returns for the two companies are displayed in Table 9-1.

Note several things about the table. First, the realized returns of Super Tech tend to be both higher in good times and lower in bad times and therefore much more volatile. Second, the realized returns of the two companies sometimes move in *opposite* directions. These two effects—volatility and co-movements—are known in the parlance of statistics as *variance* and *covariance.*

Note that a *positive* relationship or covariance between the two securities *increases the variance of the entire portfolio.* That is not a good thing if you are looking to diversify your risk. On the other hand, a *negative* relationship or covariance between the two securities *decreases* the variance—and the risk—of the entire portfolio.

T A B L E   9-1

The Expected Returns of Super Tech versus Defensive Staple

	Super Tech Expected Returns(%)	Defensive Staple Expected Returns (%)
Depression	−20	5
Recession	10	20
Normal	30	−12
Boom	50	9

This important result seems to square with common sense. If one of your securities tends to go up when the other goes down, or vice versa, your two securities are offsetting each other. You are achieving what is called a *hedge* in finance, and the risk of your entire portfolio will be lower. However, if both your securities rise and fall together, you are not hedging at all! Hence, the risk of your entire portfolio will be higher.

This concept of hedging is important because one way to diversify nonsystematic stock market risk will be to invest in the stocks of companies in different industry sectors. For example, an investor who holds Super Tech and another company in the same semiconductor sector generally will be less diversified than an investor who holds one stock in one sector like chips and another stock like Defensive Staple in a sector like drugs.

The broader point here is that the variance of a portfolio depends on *both* the variances of the individual securities *and* the covariance between the two securities. That means that, in seeking a diversified portfolio, an investor ultimately cares about the *contribution* of each security to the expected return and risk of the portfolio—that is, the systematic risks.

Mathematically, the beta may be expressed this way:

$$\beta_i = \frac{\text{Cov}(R_i, R_M)}{\sigma^2(R_M)}$$

This means the beta of asset i is the covariance between the return of the asset i (which we take here to mean an individual stock) and the return on the broad market, divided by the variance σ^2 of the broad market. *Intuitively, all this formula says is that the risk of holding any individual stock is a function of its relationship to movements in the broad market and other stocks!*

Figure 9-5 is a graphic description of the CAPM. It illustrates one of the most famous figures in corporate finance—the so-called *security market line* as it is defined by the beta. This figure captures the relationship between the expected return on an individual security and the beta of that security as calculated by the CAPM. Note that the vertical axis measures the expected return on the security, the horizontal axis provides the beta, and the upward sloping security market line (SML) is a graphic depiction of the capital asset

F I G U R E   9-5

The Security Market Line and Beta

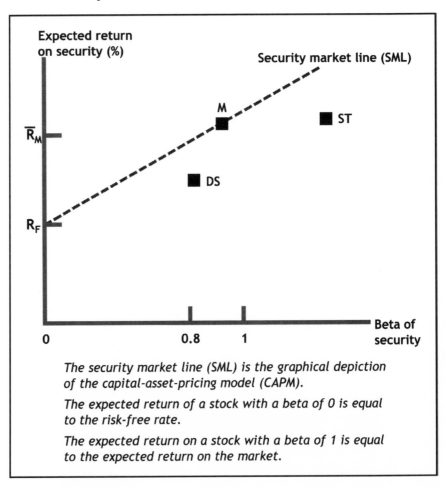

The security market line (SML) is the graphical depiction
of the capital-asset-pricing model (CAPM).

The expected return of a stock with a beta of 0 is equal
to the risk-free rate.

The expected return on a stock with a beta of 1 is equal
to the expected return on the market.

pricing model. Note that Super Tech (ST) has a beta significantly higher than one while the beta of Defensive Staple (DS) is less than one.

Observe now that the SML slopes upward. This reflects two assumptions. The first is that the expected return on investing in the stock market will be higher than the risk-free rate—an assumption, by the way, supported by the fact that the average return on the market portfolio for more than 70 years has been 9.5 percent above the risk-free rate. The second is that if beta is an appropriate measure of risk, high-beta securities should have an expected return above that of low-beta securities.

To summarize, we can say that the contribution of a security to the risk of a large, well-diversified portfolio is proportional to the covariance of the security's return with the market's return. This contribution, when standardized, is called the beta. The beta of a security can therefore be characterized as the responsiveness of its return to that of the market. Although there is much more heavy mathematical lifting in actual MBA finance classes, it should nonetheless be intuitively clear that CAPM can be used to calculate the cost of capital or discount rate needed to make capital budgeting decisions. It is simply the expected return based on the beta of the company's security.

Finally, please note that while the CAPM is part of the bread and butter of corporate finance, it has weaknesses. That is why there are important alternative models used to estimate the cost of capital such as the *Arbitrage Pricing Theory* model.

THE OPTIMAL PORTFOLIO FOR THE INDIVIDUAL INVESTOR

We now turn to the second big question of corporate finance: How do you design "diversified" and "efficient" portfolios that maximize return for a given level of risk?

For any given investment, there is a trade-off between the expected return from that investment and the possible risk of failing to achieve that return. Investors will choose some combination of assets that maximizes their expected return for a given level of risk.

The Opportunity Set

The first task of constructing the optimal portfolio is defining the *opportunity set* or *feasible set* of investments that can be chosen. Examining, for simplicity's sake, an all-equity opportunity set comprising just two companies—Super Tech and Defensive Staple—Figure 9-6 illustrates the different combinations of the stocks investors can hold. The figure's vertical axis represents *expected returns*. That is the reward we are seeking. The horizontal axis shows the *standard deviation* of the portfolio's return. This is the measure of risk, and it is simply the square root of the portfolio's variance.

Point A indicates a portfolio consisting entirely of the stock of the relatively less risky Defensive Staple. It has a low expected return of 5.5 percent and a collateral measure of risk of 11.50. In contrast, Point B indicates a portfolio consisting of the much more risky Super Tech. This higher risk is indicated both by a much higher standard deviation of 25.86 and an expected return more than *triple* that of Defensive Staple.

FIGURE   9-6

The Optimal Portfolio in a Two-Stock World

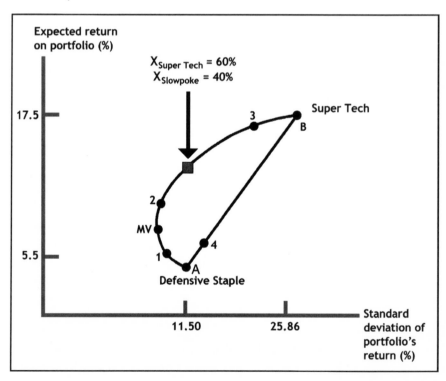

The straight line between Point A and B is drawn under the assumption that the correlation between Super Tech and Defensive Staple is exactly one. In other words, the returns of the two companies move in lockstep. As a practical matter, that means there can be no benefits from diversifying one's holding between the two stocks—or no *diversification effect*.

The curve above the straight line reflects the assumption of a negative correlation between the returns of the two companies. (In this example, we calculate it to be -0.1639.) This negative value means, of course, that the returns of these two companies tend to move in opposite directions so that there will be a *diversification effect* and an opportunity to *hedge*. The points along the curve offer the best combinations of expected return in exchange for anticipated risk. This is the *efficient frontier* for this portfolio.

The Diversification Effect and Efficient Frontier

To fully understand the diversification effect, compare points 1 and 4 in the figure. In both cases, these points represent a portfolio consisting of 90 percent Defensive Staple and 10 percent Super Tech. However, point 1 assumes a diversification effect and point 4 does not.

Moving up the curve from point 1, there is a point marked "MV" for *minimum variance*. This represents the combination of the two stocks that yields the *lowest possible risk*. Interestingly, in this example, MV lies to the left of Point A—between those two points the curve is actually "backward bending." This means that Defensive Staple is a very low risk security, and an investor can actually further reduce risk exposure by selling some of that stock and replacing it with the much higher risk Super Tech! This is the *diversification effect* in all of its glory, and it is one of the most important conclusions in corporate finance!

Finally, note that no investor would want to hold a portfolio with an expected return less than the minimum variance portfolio. For example, no investor would choose portfolio 1 even though it is feasible and on the efficient frontier. Such portfolios are said to be *dominated* by the minimum variance portfolio. That is, although the entire curve from Defensive Staple to Super Tech is called the feasible set, only the portion of the curve from MV to Super Tech constitutes the true *efficient frontier*.

In MBA classes, students learn to generalize this analysis to a more realistic set of assumptions. They also learn about the last key concept concerning the construction of the optimal portfolio, the so-called *separation principle.* According to this principle, the investment decision is actually a two-step process in which the investor first calculates the efficient set of risky assets and then blends a particular portfolio of those assets with risk-free assets, such as Treasury securities, based on his or her level of *risk aversion.*

There is also much more MBA students learn about the mathematical and statistical relationships between concepts like the variance, covariance, correlation, and standard deviations as well as the very important relationship between unsystematic risk and diversification. However, your key takeaway point here is that by learning how to appropriately value capital budgeting projects, you also learn how to build portfolios of financial assets in a way that minimizes risk for a given expected reward.

CAPITAL FINANCING AND CAPITAL STRUCTURE

We turn now to the third big question of corporate finance: How do you determine the optimal *capital structure* or ratio of debt and equity financing for the firm and its capital projects? Let us begin with an examination of capital structure.

Capital Structure

Suppose that Super Tech's corporate executive team has used DCF analysis to value an investment in a new semiconductor fabrication plant, and the project has gotten the positive NPV green light. Super Tech's CFO must now figure out how to pay for that project in such a way as to maximize the value of the firm. The CFO's decision will depend upon two key concepts: the *value of the firm* and the *weighted average cost of capital.*

The first concept is really an equation. It says that the value V of any company such as Super Tech may be written as:

$$V = D + E$$

where D equals the value of the bonds issued by the firm and E is the value of the firm's equity or stock. As profit-maximizers, the corporate executive team must choose a *debt-to-equity ratio*—that is, some combination of bond- and equity-financing—that maximizes the value of *V.*

Note that companies in different sectors tend to systematically favor different capital structures. For example, industry sectors such as building construction, hotels and lodging, and air transport all favor higher debt-to-equity ratios and rely heavily on bond-financing to fuel growth. On the other hand, companies in the drug and chemical, electronics computer sectors tend to avoid heavy leverage, preferring instead to fuel their capital investment needs primarily by issuing new stock. What might account for these radically different and apparently *systematic* capital structures across different sectors of the economy? The answer to this intriguing question lies at the very heart of corporate finance. To answer it, we must first define the *weighted average cost of capital* and then acquaint ourselves with the famous "M&M Propositions."

The Weighted Average Cost of Capital

Up to now, we have focused only on the cost of equity capital, which we learned to estimate using the CAPM model. However, since real world companies use both debt and equity, we must expand our definition of the cost of capital to include that of debt financing and introduce the weighted average cost of capital. This may be expressed as:

$$r_{WACC} = \frac{S}{S+B} r_S + \frac{B}{S+B} r_B (1 - T_C)$$

where r_{WACC} is the weighted average cost of capital and r_S is the cost of stockholders' equity. Ignoring taxes, the cost of debt is simply the borrowing rate r_B. However, with corporate taxes, the appropriate cost of debt is $(1 - T_C)$ r_B, where T_C is the tax rate. S and B represent the market values for the stocks and bonds of the firm. Finally, the "weight" for equity is $S/(S + B)$ while the debt ratio is $B/(S + B)$. Thus, for example, if the cost of equity, r_S, is 15 percent, the weight for equity is 50 percent, the cost of debt, r_B, is 5 percent, the debt ratio is 50 percent, and the tax rate is zero, then r_{WACC} equals 10 percent.

As a rule, the cost of debt capital is less than that of equity because debt tends to be less risky. This is primarily because, under corporate law, bondholders take precedence over stockholders when it comes to claims on the firm's assets. Bondholders always get their interest payments first. Only if there is cash left over will shareholders get their dividends. Moreover, if the firm goes bankrupt and is liquidated, bondholders must be compensated before stockholders.

The M&M Propositions

Because debt capital is cheaper, finance scholars originally believed that it was better to rely on it for financing needs. That was, however, until the

1950s when two Nobel laureate economists, Franco Modigliani and Merton Miller, first articulated a set of theoretical propositions, known as the *M&M Propositions*.

- *Proposition I*: In the absence of taxes or the consideration of bankruptcy costs, the value of the unlevered firm is the same as the levered firm.
- *Proposition II*: A firm cannot lower its weighted average cost of capital by increasing its debt load—even though the cost of debt is lower than that of equity.

Note that these two propositions imply something quite startling, namely that the value of the firm is *independent* of capital structure. Therefore, it does not matter what capital structure managers choose; this can have no impact on the value of the firm!

As for how Modigliani and Miller came to such a conclusion, let us take the propositions one at a time, starting with the perhaps more intuitive Proposition II. The argument here is that as a firm becomes more levered, the returns to equity holders become more risky because bondholders have first claim on the cash flow. Thus, the benefits of a lower cost of debt will be offset by increases in the cost of equity. Interestingly, the proposition predicts that costs will *exactly* offset the benefits.

The first proposition is perhaps less intuitive. It rests on a so-called *arbitrage* argument. Here is the logic of it via a well-known example.

Consider a dairy farmer faced with the choice of either selling milk whole, or skimming it and selling both cream and low-fat milk. If he can sell the cream at a substantially higher price than whole milk and the low-fat milk at an only slightly lower price, he may well experience a net gain from the separation.

In such a case, however, we would expect arbitrageurs to step in and buy the whole milk, perform the skimming operation themselves, and resell the cream and low-fat milk separately. The result would be increased competition among the arbitrageurs to obtain the whole milk, and the price would be bid to the point where separation was no longer more profitable.

In a capital structure context, the arbitrage process envisioned by Modigliani and Miller involves consumers using *homemade leverage* to undo the effects of corporate leverage. They do so by buying or selling shares of the stock using borrowed funds, that is, by buying stocks "on margin."

The Problem With the M&M Propositions

In the center lane of life where theory often crashes into reality, the original M&M propositions faced a very real problem. Unfortunately, they neither predicted nor explained the systematic differences in capital structure one observes across different industry sectors that we alluded to earlier. Indeed, the propositions imply that such variations are the result of random decisions by managers rather than logical, value-maximizing choices. Modigliani and Miller bridged this gap between theory and reality by taking into account the effects of both taxes and bankruptcy costs.

The Tax Shield

Under the corporate tax law in the United States, the Internal Revenue Service treats interest payments going to bondholders differently than it does earnings going to stockholders. Indeed, *interest on debt totally escapes corporate taxation*—it is directly expensed. In contrast, earnings after the deduction of interest are taxed, for example, at a 35 percent rate. The result of this tax shield for interest is that by increasing leverage, business executives can increase the value of the firm. This is illustrated in Figure 9-7.

This figure shows that because the levered firm pays less in taxes than does the all-equity firm, the sum of the debt plus the equity of the levered firm is greater than the equity of the unlevered firm. This leads us back to our point of intuitive origin: because debt is cheaper (albeit this time through a tax shield effect), the value of the firm will be maximized only if it is completely levered.

While this theory seems to comport better with reality, it does not quite get at the whole story. Indeed, there must be some constraints on high leverage because, the superiority of debt financing notwithstanding, we never observe completely leveraged firms. Why? The answer lies in such factors as *bankruptcy risks* and so-called *agency costs* that act as a brake or constraint on leverage.

The Bankruptcy and Agency Costs Brake

In the case of *bankruptcy risk*, the higher the leverage of the firm, the greater its fixed obligations to service its debt. Thus, for example, in any kind of industrial sector in which sales revenue and earnings are highly cyclical, the highly or completely levered firm runs the high risk of encountering a recessionary patch in which it will not have the cash flow to pay its debts. That, in turn, means that as the firm approaches 100 percent leverage, its cost

F I G U R E   9–7

Two Pie Models of Capital Structure Under Corporate Taxes

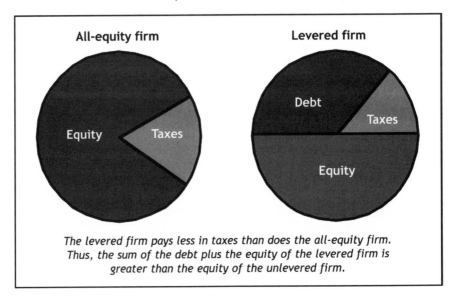

*The levered firm pays less in taxes than does the all-equity firm.
Thus, the sum of the debt plus the equity of the levered firm is
greater than the equity of the unlevered firm.*

of debt rises to a point where using additional debt financing is no longer optimal. As a practical matter, this means that debt capital grows ever more risky and expensive as any firm becomes more levered—thereby discouraging its use after a certain point.

In addition to bankruptcy risks, there are so-called *agency costs*. When a firm has debt, conflicts of interest can arise between stockholders and bondholders. Because of this, stockholders, as represented by corporate managers, may be tempted to pursue selfish strategies at the expense of bondholders. Leverage, in this context, is important because it can provide perverse incentives for managers to take large risks or under-invest or "milk the property." Each of these actions makes debt financing more risky, thereby increasing its costs and reducing its use.

Modigliani and Miller amended their propositions to take into account the tax shield as well as the risks of bankruptcy and agency costs:

* *Proposition I*: Since corporations can deduct interest payments but not dividend payments, corporate leverage lowers tax payments.

♦ *Proposition II*: The cost of equity rises with leverage because the risk to equity rises with leverage.

As it turns out, the revised propositions go a long way towards explaining systematic differences in the capital structures of different firms.

SHORT-TERM CASH FLOW MANAGEMENT

Our fourth and final big question of corporate finance moves from longer term issues of capital budgeting, portfolio design, and capital financing to short-term financial management. The overarching question is this: How do you determine the profit-maximizing levels of short-term production inputs, product inventory, and to other "current assets" while managing short-term cash and credit balances? Typically, these short-term decisions involve cash flows within a year or less and revolve around more specific questions such as:

♦ How much raw material and how much inventory of other "production inputs" should be kept on hand for the production process?

♦ What should be the target level of inventory on hand to meet product demand?

♦ What is a reasonable level of cash to keep on hand in the bank to pay bills?

♦ Should cash or credit terms be offered and how much credit should be extended to customers?

♦ How (and how fast) should cash be collected?

The Operating Cycle and the Cash Cycle

To begin to answer these questions, we must distinguish between the *operating cycle* of a firm and its *cash cycle*. This is because the firm's short-run operating activities create patterns of cash inflows and cash outflows that are both *unsynchronized* and *uncertain*.

They are unsynchronized because the payments of cash for raw material does not happen at the same time as the receipt of cash from selling the product. They are uncertain because both future sales and costs are not known with certainty to the management team. The result, as we shall now see in Figure 9-8, is that a company can face "gaps" between short-run cash

F I G U R E   9-8

The Cash Flow Time Line and Short-Term Operating Activities of a Typical Manufacturing Firm

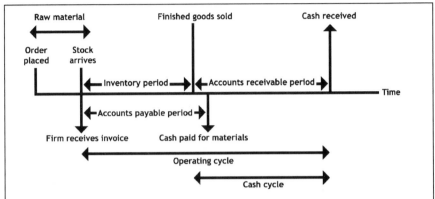

The *operating cycle* is the time period from the arrival of stock until the receipt of cash. (Sometimes the operating cycle is defined to include the time from placement of the order until arrival of the stock.) The *cash cycle* begins when cash is paid for materials and ends when cash is collected from receivables.

outflows and inflows that create the need for short-term financial management.

The figure shows the short-term operating activities and cash flows of a typical manufacturing firm depicted along a *cash flow time line*. In the figure, any "gap" between the cash inflows and cash outflows creates the need for short-term financial planning.

Note that a company can fill such gaps either by borrowing or holding a liquidity reserve for marketable securities. Perhaps more importantly, the executive team can shorten the gap by changing its policies regarding the amount of raw materials purchased, the inventory held, and/or the length of the accounts payable and receivable periods.

Choosing the Tools and Tactics

As for how executives actually go about the business of choosing just what to do in each of these areas, well, that is where our next important tool of corporate finance comes in. As a prelude to introducing this tool, allow us to observe that in virtually every field in business, you will encounter some type of figure or graph or set of equations that illustrate how to "optimize" the relevant decision at hand based on a calculus that weighs the costs of a particular policy against its benefits.

In the field of economics, for example, such "cost–benefit" analysis can be used to examine important public policy issues such as the level of defense spending and environmental protection. In corporate finance, we can use a similar type of analysis to examine all three of the major policies of short-term finance—those regarding the level of *current assets* as well as *cash and credit balances*. In this way, the optimal combination of tactics can be arrived at through an analysis of all three of the major policies of short-term finance—those regarding the level of current assets as well as cash and credit balances.

Figure 9-9 provides a picture of a typical manufacturing firm facing just such an optimization problem. In weighing the *carrying costs* of holding current assets against the *shortage costs*, the executive team must decide upon the quantity of raw materials and other production inputs it needs to have on hand for its production process. The team must also decide how much product to produce and hold in inventory in anticipation of order flow.

In the figure, the upward sloping "carrying cost" line indicates that the more production inputs and product inventory the company holds, the higher will be the costs of doing so. There are two reasons for this. First, the rate of return on current assets such as supplier inputs or product inventory is low relative to other assets of the firm because these current assets are quite literally "sitting around." That means there is an *opportunity cost* associated with these current assets equal to the return that could have been earned if the firm's capital had been deployed elsewhere. Secondly, there is a cost associated with simply warehousing the inventory of current assets.

Despite these costs, however, an appropriate amount of production inputs and product inventory must be carried because there are also costs associated with any shortage. In the figure, the *shortage costs curve* slopes downward. Again, there are two reasons for this.

Most obviously, there are costs related to the firm's safety reserves. For example, if a firm winds up with no inventory—or a "stock out" as it is referred to in the trade—it will not only lose sales but also customer goodwill. By the same token, if it runs short of production inputs, its production schedule will be disrupted. Thus, there are obvious benefits to holding more assets.

More subtly, there are also *trading costs* and *order costs*. For example, trading costs can arise when a firm runs out of cash—a "cash out"—and is

FIGURE   9-9

Carrying Costs and Shortages Costs for Current Assets

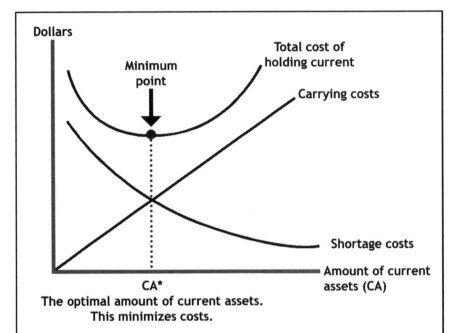

Dollars

Minimum point

Total cost of holding current

Carrying costs

Shortage costs

Amount of current assets (CA)

CA*

The optimal amount of current assets. This minimizes costs.

Carrying costs increase with the level of investment in current assets. They include both opportunity costs and the costs of maintaining the asset's economics value.

Shortage costs decrease with increase in the level of investment in current assets. They include trading costs and the costs of running out of the current asset (for example, being short of cash).

forced to sell marketable securities, borrow, or even default on its obligations. Order costs can arise when a firm produces too little inventory in any given production run and has to incur additional production setup costs for more runs to meet demand.

Looking more closely at the figure, it should become readily apparent why framing the short-run finance question in this fashion is so useful. In fact, the figure suggests a very easy answer. The top curve, which represents the total costs of holding current assets, is determined by adding the carrying costs and shortage costs. The minimum point on this curve occurs where the carrying costs intersect the shortage costs and that defines the optimal amount of current assets to hold. The intuitive conclusion is this: Having a lot of raw materials on hand ensures smooth production and having a lot of inventory ensures product will be on hand to sell when it is demanded. But a company can have too much of either asset and that will incur costs. A happy medium must be found and clearly can be found using the above-discussed tool.

Note that this kind of analysis can be used to answer several other burning questions of short-term corporate finance concerning appropriate levels of cash balances and credit policy.

Cash Management

Let us talk now about cash management. Firms hold cash for two basic reasons. One is to satisfy the *transactions motive*. Cash is collected from sales from operations, sales of assets, and new financing. Cash is also disbursed to pay wages and salaries, trade debts, taxes, and dividends.

The second reason to hold cash is for *compensating balances*. In exchange for receiving services from commercial banks, a firm is typically required to keep a minimum level of cash on deposit. This, of course, creates an opportunity cost in the form of foregone return that could have been realized had the cash been invested in some manner.

To manage the firm's cash, the firm's executive team must determine the appropriate target cash balance, collect and disburse cash efficiently, and appropriately invest excess cash in marketable securities that earn a return.

Determining the appropriate target cash balance involves a cost–benefit optimization—such as the one conducted above for current assets. In this case, this optimization involves a trade-off between the benefits and costs of liquidity, that is, of holding cash. Some of the *benefits of liquidity* include being able to pay one's bills as needed and retaining customer, employee, and creditor goodwill. The *costs of liquidity* are primarily the opportunity costs of idle cash not earning a higher return.

As it is taught in MBA classes, the value the firm derives from holding its optimal cash balance is equal to the foregone interest that could have been derived from investing the cash in Treasury bills. Or to put it another way, a firm should increase its holdings of cash until the NPV from doing so is zero.

Once optimal liquidity is determined, the executive team seeks to collect and disburse cash as efficiently as possible. Techniques aimed at accelerating collections that are taught in business schools include "lockbox processing," "concentration banking," and wire transfers. MBA students also learn how to delay disbursements by playing the "float game" and setting up zero-balance accounts. The fundamental idea here is "collect early and pay late," a dictum that can, of course, sometimes tempt executives to unethically and illegally manage their cash to corporate advantage.

The third cash management mandate for the corporate executive is to invest idle cash in short-term marketable securities that will earn the firm a return. Typically, these securities can be bought and sold in the money market, have very little risk of default, and are highly marketable. They range from U.S. Treasury notes and commercial paper to Eurodollar certificates of deposit.

Credit Management

When a firm sells goods and services, it can either receive cash immediately or extend credit to its customers and be paid at a later time. While cash in hand seems obviously to be the better choice, granting credit can be a very effective way to increase sales while building customer goodwill. Typically, a company's *credit management policy* has three components:

1. *Terms of the sale:* The firm determines the credit period, any cash discount, and the type of credit instrument it will allow.
2. *Credit analysis:* The firm uses a variety of devices to determine the probability that customers will pay and sorts customers into higher and lower risk categories.
3. *Collection policy:* The firm decides how to collect the cash when bills come due.

As with both the current asset and cash management decisions, there is a "cost–benefit" optimization approach for addressing each aspect of extending credit. For example, the carrying costs of credit include the delays in actually receiving the cash, the losses when customers do not pay, and the actual costs of managing what can often be rather complex credit operations. In contrast, the benefits include the additional sales that result from extending credit, which can be thought of as recouping the opportunity costs (in terms of lost sales) that would arise from refusing credit.

Figure 9-10 is simply a variation of the analysis used in Figure 9-9 to highlight the current asset problem. The executive team can use this analytical variation to determine the optimal amount of credit to extend.

FIGURE 9-10

The Costs of Granting Credit

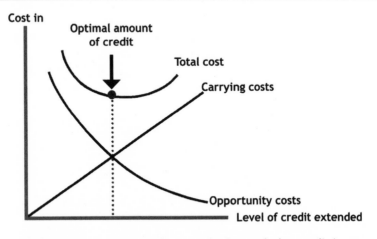

Carrying costs are the costs that must be incurred when credit is granted. The are positively related to the amount of credit extended.

Opportunity costs are the lost sales from refusing credit. These costs drop when credit is granted.

In the figure, carrying costs, the costs that must be incurred when credit is granted, are positively related to the amount of credit extended. Opportunity costs—the lost sales from refusing credit—drop when credit is granted. Again, the optimal level of credit is indicated by the intersection of the two lines.

Of course, just as with current-asset and cash-management policies, any given firm's optimal credit policies will depend upon the characteristics of the firm. As MBA students learn, firms with excess capacity, low variable operating costs, high tax brackets, and repeat customers generally should extend credit more liberally than others.

CONCLUDING REMARKS

We began this chapter with the goal of providing you with an overview of the four big questions of corporate finance—long-term capital budgeting, optimal portfolio design, capital financing, and short-term financial management. In a typical MBA program, there will be much more work to do.

Indeed, in addition to further analyzing these four big questions, corporate finance students also have the opportunity to examine a variety of other highly interesting issues. These range from an analysis of options and futures, warrants and convertibles, and derivatives and hedging risks to mergers and acquisitions, bankruptcy, and international corporate finance. We wish you well and urge you, in the spirit of this book, to always try to see the big picture forest before examining the individual trees.

PART FOUR

The Organizational and Leadership MBA

CHAPTER 10

Organizational Behavior— The Power of People and Leadership

Steven L. McShane and Mary Ann Von Glinow*

INTRODUCTION

> Take away my people but leave my factories, and soon grass will grow on factory floors. Take away my factories but leave my people, and soon we will have a new and better factory.

Andrew Carnegie

Among many MBA students, organizational behavior (OB) is the Rodney Dangerfield of the core curriculum—it does not get much respect. Why is this so?

On the surface, the world of business seems to be about *specialization*— and particularly specialization in core functional areas such as finance, marketing, and operations management. Of course, if you specialize in one of these areas, you will have a corresponding job title like Chief Financial Officer, Director of Marketing, and so on. But who ever heard of a career path leading to "vice-president of Organizational Behavior" or "Chief OB Officer"?

---

*Steven L. McShane is Professor of Management in the Graduate School of Management at the University of Western Australia. He has served as president of the Administrative Services Association of Canada, which is the Canadian equivalent of the Academy of Management, and director of graduate programs in the business faculty at Simon Fraser University. Mary Ann Von Glinow is Professor of Management and International Business at Florida International University. She is a past president of the Academy of Management, and a Fellow of the Academy and the Pan Pacific Business Association. This chapter is based on S. McShane and M. Von Glinow, *Organizational Behavior*, third eition, Irwin McGraw-Hill, 2005.

Yet, spend enough time in the workplace and you will eventually discover that people in every specialization work best when they tap into this gold mine of knowledge called organizational behavior. Organizational behavior not only helps you to understand, predict, and influence the behavior of others, it is also the platinum key to effective leadership. In other words, everyone needs to become a Chief OB Officer if they want to excel in their specialization or lead others from the top ranks of the organization.

F I G U R E   10-1

The Big Questions and Key Concepts of Organizational Behavior

The Big Questions

What are the sources of individual behavior and personality? How do values and personality affect behavior and performance? How do emotions and attitudes influence workplace behavior? How do we motivate employees? What constitutes fairness and justice in compensation, job assignments, and promotions?

Why are teams important? How do organizations create effective teams? Why do teams sometimes fail? How can teams make more effective decisions? What are the characteristics of effective leaders? What do "transformational leaders" do that makes organizations successful?

How can we decipher an organization's culture? Does organizational culture affect corporate performance? How can an organization develop a strong culture? How can leaders effectively change organizations?

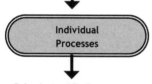

Individual Processes

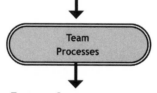

Team Processes

Organizational Processes

- Behavior and Performance
  - The MARS Model
- Personality and OB
  - The CANOE Model
- Workplace Emotion/Attitudes
  - EVLN Model
  - Job Satisfaction and Performance
  - Emotional Intelligence
- Motivation
  - Needs Hierarchy Theory
  - Innate Drives Theory
  - Goal Setting
- Organizational Justice

- Teams vs. Groups
- Self-directed Work Teams (SDWTs)
- Four Team Processes
  - Roles, Norms, Development, and Cohesiveness
- Why Teams Sometimes Fail
  - Social Loafing and Groupthink
- Team Decision Making
- Effective Leadership Perspectives
  - Leadership Competencies
  - Contingency Leadership
  - Transformation Leadership

- Organizational Culture
  - Deciphering Corporate Culture and Cultural Artifacts
  - Culture and Performance
  - Maintaining a Strong Culture
  - Organizational Socialization
- Organizational Change
  - Sources of Resistance
  - Increasing Urgency to Change
  - Minimizing Resistance
  - Role of Communication, Training, Employee Involvement, Negotiation, and Coercion

The Key Concepts

So just what exactly is organizational behavior? Perhaps the best way to see the big OB picture is to start with Figure 10-1. It illustrates some of the most important big questions and key concepts in the field. From Figure 10-1, you will see that your OB studies are typically divided into three albeit highly interrelated levels of analysis—the *individual, teams* and *groups*, and the broader *organization*.

Individual processes typically focus on how individuals behave. This matters because, as you will learn, individual processes dealing with values, personality, motivation, and job satisfaction can all affect a company's performance.

The *team* and *group level processes* look at the way people interact. This includes not only issues of team development and effectiveness but also various perspectives on the perennial management question: <u>What makes for good *leadership*</u>?

Finally, *organizational processes* take a big picture look at what happens in companies. Two pieces of this big picture that we will look at in this chapter are *organizational culture* and *organizational change*. You will see how a healthy organizational culture can lead Southwest Airlines and other firms to peak performance, while a pernicious culture can send Enron and other firms down the road to ruin and disgrace. You will also learn specific strategies to understand and improve the challenges of changing organizations.

With that as our overview, let us dive into the first element in Figure 10-1, namely, individual processes. And let us start with some "OB speak"—a tongue-in-cheek reference to the technical jargon of the field.

INDIVIDUAL BEHAVIOR AND PROCESSES

In this section, our goal is not to catalog and explain all of the theories and models of individual behavior in exhaustive detail. Rather, we want to highlight the really big concepts that make the most difference in individual behavior. Here are some of the big questions we OB professors ask about the individual and why we do so:

1. We ask the question "What are the sources of individual behavior and performance?" because guiding employee behavior is one of the main keys to effective organizations.

2. We ask the question "How do values and personality affect behavior and performance?" because if leaders better understand these stable individual characteristics, they will do a better job of hiring the right people and putting them into the right jobs.

3. We ask the question "How do emotions and attitudes, particularly job satisfaction, influence workplace behavior?" because attitudes and emotions have a complex and pervasive effect in how people act at work.

4. We ask the question "How do we motivate employees?" because highly motivated employees are a key ingredient in corporate and organizational success.

5. We ask the question "What constitutes fairness and justice in areas such as compensation and job assignments and promotions?" because companies that treat their employees unfairly are likely to fare far worse than other companies that tend to these issues.

Individual Behavior and Performance

A very useful starting point is the *MARS model* illustrated in Figure 10-2. Of course, we are not referring to the planet MARS; rather, MARS is an acronym for the four main factors that directly influence employee behavior and

F I G U R E   10-2

MARS Model of Individual Behavior and Results

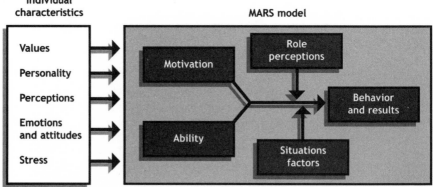

resulting performance—Motivation, Ability, Role perceptions, and Situational factors.

The MARS Model

The left-hand side of the figure identifies individual characteristics: values, personality, perceptions, emotions and attitudes, and stress. These feed into the four elements of the MARS model and the resulting behavior and results.

Motivation represents the forces within a person that affect his or her direction, intensity, and persistence of voluntary behavior. Ability includes both the *natural aptitudes* and *learned capabilities* required to successfully complete a task. The challenge here is to hire people with the right abilities, or to train them so they develop learned capabilities.

Role perceptions represent how well a person understands what the job involves, such as what tasks to perform and their relative importance. The fourth element of the MARS model, called Situational factors, includes conditions beyond the employee's immediate control that can constrain or facilitate his or her behavior and performance. Some conditions, such as budgets and tools, may be within the supervisor's control; other factors, such as the consumer preferences that you learned about in your marketing chapter or economic conditions that you learned about in your macroeconomics chapter, are beyond management control.

The MARS model highlights the key drivers of behavior, but we also need to touch base with the different types of behavior. First, there is *task performance*, which refers to goal-directed behavior under the individual's control that supports the organization's objectives. Another type of behavior, called *organizational citizenship*, includes any behavior that extends beyond expected task performance, such as tolerating impositions or helping others with their work.

A third type of behavior is *joining and staying with the organization*. After all, if qualified people do not join and stay with your organization, neither task performance nor organizational citizenship behaviors will occur. Fourth, organizations need employees to *maintain work attendance*, that is, they need to show up for work at scheduled times. The fifth category, called *counterproductive work behaviors* (CWBs), includes voluntary behaviors that potentially harm the organization. These CWBs include verbal abuse, threats, work sabotage, and theft.

The all-important MARS model and five types of individual behavior provide a solid foundation for the rest of our discussion of individual behavior, including values, personality, emotions and attitudes, motivation, and organizational justice.

Values in the Workplace

Whether you work in the back office or the top floor of corporate headquarters, you will hear a lot of talk these days about values. In OB speak, *values* are stable, evaluative beliefs that guide our preferences for outcomes or courses of action in a variety of situations. They are perceptions about what is good or bad, right or wrong. There are dozens of values, and each of us arranges these values in a hierarchy of importance. Some of us value independence; others prefer tradition. We might value power and personal success, or we might prefer benevolence and concern for others.

Values shape what motivates us and how much we appreciate various work experiences. Values also account for considerable stress and conflict when they clash with the values of other people or the organization's values. Perhaps you value innovation, whereas coworkers cling to more conservative values. Or maybe senior management in the company pushes employees to cut costs whereas you place a higher value on the welfare of customers and the community where the company operates. These values clashes are not unusual. Surveys indicate that many employees experience conflict between their own and their company's values.

Anyone who has worked in other countries knows that values also differ across cultures. In some countries, employees comfortably conform to what the boss says, whereas employees in other countries do not think the boss is anyone special. In some cultures, people value duty to the groups to which they belong; people in other cultures pay more attention to their independence and personal control over their lives. The key point we are trying to make is that values differ between individuals, between employees and the companies that employ them, and across cultures. In each situation, different values can lead to conflict, which sometimes undermines corporate success and employee well-being.

Ethical Values

Values are also at the heart of ethical decision making. After all, our values are our inner voices telling us what is right or wrong. They point out what we should and should not do. They tell us what is ethical. Everyone has ethical values, but you would not know it from the way that some people act.

Indeed, accounting fraud, bribery, and other corporate wrongdoing seem to make the headlines almost every week.

Why do good people do bad things? It is quite common to blame the situation for unethical conduct. Executives caught in accounting fraud blame their actions on intense pressure from shareholders to produce good financial numbers.

A second explanation of why people engage in unethical behavior is that they do not believe the issue demands the application of ethical principles. Most of us believe that fudging corporate accounts is an important ethical concern, but some people do not see any harm in this practice. A third explanation for unethical conduct is that people vary in their ethical sensitivity. If you are not an accounting expert, for instance, you might be less aware of violating accounting rules.

Personality and OB

We said earlier that values are stable; they change very slowly over a person's life. Another stable characteristic is the individual's personality. In OB speak, *personality* refers to the relatively stable pattern of behavior and consistent internal states that explain a person's behavioral tendencies. Our personality is stable because it is shaped early in life. Some psychologists even suggest that our personality is hard-wired before we are born.

The CANOE Model

There are dozens of personality traits. Fortunately, psychologists have organized most of them into five dimensions with the handy acronym CANOE.

Conscientiousness refers to people who are careful, dependable, and self-disciplined, and every executive team loves to hire conscientious people. This is because people with low conscientiousness tend to be careless, less thorough, more disorganized, and irresponsible.

Agreeableness includes the traits of being courteous, good-natured, empathetic, and caring. People with low agreeableness tend to be uncooperative, short-tempered, and irritable, so it is useful to screen these personality types out.

Neuroticism characterizes people with high levels of anxiety, hostility, depression, and self-consciousness. In contrast, people with low neuroticism (high emotional stability) are poised, secure, and calm.

Openness to experience is the most complex and has the least agreement among scholars as to its desirability. It generally refers to the extent that people are sensitive, flexible, creative, and curious. Note that those who score low in this dimension tend to be more resistant to change, less open to new ideas, and more fixed in their ways.

Extroversion characterizes people who are outgoing, talkative, sociable, and assertive. The opposite personality type is *introversion*, which refers to those who are quiet, shy, and cautious. Guess which type you would want on your sales force?

Personality makes a difference in the workplace—if it did not, we would not mention it in this chapter. Conscientious employees set higher personal goals for themselves, are more motivated, and have higher performance expectations than do employees with lower levels of conscientiousness. People with high emotional stability tend to work better than others in high-stress situations. Those with high agreeableness can handle customer relations and conflict-based situations more effectively. Champions of organizational change seem to place well along the positive end of all five personality dimensions.

Workplace Emotions and Attitudes

Values and personality are the bedrock of individual behavior. They are the most stable elements in each of us. Much less stable, but equally important for individual behavior, are *emotions* and *attitudes*.

In OB speak, emotions are psychological and physiological episodes experienced toward an object, person, or event that create a state of readiness. Sadness, joy, anger, and contentment are emotions that we experience at work. These emotions are temporary and are usually apparent through our behavior (smiling, frowning, nervousness).

Emotions play a vital role in our attitudes toward our jobs and the workplace. As we see in Figure 10-3, attitudes represent the cluster of beliefs, assessed feelings, and behavioral intentions toward a person, object, or event. Attitudes are *judgments*, whereas emotions are *experiences*. Attitudes involve logical reasoning, whereas we sense emotions. We also experience most emotions briefly, whereas our attitude toward someone or something is more stable over time.

Think about your attitude toward your boss. You might believe that your boss makes fair decisions and is generous towards staff. These *beliefs* affect your *feelings* toward your boss, that is, your evaluation of whether your

F I G U R E   10-3

Model of Emotions, Attitudes, and Behavior

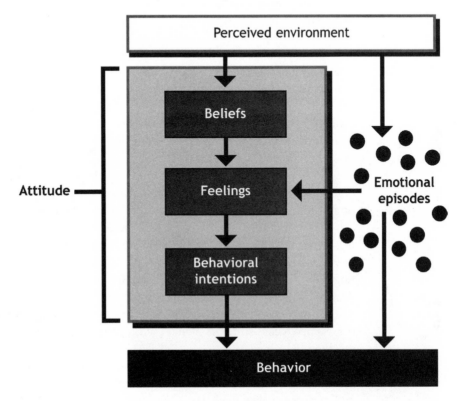

boss is good or bad overall. Your evaluation of your boss leads to *behavioral intentions*—what you are motivated to do toward your boss. If you dislike your boss, you might be motivated to quit your job, ask for a transfer to another department, or complain to top brass about your boss. These behavioral intentions then influence your behavior.

Figure 10-3 also shows how emotions shape our attitudes—and they do so in a very big way! The emotional part of our brain bombards the rational part of our brain with messages of delight, anger, surprise, contentment, and other emotions in reaction to various events at work. If you experience a lot of positive emotions at work, for example, you eventually tend to form very positive attitudes toward work. You form positive feelings, which, in turn, increase your motivation to stay and possibly perform your job better (or engage in organizational citizenship). If you experience a lot of negative emotions at work, then you tend to develop a negative evaluation of work, which motivates you to quit, complain, or possibly engage in counter-productive work behaviors.

Job Satisfaction and the EVLN Model

Organizational behavior experts have studied many attitudes, but one that stands out above the rest is *job satisfaction*—a person's evaluation of his or her job and work context. How much we like or dislike our job and work context has an important effect on how we act. The *exit-voice-loyalty-neglect* (EVLN) model identifies four ways that employees respond to dissatisfaction.

Exit refers to searching for other employment, actually leaving the organization, or transferring to another work unit. Exit occurs when people do not think they can change the source of the dissatisfaction.

Voice includes any attempt to change, rather than escape from, the dissatisfying situation. Trying to solve a problem with management is a form of voice, but so are more confrontational actions, such as filing grievances. Engaging in counterproductive behavior to get attention is the most destructive form of voice.

Loyalty applies to employees who patiently wait. Some people say these employees "suffer in silence" while the problem works itself out or gets resolved by others.

The fourth way that employees react to job dissatisfaction is called *neglect*. This refers to reducing work effort, paying less attention to quality, and increasing absenteeism and lateness. Note that either loyalty or neglect can occur when employees do not think they can change the problem but also do not have other employment opportunities.

Job Satisfaction, Performance, and Customer Satisfaction

Regarding job satisfaction and performance, one of the oldest sayings in the business world is that "a happy worker is a productive worker." But is this cliché really true? Chances are that your MBA class will vigorously debate this issue. Interestingly, OB experts have flip-flopped on the answer for several decades.

Here is what we can say based on the best research so far. It seems that there is at least a moderate relationship between job satisfaction and performance. However, the effect of job satisfaction on job performance is really a lot more complex than the "happy worker" statement suggests.

For example, the EVLN model above shows that some dissatisfied employees might continue to be productive workers while they either complain (voice) or look for another job (exit).

Job satisfaction also has an important influence on *customer satisfaction*. Here is how the logic works. First, good organizational practices lead to job satisfaction, which (as we found in the EVLN model) lowers turnover. With lower turnover, customers get better service with experienced, familiar staff. Also, happy employees tend to put customers in a better mood (smiling employees creates smiling customers). The result is more satisfied customers, which increases revenue growth and profits.

Emotional Intelligence

Now that we have the basics on workplace emotions and attitudes, it is time to look at one of the hottest topics in OB these days: *emotional intelligence* (EI). Emotional intelligence is the ability to perceive and express emotion, assimilate emotion in thought, understand and reason with emotion, and regulate emotion in oneself and others. Table 10-1 illustrates the four main

T A B L E   10-1

Model of Emotional Intelligence

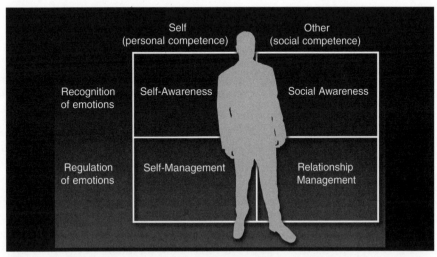

(*Sources*: D. Goleman, R. Boyatzis, and A. McKee, Primal Leadership, Harvard Business Press, Boston, 2002, Chapter 3; D. Goleman, "An EI-Based Theory of Performance," in *The Emotionally Intelligent Workplace*, ed. C. Cherniss and D. Goleman, Jossey-Bass, San Francisco, 2001, p. 28.)

elements of emotional intelligence, which consists of how well we recognize and regulate our own emotions and the emotions of others.

Self-awareness refers to having a deep understanding of our own emotions as well as strengths, weaknesses, values, and motives. Self-aware people also recognize their intuition or gut instincts.

Self-management is all about controlling or redirecting our emotions. We keep disruptive impulses in check, maintain the drive to perform, and remain optimistic even after failure.

Social awareness, the third element of emotional intelligence, is mainly about *empathy*—having understanding and sensitivity to the feelings, thoughts, and situation of others. In this regard, socially aware people are usually better at customer service, and can sense organizational politics.

The final and most challenging element of EI is *relationship management*, which refers to managing other people's emotions. This includes everything short of walking on water, such as inspiring others, managing change, resolving conflict, cultivating relationships, and supporting teamwork. That is a tall order; one that few people have mastered!

Emotional intelligence makes a difference, as we see in Snapshot Application 10-1. The U.S. Air Force discovered that recruiters with high emotional intelligence were better at their jobs. Other evidence reports that people with high EI scores are better at interpersonal relations, serving

S N A P S H O T   A P P L I C A T I O N   10–1

U.S. AIR FORCE DISCOVERS THE BENEFITS OF EMOTIONAL INTELLIGENCE

Each year, the U.S. Air Force hires about 400 recruiters, and each year up to 100 of them are fired for failing to sign up enough people for the service. Selecting and training 100 new recruiters costs $3 million, not to mention the hidden costs of their poor performance. In response to this dismal situation, the head of Air Force recruiting decided to give 1,200 recruiters a new test that measured how well they manage their emotions and the emotions of others.

From this experiment in "emotional intelligence," the Air Force discovered that the top recruiters were better at asserting their feelings and thoughts, empathizing with others, feeling happy in life, and being aware of their emotions in a particular situation. The next year, the U.S. Air Force hired new recruiters partly on their results of this emotional intelligence test. The result—only eight recruiters got fired or quit a year later.

customers, and becoming leaders. In fact, EI is one of the most important elements of *effective leadership*, which we discuss later in this chapter.

Motivation

Let us turn now to the subject of motivation in the workplace. In OB speak, motivation refers to the forces within a person that affect his or her direction, intensity, and persistence of voluntary behavior. In other words, we are motivated to achieve a particular goal (direction), at a particular level of effort (intensity), for a particular length of time (persistence).

Most employers—92 percent of them, according to one recent survey—agree that motivating employees has become a lot more challenging. One reason is that globalization has dramatically changed the jobs that people perform and resulted in numerous forms of corporate restructuring and downsizing. Also, the "one size fits all" approach to motivation does not work as well as a few decades ago because the workforce is far more diverse. Still, by understanding a few key theories, we can develop a more motivated workforce.

Maslow's Needs Hierarchy

The granddaddy of motivation theories—the one that most people have heard about—is psychologist Abraham Maslow's *needs hierarchy theory*. Developed several decades ago, this theory places basic needs in a hierarchy of importance. *Physiological* needs—things like food, air, water, and shelter—are the bottom rung of Maslow's hierarchy. Next comes *safety* needs for things like a secure and stable environment and the absence of pain, threat, or illness.

Belongingness includes the need for love, affection, and interaction with other people, while *esteem* includes self-esteem through personal achievement as well as social esteem through recognition and respect from others. And at the top of the hierarchy is *self-actualization*, which represents the need for self-fulfillment—a sense the person's potential has been realized.

Maslow believed that when we satisfy a lower level need, the next need above it in the hierarchy becomes most important. For instance, when you have enough food and shelter that your physiological needs are satisfied, you become more energized to satisfy your safety needs.

Needs hierarchy theory sounds logical, but unfortunately does not reflect reality. The problem is that Maslow (and other needs theorists in his day) believed that everyone places their needs in the same hierarchy.

Apparently, according to research, we do not. Sure, most of us probably scramble for food and shelter before trying to make friends, but not everyone places status above safety, or self-actualization before belongingness. In short, the world's most popular motivation theory should not be so popular!

Innate Drives Theory

If Maslow's needs hierarchy does not work, what does? Researchers have found that everyone has a core set of hard-wired drives. Two Harvard business school professors, Paul Lawrence and Nitin Nohria, recently organized this emerging knowledge into an elegant model that includes four innate drives: the drives to acquire, bond, learn, and defend.

Everyone has a *drive to acquire*, which includes the drive to seek, take, control, and retain objects and personal experiences. This drive is insatiable because the purpose of human motivation is to achieve a higher position than others, not just to fulfill one's physiological needs. The *drive to bond* involves the motivation to form social relationships and develop mutual caring commitments with others. This drive is essential for the success of organizations because it motivates people to cooperate with each other.

The *drive to learn* recognizes that all of us have some degree of curiosity about the world in which we live, particularly when what we see is inconsistent with previous beliefs. Finally, the *drive to defend* is the drive to protect our physical self as well as our relationships, acquisitions, and belief systems. It creates a "fight or flight" response in the face of personal danger and threats to the things in which we believe.

Motivation Through Goal Setting

Now that we have straightened out past confusion about employee needs, let us look at *goal setting*, a theory that has a rock solid reputation at motivating employees and improving their performance. Goal setting potentially improves performance in two ways: (1) by motivating employees to be successful and (2) by clarifying role perceptions so employees know where to direct their effort.

Goal setting does not involve just telling employees to "do your best." Instead, goal setting is most effective under six conditions:

1. Setting specific goals such as "increase sales by five percent over the next six months."

2. Setting goals that are relevant to the individual's job and within his or her control.

3. Setting challenging goals whereby employees experience self-actualization when the goals are achieved.

4. Ensuring that employees are committed to their goals.

5. Allowing employees to participate in setting goals when goal commitment is otherwise low.

6. Providing feedback relevant to the set goals.

Organizational Justice

Let us complete our review of individual processes by describing something that strikes everyone's emotions: *organizational justice*. Corporate leaders and OB scholars alike have long known that to maximize employee motivation, satisfaction, and loyalty, they need to treat people fairly. This seems simple enough, but organizational justice is an elusive goal. All of us experience unfairness at work, sometimes quite often.

Distributive versus Procedural Justice

To improve organizational justice, we need to first recognize that fairness has two components: distributive and procedural justice. In OB speak, *distributive justice* is perceived fairness in the outcomes we receive relative to our contributions and the outcomes and contributions of others. If you get paid less than a coworker who does not seem to be any more productive than you are, then you probably feel distributive injustice.

Let us take this example further. Suppose that you also believe the manager who decided to pay the coworker more money is biased (a friend of the coworker), did not look closely at your job performance, and will not give you the chance to complain about this unfair situation. Under these conditions, you would REALLY feel a sense of injustice because you are also experiencing *procedural injustice*. Procedural injustice refers to the fairness of the procedures used to decide the distribution of resources. The manager's bias, lack of access to information when making the decision, and your lack of opportunity to appeal the decision are three conditions that make people feel procedural injustice.

What does this say for managerial practice? First, leaders need to distribute pay, promotions, time off, recognition, and other rewards fairly.

Secondly, leaders need to know what employees value as rewards (for example, pay, promotions, and recognition) as well as what contributions employees think are most important (for example, performance, experience, seniority). But equally important, leaders need to create a workplace where employees believe that the decision-making process is fair. In other words, the executive team should be mindful of both distributive *and* procedural justice.

TEAM PROCESSES AND LEADERSHIP

Let us turn now to the second major OB theme: *teams* and *leadership*. In OB speak, *teams* are groups of two or more people who interact and influence each other, are mutually accountable for achieving common goals associated with organizational objectives, and perceive themselves as a social entity within an organization. Work teams exist to fulfill some purpose.

At this point, we need to distinguish "teams" from "groups." All teams are groups, but not all groups are teams. Employees gathered in the same area to watch a ceremony are called a "group," but they do not necessarily have any interdependence or common organizational goals. Most OB research is focused on teams, that is, groups with an organizational objective.

Why Teams are Important

So why are teams important? Experts say that teams, not individuals, have become the building blocks of organizations. As Snapshot Application 10-2 describes, Wall Street brokerage firms have recently paid much more attention to teamwork rather than individual "star" performance.

So why are teams effective? One important reason is that, under the right conditions, teams tend to be better than lone individuals at making decisions. Team members are also more likely to discover problems or opportunities. They create *synergy* by pooling their knowledge to form new alternatives. And they are often better than individuals at choosing the best alternatives because the decision is reviewed by people with diverse perspectives.

Another reason for the popularity of teams is that people working together have more knowledge to serve customers. For instance, the Wall Street brokerage teams in our Snapshot Application provide more expertise than any individual alone can provide.

S N A P S H O T   A P P L I C A T I O N   10-2

WALL STREET EMBRACES THE POWER OF TEAM WORK

Wall Street brokerage firms are placing more emphasis on teams rather than individuals to serve clients more effectively. For example, almost all private client brokers at Credit Suisse First Boston are assigned to teams while Bear, Stearns, and Company organizes staff into specialized teams. When asked about star performers in investment funds, an executive at Templeton Emerging Markets Fund quickly replied that "funds are actually run by teams of people and do not depend on one person."

Interestingly enough, many Wall Street firms are still struggling to make teams work. Nonetheless, a few are reaping the rewards of the team approach.

A case in point is UBS PaineWebber. Its brokers that were trained in a team development program generated 19 percent more revenues and 9 percent more assets than all other UBSPW advisors. The main reason for this improved performance, according to UBSPW executives, is that properly trained teams offer clients better product and service knowledge.

Still a third benefit of teams is that they can complete more challenging tasks than lone individuals. For example, teams can build entire computer systems whereas few individuals can accomplish such a complex task. These larger challenges tend to energize employees, while working together satisfies the drive to bond.

Self-Directed Work Teams

Many firms around the planet are leveraging the benefits of teamwork through *self-directed work teams* (SDWTs). These "high-performance" teams complete an entire piece of work requiring several interdependent tasks and have substantial autonomy over the execution of these tasks.

For example, at the Collins & Aikman auto parts plant in Americus, Ga., SDWTs are responsible for quality assurance as well as safety reviews and compliance, environmental compliance, daily job assignments, and training. In many operations, such as Harley-Davidson's motorcycle production plant in Kansas City, self-directed work team members are their own supervisors.

While SDWTs require managers to give up control, under the right conditions, they are incredibly effective. Canon, the Japanese camera and copier company, introduced SDWTs a few years ago and now claims that a team of a half-dozen people can produce as much as 30 people in the old assembly line system. However, the watch phrase here is "under the right conditions." Such SDWTs and other teams require the right environment, team design, and team processes. These observations lead us to our next big question: "How do organizations create effective teams?"

A Model of Team Effectiveness

Most corporate executives have struggled to find the answer to this question. Fortunately, Figure 10-4 provides a useful template that leads us to an answer. Starting with the left side of the model, we see that successful teams require the right type of environment. They need effective communication systems and an external environment that encourages them to work together. Teams also blossom with team-friendly leaders, physical space, organizational structure, and rewards.

For instance, American Skandia rewards the best customer service representatives with an individual bonus. But recognizing that individuals rarely accomplish work alone, the Swedish insurance company also rewards the employee's team for that individual's achievement.

F I G U R E   10-4

A Model of Team Effectiveness

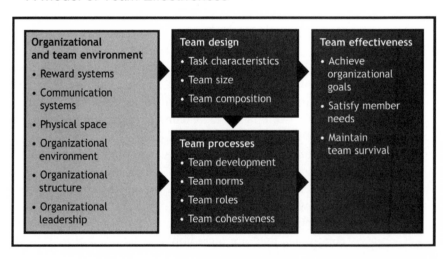

Note, however, that even with the right environment, teams fall apart if they are not designed properly. In this regard, teams work best when the assigned tasks are structured (not too fuzzy) and require team members to work together rather than alone much of the time.

Teams also work best if they are not burdened with too many members. Along with tasks and team size, effective teams are designed with members who possess the required skills as well as the ability and motivation to work together. For some tasks, teams should also consist of people with diverse backgrounds so they do not all think alike.

Four Team Processes

The team's environment and design are just the starting points. The real heart of team effectiveness consists of four team processes: *roles*, *norms*, *development*, and *cohesiveness*. Let us look briefly now at each of these four processes.

First, a high-performing team must ensure that each of the required team roles are covered. That is, someone must encourage the team to explore opportunities; another person smoothes over internal conflict, and so on. At the same time, high-performance teams also establish *norms*—informal rules and expectations—that are consistent with the team's and organization's objectives.

A third important process is *team development*. Team members must pass through several stages of development before emerging as an effective work unit. They typically begin by politely learning about each other. They then become more combative when resolving roles and norms. Eventually, a consensus forms around group objectives and team members coordinate their work more efficiently.

Note that while team development takes time, the process is vital. Consider that a few years ago, NASA studied the effects of fatigue on pilots returning from multiday trips. As one might expect, fatigued pilots made more errors in the NASA flight simulator. But the truly amazing finding was that *fatigued crews who had previously worked together made fewer errors than did rested crews who had not previously flown together!*

Team cohesiveness is the fourth important process of team effectiveness. Indeed, the best performing teams are typically highly cohesive. *Team cohesiveness* occurs when team members feel attracted to the team and motivated to remain members. This motivation energizes team members to work harder for the team's goals. As long as team norms are consistent with organizational objectives, the team will achieve corporate objectives more effectively. On the other hand, if the team's norms are counterproductive–such as encouraging absenteeism or working slowly—then high cohesiveness will make the team less productive.

Teams become cohesive when their members have similar backgrounds and beliefs, interact with each other fairly regularly, are challenged to become team members, and face external challenges, such as competition from other teams or organizations. Team cohesiveness is also higher when teams are successful and where the team is as small as possible to complete the task effectively.

Why Teams Sometimes Fail

Note that while teams can be highly effective, they are not always the panacea for every problem. One reason is that corporate executives may be so "wowed" by teams that they install them in situations where an individual could do the job faster and better.

A second reason is that some members tend to engage in *social loafing*. This occurs when a person exerts less effort and performs at a lower level when working in a group then when working alone.

Organizational behavior scholars have identified several ways to minimize social loafing, such as measuring individual performance, giving team members unique (rather than pooled) tasks, and hiring people who are inherently motivated to perform the work. Still, social loafing seems to be an unfortunate side effect of teamwork.

A third problem is that corporate leaders often install teams without restructuring the workplace to support teamwork. Remember the organizational and team environment part of the team effectiveness model introduced earlier? Unless rewards, leadership, physical space, communication, and other conditions are properly aligned to teamwork, teams may be more costly than individuals working alone.

Still a fourth problem with team decision making is one that you may have heard about—so-called *groupthink*. Groupthink is the tendency of highly cohesive groups to value consensus at the price of decision quality. Team members may also be reluctant to mention ideas that seem silly because they believe (often correctly) that other team members are silently evaluating them. Similarly, team members may pressure each other to conform to the status quo, which discourages individuals from suggesting groundbreaking ideas.

Our bottom line here is that teams are all around us in organizations today. We have seen that teams are potentially a great source of organizational success as well as personal need fulfillment. But teams can also become difficult to manage. That is why it takes *effective leadership* to make teams work well—a subject to which we will next turn.

Effective Leadership

> The ability to motivate and guide people toward a goal is the essence of leadership.
>
> Robert J. Shiver

The world has changed. So has our concept of effective leadership. Based on interviews with 6,000 executives and employees in several countries, a recent study shows that effective leaders subordinate their own egos and, instead, nurture leadership and others throughout an organization. The emerging reality is a far cry from the "command-and-control" leaders of yesteryear that took center stage and pretended to have all the answers. Indeed, this traditional Pattonesque leadership style is withering even in the military where it once flourished.

So just what *is* leadership? A few years ago, 54 scholars from 38 countries reached a consensus that *leadership is the ability to influence, motivate, and enable others to contribute to the effectiveness and success of the organizations of which they are members.* Even with this unified definition, we need to be aware that there are several perspectives on leadership. In this section, we will introduce three of the main perspectives: *leadership competencies, contingency leadership,* and *transformational leadership.*

The Leadership Competency Perspective

Let us start with the *leadership competency perspective* and one of the big questions that scholars have asked since the beginning of time: "What are the characteristics of effective leaders?"

The ancient Egyptians demanded authority, discrimination, and justice from their leaders while the Greek philosopher Plato called for prudence, courage, temperance, and justice. Over the past century, leadership experts have investigated a long list of possible leadership traits. Perhaps surprisingly, however, these literally hundreds of studies have not been able to put together a common list of traits.

Within this context, and in spite of the lack of consistent findings in early leadership studies, a few OB scholars now see that the leadership competency perspective illustrated in Table 10-2 may have some merit.

T A B L E   10-2

Seven Competencies of Effective Leaders

Leadership Competency	Description
Emotional intelligence	The leader's ability to perceive and express emotion, assimilate emotion is thought, understand and reason with emotion and regulate emotion in oneself and others.
Integrity	The leader's truthfulness and tendency to translate words into deads.
Drive	The leader's inner motivation to pursue goals.
Leadership motivation	The leader's need to socialize power to accomplish team or organizational goals.
Self-confidence	The leader's belief in his or her own leadership skills and ability to achieve objectives.
Intelligence	The leader's above-average cognitive ability to process enormous amounts of information.
Knowledge of the business	The leader's understanding of the company's environment to make more intuitive decisions.

(*Sources*: Most elements of this list were derived from S.A. Kirkpartrick and E.A. Locke, "Leadership: Do Traits Matter?" *Academy of Management Executive* 5 (May 1991), pp. 48–60. Several of these ideas are also discussed in: H.B. Gregersen, A.J. Morrison and J.S. Black, "Developing Leaders for the Global Frontier," *Sloan Management Review* 40 (Fall 1998), pp. 21–32; R.J. House and R.N. Aditya, "The Social Scientific Study of Leadership: Quo Vadis?" *Journal of Management* 23 (1997), pp. 409–73.)

Please take a few minutes to examine this table carefully, which is as revealing as it is concise.

For instance, *integrity* is a leadership competency. This helps explain why so many people question business leaders in this age of accounting fraud and other forms of ethical misconduct.

Notice, too, that *emotional intelligence* is a characteristic of effective leaders. As we learned earlier in this chapter, emotional intelligence is the ability to perceive and express emotion, assimilate emotion in thought, understand and reason with emotion, and regulate emotion in oneself and others. These emotional intelligence competencies are vital if leaders hope to influence and support followers. Other leadership competencies include drive, motivation, self-confidence, intelligence, and knowledge of the business.

Knowing the competencies of effective leaders enables companies to hire people who are best equipped to serve in formal leadership roles. But possessing the right skills, knowledge, and personality is not the same thing as being a great leader. Competencies only indicate a person's *potential*. What really counts is what leaders do—their *behaviors*. And that is where the *contingency perspective* of leadership comes into the picture.

Contingency Perspective of Leadership

About half a century ago, OB experts started looking more closely at the behaviors of leaders. From this research, they have identified two clusters.

One cluster represents *people-oriented behavior,* which includes showing trust in and respect for subordinates, demonstrating a genuine concern for their needs, and having a desire to look out for their welfare. The other cluster centers around *task-oriented behavior.* Task-oriented leaders assign employees to specific tasks, clarify their work duties and procedures, ensure that they follow company rules, and push them to reach their performance capacity.

After debating whether leaders are more effective with a people-oriented or task-oriented leadership style, OB experts have concluded that the best leadership style *depends on the situation.* This view is known as the *contingency perspective of leadership.*

According to various contingency theories of leadership, the people-oriented style works best when employees experience stress and lack supportive team members. The task-oriented leadership style works best for followers who are inexperienced, lack confidence in their abilities, work in teams with counterproductive norms (that is, which do not support company goals), and work on complex or ambiguous tasks. In contrast, task-oriented leadership is *ineffective* when employees are skilled and experienced because they feel resentful at being overmanaged.

Most contingency leadership theories assume that effective leaders are able to adapt their styles to the immediate situation. This, of course, is more difficult to do than it sounds. Most of us have a preferred leadership style, and it takes considerable effort to learn when and how to alter our style to match the situation. In fact, some experts suggest we need to assign leaders who prefer one style to jobs that match that style.

The contingency perspective of leadership has a strong supervisory focus because it recommends the best style to improve employee performance and satisfaction. But OB scholars realized not long ago that this perspective is really about "managing" employees, not about "leading" them into the future. To understand leadership as a source of change, we need to pay attention to the transformational perspective of leadership.

Transformational Perspective of Leadership

The third, and perhaps the currently most popular, perspective on leadership is that of the *transformational perspective.* To give a real flavor for this leadership style, you may want to look at Snapshot Application 10-3

A TRANSFORMATIONAL LEADER SLEDGEHAMMERS HIS WAY TO CHANGE

In the 1980s, Zhang Ruimin, the newly appointed chief executive of the Haier Group, was so incensed by the poor quality of the products built at the company's factory in the Chinese port city of Qingdao that he picked up a sledgehammer and smashed several washing machines. Zhang had just taken over the state-owned appliance manufacturer and saw the need for radical change.

Today, the legendary sledgehammer is displayed in a glass case on Haier's shop floor, which has been transformed in Qingdao into a model of modern efficiency. Thousands of employees dress in clean uniforms and work in pristine workshops while a fully automated logistics center and advanced research and development program help to produce superior quality appliances.

Because of the transformational leadership qualities of Zhang, the Haier group has become China's first truly multinational company, with plants around the world. By relying on Japanese quality control and American-style management practices, Zhang's dream of making Haier a global brand is becoming a reality.

before moving on. It tells a fascinating tale about Zhang Ruimin—who quite literally smashed his way in China to constructive change.

Zhang Ruimin of Haier Group, Herb Kelleher of Southwest Airlines, Carly Fiorina of Hewlett-Packard, Richard Branson of Virgin Group, and other transformational leaders dot the corporate landscape. But identifying transformational leaders is just a small step toward answering another big question in OB: "What do transformational leaders do that makes organizations successful?"

The hallmark of transformational leaders is that they are *agents of change*. They create a vision, communicate that vision, model the vision, and build commitment to the vision. Through the behaviors related to each of these activities, transformational leaders move the organization to a new and better set of organizational practices. Because transformational leadership can be so important, let us look at four types of behavior that help define this type of leadership.

First, effective transformational leaders help shape a corporate vision—a desirable image of the company's future. This vision might originate from the leader or from others, but the leader orchestrates the development and refinement of this future state. No matter how vague, a strategic vision establishes a goal post and direction for the company and its employees.

Secondly, transformational leaders communicate this vision in ways that make it appealing and motivating. They frame their messages around a grand purpose with emotional appeal that captivates employees and other corporate stakeholders.

Thirdly, transformational leaders model the vision. They "walk the talk," by doing things that symbolize the vision and by acting consistently with that vision.

Finally, transformational leaders build commitment to the vision through their communication and modeling, as well as through their "authenticity" as leaders.

Note that all four elements of transformational leadership apply to leaders at *all* levels in the firm, from first line supervisors to the chief executive officer. After all, every level of the organization needs change.

Note also that there is a fair bit of confusion between transformational leadership and *charismatic leadership*, so allow us to clarify this matter. Charismatic leaders possess personal power; we are attracted to people with charisma based on their persuasiveness and "presence." In contrast, transformational leadership describes a set of behaviors to change organizations.

While charismatic leaders might be transformational leaders, this is not always so. On the contrary, charismatic leaders tend to make followers dependent on them, whereas transformational leaders empower employees through their involvement in the change process. Some very recent writing also points out how some charismatic leaders do not change the organization at all. Instead, they use their personal power merely to give themselves more salary and perks while the company sinks. Thus, we should never confuse charisma with transformational leadership.

ORGANIZATIONAL PROCESSES

Let us turn now to two very important organizational processes. These have to do with the critical concepts of *organizational culture* and *organizational change*.

Organizational Culture

Open any major newspaper today and you will probably find the phrase "corporate culture" mentioned somewhere. One company's corporate culture is identified as the main culprit for its unethical conduct. Another firm's success is attributed to its deeply held culture that values customer service.

Organizational culture may seem like a "touchy-feely" concept that is difficult to grasp, but it is constantly on the minds of senior executives. In OB-speak, organizational culture is the basic pattern of shared assumptions, values, and beliefs that are considered to be the correct way of thinking about and acting on problems and opportunities facing the organization.

Organizational culture defines what is important and unimportant for the company. For example, Wal-Mart embraces a culture of frugality and efficiency. It has Spartan waiting rooms for suppliers, visitors buy their own coffee and soft drinks, and employees sit at inexpensive desks.

In contrast, SAS Institute has one of the most employee-friendly cultures on the planet. Located on a 200-acre campus in Cary, North Carolina, the world's largest privately held software company offers free on-site medical care, unlimited sick days, heavily subsidized day care, personal trainers, and inexpensive gourmet cafeterias. Both Wal-Mart and SAS Institute are incredibly successful, yet both have quite different corporate cultures.

Deciphering Corporate Culture

To help you visualize the meaning of organizational culture, take a look Figure 10-5. This figure will help us answer one of the big questions in organizational behavior, namely: "How can we understand or decipher an organization's culture?"

We see in the figure that organizational culture rests on a set of beliefs, values, and assumptions that are below the surface and largely unseen. However, above the surface, we can nonetheless discern various *artifacts* of the culture, as embodied in elements such as *physical structures, language, rituals* and *ceremonies*, and *stories* and *legends*.

For instance, although we cannot see Wal-Mart's culture, we can nonetheless observe evidence of its culture above the surface through its *physical structures*—modest buildings and office furniture. In a similar vein, employees at The Container Store compliment each other about "being Gumby"; this type of *language* reflects the company's culture of being as flexible as the once-popular green toy. That is, employees will go outside their regular job to help a customer or another employee.

As for *rituals*, these are the programmed routines of daily organizational life that dramatize the organization's culture, whereas

FIGURE   10-5

The Artifacts and Elements of Organizational Culture

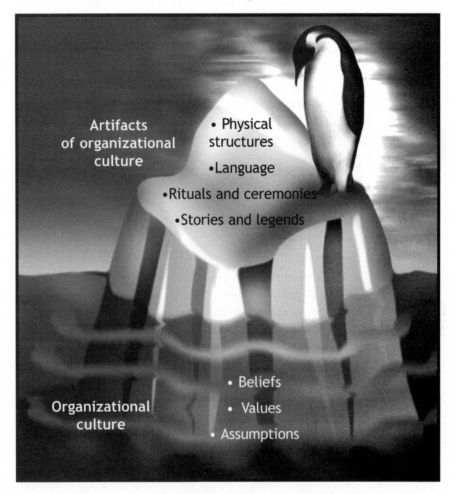

ceremonies are simply more formal artifacts and rituals. Consider a recent annual meeting of Brown & Brown, Inc., the Daytona Beach, Florida, insurance company. Managers of poorly performing divisions were led to a podium by employees dressed as medieval executioners, while a funeral dirge played over loudspeakers. "It does sound a bit harsh, but that's the culture," says Brown & Brown's CEO.

The fourth category of cultural artifacts consists of *stories* and *legends*. For example, "Malice in Dallas" is a legendary story that almost every Southwest Airlines employee knows. It is about how Southwest CEO Herb Kelleher decided to settle a dispute with another company by challenging the other company's CEO to an arm wrestling contest. This tale aptly communicates one of the maverick airline's core values—that having fun is part of doing business.

Culture and Performance

One of the biggest questions in organizational behavior is this: "Does organizational culture affect corporate performance?" While some OB scholars and many top executives have argued that a strong corporate culture is good for business, the relationship is actually a little more complex. A *strong organizational culture* exists when most employees across all subunits adopt the dominant values, beliefs, and assumptions.

To figure out how a strong culture relates to organizational effectiveness, let us first understand how it potentially benefits organizations. First, corporate culture is a deeply embedded form of social control that influences employee decisions and behavior. Culture is pervasive and operates unconsciously. You might think of it as an automatic pilot, directing employees in ways that are consistent with organizational expectations and broader strategic goals.

Secondly, corporate culture is the "social glue" that bonds people together and makes them feel part of the organizational experience. Employees are motivated to internalize the organization's dominant culture because it is consistent with their drive to bond. This social glue is increasingly important as a way to attract new staff and retain top performers.

Finally, a strong corporate culture helps employees better understand their organization. It also allows them to communicate more efficiently and reach higher levels of cooperation with each other because they share common mental models of reality.

So far, so good. But if a strong culture has all of these benefits, *why are companies with strong cultures not always more successful?*

One reason is that a business might have the *wrong culture* for the situation. For example, a frugal culture works great when price competition makes a difference, which explains Wal-Mart's success. But a frugal culture might be a disaster at SAS Institute, which competes with IBM and Microsoft for a short supply of highly skilled talent.

Note also that a very strong culture can be a problem because it stifles dissent. This prevents employees with different views from voicing their opinions, and ultimately makes it difficult for companies to change their culture over time.

Maintaining a Strong Culture

Assuming that a company has the right culture for the situation, we need to answer another big OB question: "How can we develop and maintain a reasonably strong culture?" There are several ways, actually.

First, founders and transformational leaders can play a big role because they can emphasize a corporate vision that reinforces certain cultural values. Leaders also form and rearrange systems and structures that shape and change corporate culture. In this regard, reward systems represent a particularly important organizational system that reinforces a specific corporate culture.

Secondly, because an organization's culture is embedded in the minds of its employees, maintaining a stable workforce is another way to maintain a strong culture. On this point, it is useful to note that corporate cultures can literally disintegrate during periods of high turnover and precipitous downsizing because the corporate memory leaves with these employees.

Thirdly, *organizational socialization* is another popular strategy to build a strong culture. This refers to the process by which individuals learn the values, expected behaviors, and social knowledge necessary to assume their roles in the organization. By communicating the company's dominant values, job candidates and new hires are more likely to internalize these values quickly and deeply.

More broadly, organizational culture is learned, so an effective network of cultural transmission is necessary to strengthen the company's underlying assumptions, values, and beliefs. Thus, a strong culture requires frequent opportunities for interaction so employees can share stories and re-enact rituals.

Finally, companies can further strengthen and maintain their culture by hiring people whose values are consistent with the organizational culture.

Organizational Change

Now that we have looked closely at the key concept of organizational culture, let us turn to another set of very important organizational processes, those having to do with *organizational change*. Put simply, companies cannot survive if they do not change, because eventually they will not provide products or services that customers want, they will not be able to secure the resources necessary to make those products or services, and they will not remain competitive with other firms in the efficient transformation of inputs to outputs. That is why OB scholars pay a lot of attention to why companies have difficulty changing as well as to various strategies that help them change more smoothly.

In this final section, we will briefly highlight the main sources of resistance to change and how to overcome them. Together, this information answers the last big question we will address, namely: "How can leaders effectively change organizations?"

Sources of Resistance to Change

To understand the problem of resistance to change, consider the situation faced by BP Norge a few years ago. This Norwegian subsidiary of British Petroleum tried to introduce self-directed work teams (SDWTs) on its drilling rigs, but its executive team was met by a wave of complaints.

For example, some employees claimed that previous attempts to create SDWTs had not work. Others complained that SDWTs required more responsibility so they wanted more status and pay. Still others were worried that they lacked the skills to operate in SDWTs.

Unfortunately, the experience of BP Norge is not unusual. Corporate leaders invariably experience varying levels of resistance when introducing change. This phenomenon can be traced to at least six reasons:

1. *Direct costs*—In our example, some BP Norge employees resisted SDWTs because they believed they would result in higher direct costs or lower benefits than the existing situation.

2. *Saving face*—Some people resist change as a political strategy to "prove" that the decision is wrong or that the person encouraging change is incompetent.

3. *Fear of the unknown*—In our example, some BP Norge employees rebelled against SDWTs because they were worried that they could not adapt to an SDWT environment

4. *Breaking routines*—People resist organizational changes that force them out of their comfort zones and require investing time and energy learning new role patterns.

5. *Incongruent organizational systems*—Rewards, selection, training, and other control systems encourage employees to act in a certain way. If these systems do not change, employees will not change either.

6. *Incongruent team dynamics*—Team norms represent a powerful force that guides behavior. However, team norms that conflict with the desired changes may discourage employees from accepting organizational change.

Increasing the Urgency to Change and Minimizing Resistance

Given these sources of resistance, how should leaders bring about change in the organization? There are two parallel strategies. One strategy involves increasing employee motivation to change. The other strategy includes several ways to reduce the various sources of resistance to change.

Regarding the first strategy, leaders need to ensure that employees are aware of the urgency to change. The urgency to change must be real, and employees need to be aware of these forces for change in order to be sufficiently motivated to break out of their comfort zones. That is why it is important for employees to experience the very real forces for change in the external environment. These range from customer complaints and increased competition to an increasing scarcity of valuable resources.

Unfortunately, some organizational leaders will buffer their employees from the external environment, and yet they are surprised when change does not occur. Worse still, some leaders may rely on contrived threats rather than the external driving forces to support the change effort.

Note, however, that increasing the urgency to change usually is not enough to bring about change. That is because employees often "push back" when confronted with these forces for change. That is why effective change management also involves a second strategy, namely, directly dealing with the sources of resistance.

In this regard, *communication* is the highest priority required for any organizational change. It reduces the restraining forces by keeping employees informed about what to expect from the change effort, thereby minimizing fear of the unknown.

Training is likewise an important process in most change initiatives because employees need to break old routines and learn new knowledge and skills. So, too, is *employee involvement*, because participation in the change process tends to help employees save face, feel less uncertainty about the future, and develop team norms that are more supportive of the change.

Still another way to reduce resistance to change is through *negotiation*. Negotiation potentially increases support from employees who bear large direct costs from the change or who need to break routines. However, this strategy merely gains compliance rather than commitment to the change effort, so might not be effective in the long term.

If all else fails, leaders can rely on *coercion* to change organizations. Coercion includes persistently reminding people of their obligations, frequently monitoring behavior to ensure compliance, confronting people who do not change, and using threats of sanctions to force compliance. Firing people who will not support the change is an extreme step, but it is not uncommon. At the same time, coercion is a risky strategy because survivors (employees who are not fired) may have less trust in corporate leaders and engage in more political tactics to protect their own job security.

CONCLUDING REMARKS

Well, that completes our overview of the three major areas of organizational behavior: individual processes, team processes, and organizational processes. Please keep in mind that OB is a huge and indeed sprawling field. Some of the other topics you might want to read about elsewhere include: perceptions, cultural diversity, learning, knowledge management, organizational commitment, job design, reward systems, self-leadership, stress management, individual decision making, creativity, virtual team dynamics, team-building practices, communication, power and influence in the workplace, negotiation strategies, and organizational structures and design.

To close, allow us to repeat these words from the opening quotation to this chapter uttered nearly 100 years ago by the great industrialist Andrew Carnegie:

> Take away my people but leave my factories, and soon grass will grow on factory floors. Take away my factories but leave my people, and soon we will have a new and better factory.

Carnegie's statement reflects the basic message woven throughout this chapter, namely, that organizations are not buildings, or machinery, or financial assets. Rather, they are the people in them. Indeed, organizations are very much like human entities—full of life, sometimes fragile, but always exciting. Our hope is that you will find the subject of organizational behavior not only very exciting but also very useful in your career.

PART FIVE

The MBA Toolbox

CHAPTER 11

Statistics, Decision Analysis, and Modeling—How the Numbers Help Us Manage

Charles P. Bonini*

You can't manage what you can't measure.

William Hewlett

INTRODUCTION

♦ A firm marketing on the Internet has developed two alternative advertisements for displaying its product. The firm pays for the ads to be displayed on the page of an Internet browser. The firm would like to examine which of the ads is more effective in getting customers to click through to their Web page. An experiment is run in which each ad is randomly displayed. The click-throughs are recorded. The data needs to be analyzed to determine if there really is a difference or if the observed result might just be a random effect. *What tools can be used for such analysis?*

♦ An international firm has manufacturing plants at various locations around the world. Each plant has its own operating costs, and production capacities for the firm's products. The firm also has orders and needs to supply its customers around the world. And there are shipping times and costs for delivering the manufactured product. The firm wants to find the production and shipping schedules that minimize the cost of meeting the orders. This is a

---

*Charles P. Bonini is the William R. Timken Professor of Management Science at the Graduate School of Business, Stanford University. This chapter is based upon his textbook (with Warren H. Hausman and Harold Bierman, Jr.) entitled *Quantitative Analysis for Management*, ninth edition, Irwin-McGraw Hill.

complex problem, involving hundreds of decision variables. But there are other issues. The firm may wish to know if it should expand the capacity of any of the facilities or, perhaps, close some. It would also like to know which customers are most profitable and if there are any customers that have more costs than revenue. *How does this firm's executive team go about answering these questions?*

These two examples, one relating to operations and the other to marketing, highlight the over-riding importance of one of the most important core subjects in the MBA curriculum—*management analysis*. And note that while I refer to this subject as management analysis, in truth, it encompasses and includes many different names—statistics, decision analysis, and modeling, just to name a few.

F I G U R E   11-1

The Big Questions and Key Concepts of Managerial Analysis

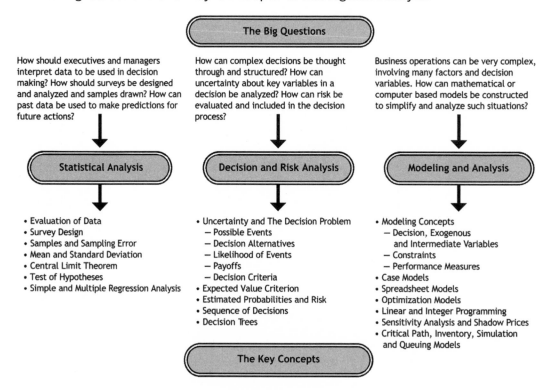

Regardless of how the subject material in management analysis is referred to in a business school's catalog, all MBA curricula have one or more modules of this topic that cover three basic areas: (1) *statistical analysis*, which involves learning about basic statistics such as means and standard deviations and powerful tools like regression analysis; (2) *decision and risk analysis*, which entails a mastery of basic concepts of probability as well as the application of tools like *decision trees*; and (3) *model building and analysis*, which involves the *simulation* or replication of complex problems and the use of complex mathematical tools such as *integer programming*.

In the remainder of this chapter, we will sequentially work our way through the big questions and key concepts presented in Figure 11-1. Before reading on, please take a few minutes to study this figure carefully as it will give you a very nice overview and map of where we are headed.

STATISTICAL ANALYSIS AND THE EVALUATION OF DATA

Properly Evaluating Data

Our first big question is: "How should executives and managers interpret data in decision making?" To answer this big question, we generally have to ask one or more smaller questions. These include: (1) How was the data obtained and what was its source? (2) What is the group represented and is there bias in the selection? (3) Is there a proper comparison? (4) Are there missing factors? (5) Is there proper graphic representation?

To illustrate why these questions are important, I want to offer up three different examples, each of which highlights slightly different problems in data evaluation. Let us start with this little excerpt from the CBS news:

> A startling number of American children in danger of starving. Dan Rather reporting. Good Evening. One out of eight children under the age of twelve is going hungry tonight ...

This "startling" comment was mistakenly based upon a study by an advocacy group that concluded that one in eight children were hungry *once* in the past year—not every night.

A slightly more challenging problem in data evaluation compares the number of automobile traffic deaths in the United States in 1963 (43,265)

T A B L E   11-1

Comparison of Performance of Two Airlines

	Alaska		America West	
Destination	**% Arrivals on Time**	**Number of Arrivals**	**% Arrivals on Time**	**Number of Arrivals**
Los Angeles	88.9	559	85.5	811
Phoenix	94.5	233	92.1	5,255
San Diego	91.4	232	85.5	448
San Francisco	83.1	605	71.3	449
Seattle	85.8	2,146	76.7	262
Overall	86.7	3,775	89.1	7,225

versus those in 2000 (44,281). From these numbers, one might conclude that driving has become less safe over those 37 years. But note that there are many more vehicles on the roads today, driving many more miles. So if one compares the number of vehicle deaths per 100 million vehicle miles the drop is dramatic, 5.41 to 1.55. Viewed in this fashion, automobile safety has increased significantly.

Now here is a third example that illustrates just how subtle the task of data evaluation can be. To set this example up, I want to ask you this seemingly paradoxical question: *Is it possible for one airline to perform better at every single airport it visits—yet still have a worse overall average record than its competitor?*

The surprising answer is *yes!* To see how this can happen, take a look at Table 11-1. Note that Alaska does indeed have a better on-time record at each destination, but its overall performance lags America West.[1] How can this be?

It is simple—albeit subtle. The weather at two particular destinations turns out to be an important missing factor. On the one hand, the great majority of America West stops are in Phoenix, with few weather problems. On the other hand, Alaska has a very significant number of flights to Seattle and San Francisco where weather is often a delay problem. So when you "weight the data" to account for the fact that Alaska flies a lot into Seattle

---

1. A. Barnett, "How numbers are tricking you," *MIT Tech Review*, October, 1994.

and San Francisco and America West flies a lot into Phoenix, the paradox is resolved.

Samples and Surveys

Let us turn now to our next big question: How should surveys be designed and analyzed and samples drawn? In fact, evaluating information based upon samples and surveys is a very important part of any statistical analysis course module.

For example, a marketing department may conduct surveys of potential customers to test new products or evaluate advertising. Operations managers may similarly take samples of incoming materials or outgoing product to determine if quality standards are being met. In either case, a *sample* is taken from some larger group, called a *population* in statistical terminology.

Now one important issue is how the sample should be selected so as not to be unrepresentative or *biased*. A second related issue is how *accurate* is the sample. If the sample is selected at *random*, there is a basic formula that determines the *sampling error*. This formula may be written:

$$\text{Sampling error} = \frac{\text{Standard deviation}}{\sqrt{\text{Sample size}}}$$

where the standard deviation is a measure of variability, and indicates how far away from the average or the mean the individual values vary.

In this regard, there is a very famous theorem in statistics called *The Central Limit Theorem*. This theorem enables one to use the above formula and what is called *Normal Distribution probabilities* for indicating probability limits for the accuracy of samples. While this may sound quite complex, the importance of this observation is that the definition of such limits has several very important uses in a managerial context.

For example, a manufacturing firm may need to make sure that the components of its product meet certain standards. If sampling is used to check on these standards, company analysts must calculate how large a sample will be necessary to assure accuracy within the specified limits. Similarly, if a marketing firm is conducting a survey of potential customers, the analysts can determine the sample size, and hence the cost of the survey necessary to estimate sales.

A very important related topic in statistical analysis is called the *Test of Hypothesis*. The idea here is to use data from a sample to prove or disprove some hypothesis.

For example, a drug manufacturer may conduct a clinical trial to prove that its new drug or medical treatment is superior to existing treatments or to a placebo. Note that the measure of sampling error is an important part of this analysis.

Regression Analysis

Let us turn now to another very important set of tools to evaluate data, that of *simple* and *multiple regression analysis*. In this regard, the ability to make predictions based upon data is another key element in statistical analysis.

In a simple example, let us suppose The Quality Kitchens Company uses promotion expenditures as a means of increasing sales. Such promotion expenditures involve special offers to supermarkets, such as offering one free case with the purchase of three cases. Figure 11-2 below shows the dispersion of the historical data as dots for the past 24 periods and an associated "regression line."

To get that line, *simple regression analysis* involves using the data to estimate an equation relating the two variables—sales and promotions. Such estimation can be done with just about any statistical package on the market today, including the ubiquitous Microsoft Excel. In the example shown, the

F I G U R E   11-2

Promotion versus Sales at Quality Kitchens

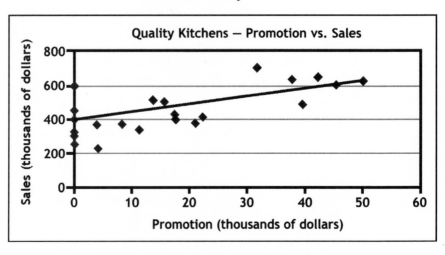

estimated regression equation is:

$$\text{Sales} = 375 + 5.0 \text{ (Promotion)}$$

This equation, and the associated linear "regression line" that can be drawn from it, shows the effect of the promotion and can be used to forecast future sales. In this case, we see that one dollar of promotion is related to five dollars in sales.

Note, however, that this is a very simple model to predict sales, and there may well be a number of other important factors involved. For example, the company may also have advertising directed at consumers and the pattern for these expenditures may overlap with those for the promotion. In addition, there may be seasonal factors to deal with along with both competitor actions and economic conditions that also may effect sales. In such cases where *many* variables may be important, *multiple regression analysis* may be both more appropriate and more valuable than simple regression.

Multiple regression is a similar approach to simple regression and estimates the effect of multiple variables on the one to be predicted. Thus, using multiple regression, Quality Kitchen's statisticians may add both advertising and a seasonal winter variable to the equation, as we see below:

$$\text{Sales} = 883 + 3.11 \text{ (Advertising)} + 5.22 \text{ (Promotion)} + 5.63 \text{ (Winter)}$$

This more textured equation shows the effect of each variable on sales taking into account the other variables effect. More broadly, regression analysis is a

S N A P S H O T   A P P L I C A T I O N   11–1

EXECUTIVE PAY ANALYSIS

Suppose you would like to investigate if the executives in your organization are overpaid or underpaid relative to other executives. There is a consulting firm that collects data for multiple firms including salaries and variables such as the level of the individual in the organization, the number of people reporting to him/her, the size and location of the organization, the sales of the division, the age and experience of the individual, and so on. For any individual, one can use the multiple regression model to estimate the salary for comparable individuals, taking into account the various variables. One can then see if the compensation is comparable.

very powerful tool that is widely used in the real world and in other courses in the business school curriculum.

For example, in the Finance chapter in this book, the authors described the "Beta coefficient" used to measure the variability of a stock price relative to the market. This beta coefficient is estimated using regression analysis on past price movements. Similarly, one important aspect of macroeconomics involves forecasting trends in various economic measures, and, again, regression is a tool used in these analyses.

To round out these ideas and underline the importance of these tools, let us finish this section with Snapshot Application 11-1.

DECISION AND RISK ANALYSIS

Let us turn now to the second major portion of the management analysis curriculum. To begin, let me observe that many of the most important executive and managerial decisions are made under conditions of *uncertainty*. That is, we do not know for sure what the outcome will be.

For example, a company may introduce a new product, but the firm's marketing executives are not sure about customer acceptance and hence about the level of sales. You may buy stock in a given company, but you are not sure if the price will rise or fall. And a company must build up inventory for an item without knowing what the demand will be.

Decision and risk analysis is the process of thinking through such decision problems. Using the tools of such analysis, strategies are determined and evaluated, expected values are determined, and the risks are evaluated.

Example   A major Georgia electric power company is considering selling power to Florida. To do so would require the construction of major transmission lines at a cost of $100 million. The executive team recognizes, however, that there are major uncertainties associated with the investment. These include the final cost, the long run power demand in Florida, the reaction of competitors, and the share of the market the company could get. A decision analysis shows that there is substantial risk associated with the initial planned strategy, and indicates that the company should gather additional information about the competitive situation. After this analysis, the executive team develops a different strategy that can be undertaken with much less risk.

The Five Factors in Decision Analysis

In dealing with any decision problem under uncertainty, there are five factors that must be taken into account:

1. The *decision alternatives* that can be undertaken
2. Any *uncertain events* that can occur
3. The *pay-offs* in profits or costs associated with each pair of events and alternatives
4. The *likelihoods* or *probabilities* that the various events will occur
5. A *decision criterion*, that is, a method for deciding among the alternatives

To illustrate how this five factors come in to play, let us suppose we have a florist in the Honolulu airport who sells a special type of floral arrangement intended for tourists returning home. The arrangements cost the florist $5 each and are sold for $15 each. The unsold floral arrangements must be discarded at the end the day. Since customers are one-time buyers, the florist does not consider any "goodwill loss" from turning away potential buyers.

Now please note that the florist, who has an MBA degree, has kept careful track of past requests and sales and thinks that this experience is representative of tomorrow's possible demand. In the past, between 10 and 17 floral arrangements have been demanded, with the frequency shown in Table 11-2. For example on 5 percent of the days, 10 arrangements were

T A B L E   11-2

Historical Demand for Floral Arrangements

Demand (Units)	Relative Frequency
10	0.05
11	0.05
12	0.10
13	0.15
14	0.20
15	0.25
16	0.15
17	0.05
Total	1.00

T A B L E   11-3

Pay-off Table—Profit in Dollars

Demand (Units)	Amount Stocked							
	10	**11**	**12**	**13**	**14**	**15**	**16**	**17**
10	100	95	90	85	80	75	70	65
11	100	110	105	100	95	90	85	80
12	100	110	120	115	110	105	100	95
13	100	110	120	130	125	120	115	110
14	100	110	120	130	140	135	130	125
15	100	110	120	130	140	150	145	140
16	100	110	120	130	140	150	160	155
17	100	110	120	130	140	150	160	170

demanded. By the same token, on 20 percent of the days, 14 were demanded, while the overall average was 14 units demanded.

In light of this data, the florist's decision problem is the number of floral arrangements to order for tomorrow. The possible *events* are the number demanded, as shown in Table 11-2. The *decision alternatives* are the number ordered, say from 10 to 17. The *likelihoods* for the various events are given in Table 11-2. The *pay-offs* associated with each combination of alternative and event are shown in the Payoff Table in Table 11-3.

For example, if the florist chooses to stock 13 units and 11 are demanded, the cost will be $65 (13 purchased times $5) and the revenue will be $165 (11 sold times $15), for a net profit of $100.

Now let us stop and assess where we are in the florist's decision process. So far, we know four of the five factors for decision making under uncertainty. But the fifth factor we must draw a bead on is the actual *decision criterion*—that is, how should the florist actually decide what to order?

The Expected Value Criterion

One very useful criterion executives and managers often use is the *expected value criterion*. In this case, *the pay-offs are weighted by the probabilities*. This is shown in Table 11-4, where the last column shows the expected value of the pay-offs and is obtained simply by multiplying the previous two columns by one another.

T A B L E   11–4

Calculation of Expected Value for Stocking 13 Floral Arrangements

Demand (Units)	Probability	Payoff	Problem X Pay-off
10	0.05	85	4.25
11	0.05	100	5.00
12	0.10	115	11.50
13	0.15	130	19.50
14	0.20	130	26.00
15	0.25	130	32.50
16	0.15	130	19.50
17	0.05	130	6.50
Total	1.00		124.75

One way to think of this concept is as a long-run average. If the florist were to stock 13 arrangements daily and the demand pattern were as given, the profit would average $124.75 per day. That is, on 5 percent of the days the profit would be $85, on 5 percent it would be $100, on 10 percent $115, and so on, with an average of $124.75.

The results of the calculations for all the alternative stocking levels are shown in Table 11-5. *If the florist were to maximize the expected profit using the expected value criterion, a stock level of 15 floral arrangements would be purchased, with an expected profit of $131.25 per day!*

T A B L E   11–5

Expected Values for All Alternative Stocking Levels

Number Stocked	Expected Value
10	100.00
11	109.25
12	117.75
13	124.75
14	129.50
15	131.25
16	129.25
17	125.00

Note please note the beauty of all this. While the *average* demand is 14 units, *the expected value is actually highest for 15 units.* This is because the profits are taken into account as well as the likelihoods.

This illustration is an example of what is called the *newsboy problem.* It is a very interesting problem that you have already encountered in your chapter on Operations and Supply Chain Management. In fact, the use of the expected value criterion underlies most so-called *inventory models* that are routinely used in most industries. But the concept can be applied to a broad range of problems in addition to inventory planning. It is also widely used in Finance.

Estimating Probabilities and Risk

Let us turn now to the subject of estimating probabilities and risk. We saw in the example above that historical frequencies gave good estimates of probabilities. An important part of any Decision Analysis course is developing approaches for including these factors.

To see how this works, let us consider this real, although much simplified, decision problem for the Blackfoot Potato-Processing Company in Idaho. This firm buys potatoes from growers and processes them into potato flakes that are then sold to food manufacturers such as Proctor and Gamble for making potato chips. Note that the company can purchase its potato requirements in one of two ways, or a combination of the two.

One method is simply to purchase the potatoes on the open market after the crop has been harvested. The other alternative is to use a preseason contract, which is a contract to purchase the growers crop when it is harvested at a price that is set "preseason." In other words, the processing company can purchase all its requirements on the open market, or all by preseason contract, or some combination. Thus, *the decision alternatives involve the different purchase options.*

In considering these alternatives, the firm's potato buyers know that while the preseason price is fixed at the decision-making time, the open market price that will occur when the crop is harvested is the uncertain factor. Indeed, the price could be anywhere from $2.50 to $5.50 per cwt (or hundred pounds) of potatoes—a very wide swath. These prices are the uncertain *events*, and there are many factors contributing to this uncertainty, including the size of the crop planted, weather conditions during the growing season, demand for potatoes, and so.

For example, in a recent year there was a major shortfall in the potato crop in Ireland, leading to major demand for exports of American potatoes. This, in turn, led to very high open market potato prices.

Now in this example we are drawing, the firm's executive team will use the data available and assign their best judgment about the *probabilities* or *likelihoods*, as was illustrated in Table 11-5 for the florist example. In this example, these estimated probabilities, along with the associated pay-offs, are illustrated in Table 11-6.

Note that in the table, only probabilities for prices of $3, $4, and $5 per cwt are shown, but in reality probabilities were assessed for a whole ranges of prices. These are *subjective* probabilities, based upon the best judgment of the management. Note also that the pay-offs are based upon the company's processing costs, sale price of potato flakes, and purchases of potatoes.

We see, then, that in management's judgment, open market potato prices are expected to be low ($4 or $5 per cwt). If the expected value criterion is used, the best decision is to purchase none in the preseason (and hence all in the open market) with an expected payoff of $640,000. But note that this is a very risky alternative, with the possibility of a loss of $800,000. Management has assessed the probability of 20 percent of this event, and may be unwilling to take on this risk. Of course, the least risky alternative is to purchase all the needed potatoes in the open market, but that would be giving up on a possible expected profit of $640,000.

Now here is what is so very interesting about this problem. There is no right "solution." Instead, the executive team must make a judgment

TABLE 11-6

Pay-off Table for Potato Processor Company

Potato Price (dollar per cwt)	Estimated Probabilities	Fraction of Potato Requirements Purchased by Preseason Contract		
		None	50%	100%
3.00	0.4	1,600	1,050	500
4.00	0.4	400	450	500
5.00	0.2	−800	−150	500
Expected Value		640	570	500

about how much risk it wishes to bear. In other words, there is a trade-off between risk and expected return, as there often is in the world of finance.

More broadly, this example illustrates that one can assess subjective probabilities for uncertain events, consider the trade-off between expected profit and risk, and come to a decision.

Sequence of Decisions and Decision Trees

Let us turn now to the concept of the *sequence of decisions* and a very powerful tool in decision analysis known as the *decision tree*. In this regard, many important decision problems involve not just a single decision, but a sequence of decisions.

For example, Merck Drug Merck is a leading firm in the pharmaceutical industry and makes major investments in drug research. It may take many years for Merck to bring a drug to market, and the process involves not only research, clinical trials, and production facilities, but also quite literally hundreds of millions of dollars.

Because many drugs fail at some stage in the process, Merck's executive team must continually cope with such risk. Accordingly, Merck has developed a decision analysis process for evaluating new drugs, including a *decision tree* approach allowing decisions about continuing or abandoning the product at various stages. Company statisticians also use sophisticated methods to evaluate probabilities of success at the various stages based upon Merck's experience. This process has proven very effective in dealing with this very complex decision problem.

Figure 11-3 illustrates a very simplified example for a new product introduction by the Merck executive team. In the tree, *square nodes* represent decisions, and *circle nodes* are events.

Now please follow the narrative along by continually referring back to the above decision tree. We see that at first, the firm must decide about introducing the product or not. If the product is introduced, there is an unknown event—whether the distributor acceptance is *Quick* or *Slow*; and note that the associated probabilities are shown in parentheses.

After learning about the speed of distributor acceptance, the executive team then has a decision to make about its marketing strategy—either to emphasize *Promotion* or *Advertising*. The final event is the sales level—either *High* or *Low*. The resulting cash flow is shown at the end of the branches on the far right.

FIGURE   11-3

Using a Decision Tree to Determine New Product Introduction

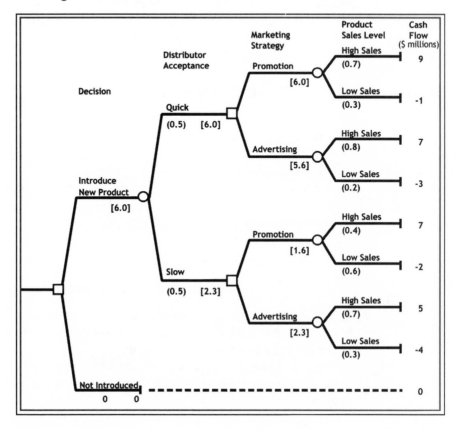

Now please note that the tree is analyzed from right to left, and the expected values are shown in brackets. Based on what you see in the figure, *what, then, do you think is the optimal strategy described by the decision tree?* Take a few minutes to study this tree to come up with your answer.

It should be readily apparent from your study that the optimal strategy is to first introduce the product. If there is Quick distributor acceptance, you should emphasize Promotion, but if there is Slow distributor acceptance, you should emphasize Advertising. The expected value of this strategy is $6.0 million.

More broadly, understanding the details of the tree structure and analysis is not critical here. Rather, the purpose is to show that complex multistage decisions can be analyzed while risk can also be assessed for the various possible strategies. That said, let us turn now to the third major area of management analysis—model building.

MODEL BUILDING AND ANALYSIS

Since most important decision problems are very complex, involving a large number of factors, it often helps to build a simplified replica of the situation. This is called a *model*.

For example, an architect, in designing a new building, will build a small physical replica to demonstrate the design. In contrast, in business situations, the model is usually a mathematical representation of the situation that may be analyzed either on a spreadsheet or using more sophisticated computer software.

Basic Modeling Concepts

In building any model there are a number of factors that are common. The first is the set of *decision variables*. These variables are the factors that are under the control of the decision maker.

Secondly, there are the *exogenous variables*. These important factors are those that are not under the control of the decision maker and must be taken as given.

Thirdly, there are certain *constraints* that limit the actions of the decision maker; and fourthly, there are *performance measures*, indicating the profit (or cost) of the possible solutions.

Finally, there may be other *intermediate variables* involved in doing the calculations for the model. Now here is an example that will help to clarify these concepts.

A maker of laptop personal computers is scheduling production for the next period. The company makes four different models of the computer, the Standard, the Excel, the Sport, and the Superba. These have different features and sell for different prices and the profits for each are shown in Table 11-7. There are two production steps—assembly and test—and each model requires different amounts of time for these operations. These requirements are also shown in Table 11-7.

T A B L E   11-7

Profit and Production Requirements for Example

	Model			
	Standard	Excel	Sport	Superba
Unit profit ($)	120	180	240	300
Assembly time (hours)	5	4	6	8
Test time (hours)	2	3	4	5

In the next period, the firm has 5,000 hours of assembly time and 3,000 hours of test time available. In addition, the Sport and Superba models require a special display screen and the supplier of these has indicated that no more than 250 are available in the next period. Finally, the firm has a contract to supply at least 200 units of the Standard model to a given distributor.

The *decision variables* in this example are the number of each model to produce. We shall label these X_1, X_2, X_3, and X_4, respectively; X_1 for the number of Standard model units, X_2 for the number of Excel units, and so on.

The *exogenous factors* are the limits on special display units and the contract for Standard models. The limits on the test and assembly time are *constraints* and, at least in this case, the exogenous factors are also constraints.

Finally, the *performance measures* are the unit profits for each model. And please note that while there are no specific *intermediate variables* given in this simplified example, they might involve the accounting calculations determining the unit profits.

Now, *the overall objective of the decision maker is to determine a production schedule to maximize profit*. The question is: How will this be done?

The answer may be found in the model and the mathematical equations given below in Figure 11-4. Let us look at this figure carefully now for the purpose of seeing the bigger modeling picture—rather than the deeper math behind it.

In the figure the first line gives the *objective*, which is to maximize the value of an equation. We also see that the second and third lines are the *constraints* on assembly and test time, respectively. The fourth line is the limit on special screens for the Sport and Superba models. And the last line

F I G U R E   11–4

Equations for the Example Model

Maximize:	$120X_1 + 180X_2 + 240X_3 + 300X_4$
Subject to:	$5X_1 + 4X_2 + 6X_3 + 8X_4 \leq 5{,}000$
	$2X_1 + 3X_2 + 1X_3 + 1X_4 \leq 3{,}000$
	$X_3 + X_4 \leq 250$
	$X_1 \geq 200$
	$X_1,\ X_2,\ X_3,\ X_4$ all ≥ 0

indicates the contract requirement relative to the standard model. Note that there is an *implicit* constraint that all of the decision variables must be non-negative, that is, one cannot "unproduce" any.

This is a *linear model*. That is, there are no variables multiplied by each other, no squares or cubes, and no "IF" statements. Rather, each expression is the sum of a constant times a variable. This type of model can be solved by a special mathematical technique previously discussed in the Operations Management chapter called *linear programming*.

This technique is widely available and is incorporated into most spreadsheet software. Using this technique, we can determine that the optimal solution for this example calls for producing 200 units of the Standard, 550 units of the Excel, 250 units of the Sport and none of the Superba, as displayed in Table 11-8. This yields an optimum profit of $183,000.

Now, in this simple example, you could, of course, find the optimal solution with a little trial and error. But consider the much more complex problems faced by a major, vertically integrated oil company. It procures crude oil from different locations each with different characteristics. It operates several refineries in different locations with capacity and storage limits. And it has to supply customers in a variety of locations with different mixes of refined products. Moreover, the refining portion of the operation has to decide on the purchases of crude, how to operate each refinery to get

T A B L E   11-8

Optimal Solution for Example Model

| Product Schedule | | | | | | |
Model	Units	Constraints	Available	Used	Slack	Shadow Prices
Standard	200	Assembly time	5,000	4,700	300	0
Excel	550	Test time	3,000	3,000	0	60
Sport	250	Available screens	250	250	0	60
Superba	0	Contract for standard	200	200	0	60

the right blend of output, and how to store and distribute the output. Most major oil companies have models to manage this decision problem, and the models involve hundreds or even thousands of variables and hundreds of constraints. In such cases, linear programming is a very effective way of dealing with these very complex problems.

Types of Models

Let us look more globally now at the various kinds of models that are the "bread and butter" of MBA management analysis classes. As we do so, let us come to understand the various conditions under which each of the models might be used. Consider, then, Table 11-9. In this table, the various models are arrayed in matrix form along the first column *vertical* dimensions of *simple, complex, and dynamic models* and along the first row *horizontal* dimensions of conditions of *certainty* and *uncertainty.*

From the table, we see that certain types of models are better suited to different types of problems. For example, for *simple problems*, the *case model* may be used. A case model is simply a model of a decision problem that is analyzed by trying out a series of cases (possible outcomes or scenarios) using different alternatives or different assumptions. Note that with such a simple model, the model is not programmed to find the "best" solution directly. Rather the manager uses the model in a trial and error process.

In contrast, many of the other types of models in Figure 11-5 are *optimization models,* in which the model uses mathematical procedures to find the optimal or best solution. One such class of models is the *decision analysis* models that we have already discussed earlier in this chapter. Other

T A B L E   11–9

Types of Models Under Certainty and Uncertainty

	Major Variables in Decision Problem	
Decision Problem	Certain	Uncertain
Simple	◆ Case models	◆ Decision analysis (including decision trees)
Complex	◆ Case models ◆ Linear and integer programming	◆ Simulation
Dynamic	◆ Inventory models ◆ Critical path models	◆ Simulation ◆ Inventory models ◆ Queuing models

optimization models range from linear programming, which we likewise have already discussed, to more complicated *integer programming, simulation, inventory, critical path,* and *queuing* models. What we are going to do now to finish out this chapter is work our way sequentially through the various

F I G U R E   11–5

The Steel-Making Process

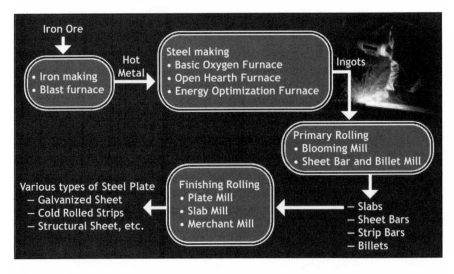

elements of the last two rows of Table 11-9 beginning with the class of models used to address complex problems under certainty and uncertainty.

Complex Problems and Linear Programming

Complex problems are those that involve a large number of important factors or variables, and they may have many alternatives to consider. For example, a firm may have several plants that produce goods for shipment to several hundred customers—as we saw in one of the opening vignettes to this chapter. The decision problem of scheduling the plants and determining which plants will supply which customers in order to minimize cost may involve hundreds of variables and constraints and may have millions of possible solutions.

One method used to solve such problems in the presence of uncertainty is that of *simulation*. Simulation is a technique for modeling large complex systems, and in any simulation, a model is designed to replicate the behavior of the system. Note that simulation models are generally analyzed on a case-by-case basis, although there some very recent software developments that allow limited amounts of optimization.

A second important class of models used to address complex problems involves both *linear programming* and *integer programming*. These widely used models are used under conditions of certainty, and they are based on mathematical techniques to find the maximum (or minimum) of an objective, subject to a set of constraints. Snapshot Application 11-2 uses the real world example of India's Tata Iron and Steel to illustrate the power of linear programming.

Integer Linear Programming

Let us turn briefly now to a variation on linear programming called *integer linear programming*. Integer linear programming is used in some decision situations where the decision variable can take on only two values—both integers rather than any fractions.

For example, a new product may be developed or not. A particular airplane may be assigned to the New York to LA route or it may not. A second shift may be operated or it may not. In such situations, a binary variable that can take on only values of zero or one may be needed—and fractional values are not feasible.

As an example of how integer linear programming may be used to solve this class of problems, consider a firm that is planning to build a new factory. The executive team has three sites under consideration, and it is up

S N A P S H O T   A P P L I C A T I O N   11-2

TATA IRON AND STEEL

Tata Iron and Steel Company is the largest producer of iron and steel products in India. The diagram in Figure 11-5 gives an overview of the steel-making process. Iron ore is converted into hot iron metal in a blast furnace and then made into steel in one of three types of furnaces. The steel emerges from the furnace as hot ingots, which are rolled in rolling mills into various semi-finished products such as so-called slabs, billets, and bars. These intermediate products can then be sold to outside firms for finishing. Alternatively, Tata can finish them on its own finishing mills into various types of steel plate, cold rolled strips, structural steel, and other products.

In recent years, Tata faced a major problem. The various furnaces and mills required substantial electric power to operate. Although Tata supplied part of its power needs from its own generating plants, much of the power was supplied by governmental agencies. These agencies were suffering major power shortages, which were passed on to Tata. When a power shortage occurred, it forced Tata to shut down a part of its operations. This turned a profitable operation when power was available to one losing money when there were shortages.

A debate emerged within the Tata executive team about what operations should be shut down when a power shortage occurred. The conventional wisdom indicated that the mill should maximize tonnage produced, and hence the finishing mills should be shut down since they were not adding tonnage but only finishing tonnage already produced. This implied a product mix with more emphasis on semi-finished products and less of finished products.

Tata employees built a very complex linear programming model for this situation that consisted of fully 770 variables and 680 equations! As indicated above, the conventional wisdom in the company favored total tonnage throughput, which meant emphasizing the semi-finished products. Note, however, that the results of the model suggested a quite different mix that entailed shutting down some primary and some finishing mills in balance. According to the model, this balancing act would result in a very significant increase in profit during the electric shortage periods—profits that were estimated at equivalent of $500,000 U.S. dollars per day!

to the team to come up with a model that will measure the profitability of this decision.

In building this model, the team's management analysts must take into account manufacturing costs, labor costs, and shipping costs for the sites.

S N A P S H O T   A P P L I C A T I O N   11-3

AIRLINE SCHEDULING

A major airline may have several types of aircraft that must be scheduled over many different routes. And the crews have to be assigned to the planes and to each leg of the flight. There are many different constraints. Crews have to be trained and certified for the particular type of craft. There are rules for how many hours a crew can fly, and how many hours between flights. And the schedule must return the crew to its home base.

Note that the crew schedule variables are binary—the crew is either scheduled on a given flight or it is not. Note also that such problems are huge, involving as many as 20,000 variables. But they are essential for airline operations, and all major airlines use integer programming models to solve them.

Note, however, that only one site can be selected. So how can this all be represented in a model?

Simply let X_1 be a variable that takes on the value of 1 if the first site is selected, and 0 otherwise. Similarly, let X_2 be the 0/1 variable for site 2, and X_3 the 0/1 variable for site three. From this specification, the constraint that only one site can be selected can be represented by the following equation:

$$X_1 + X_2 + X_3 = 1$$

As to how to find the optimal solution with integer variables in the model, this is a much more difficult computational task than with regular linear programming. Fortunately, however, modern software has been designed to handle even the largest programs. Snapshot Application 11-3 illustrates the power and importance of integer programming for the airline industry:

Models Involving Uncertainty

Okay, let us again stop and assess where we are. So far, we have covered all the models used in both simple and complex problems under certainty and uncertainty. These models have included case models, decision analysis, linear and integer programming, and simulation. Let us finish with a discussion of two additional types of models described in the bottom right box in the previously introduced Table 11-9 that deal with *uncertainty* in a *dynamic* decision context. These involve models of *queuing* and *simulation*.

Queuing Models

With respect to *queuing models*, all of us have been in situations where we have had to stand in line. It might be waiting for a teller at the bank, for a checkout at the supermarket, the check-in at the airport, or on the telephone waiting for "the next available operator."

Executives and managers who find themselves in these situations know that waiting time is a negative for customers, and wish to reduce it as much as possible. But in some situations, the arrival rate is uncertain and variable. And the service time may also be variable. For example, in a grocery story, some customers will have full shopping carts but others only a few items.

As a solution to keeping customers waiting, a manager or executive can use additional resources to make more service stations available. But there are certainly other options that should be evaluated.

For example, the service stations can be "pooled" rather than individually operated. That is what most banks and airports do, which have a single line for service and many open windows rather than a line at each window.

Another option is the "priority scheme" that can improve service. One example is the "Ten items or less" counter at the supermarket.

Ultimately, the executive team must determine the structure of the queuing system and an appropriate balance between customer waiting time and service cost. For relatively simple waiting line situations, there are mathematical queuing models than can be used for these analyses. Note, however, that if the decision situation is more complex and involves random or uncertain factors, then a *simulation model* may be built for the analysis.

Simulation Models

The particular simulation model that may be constructed may involve the flow of goods or products through several stages. Very sophisticated simulation software may also be used to construct the model. An example may help to understand such a model.

Consider, then, Figure 11-6, which represents the operations of a barge line hauling barge loads of goods from Pittsburgh down the Ohio–Mississippi river system. As you study the figure, note that these barge loads of goods arrive at the Pittsburgh port in a random fashion represented by the frequencies shown in Figure 11-6.

Note also that the destinations of these barges also vary from time to time, shown by the associated frequencies. If a barge is available, it is loaded. Otherwise the load is lost to a competitor barge line.

F I G U R E   11-6

Simulation Model of a Barge Line

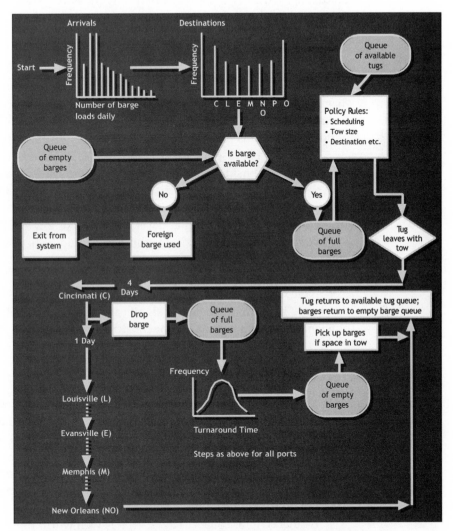

Further note that a tug will start with a tow of full barges and calls on the various ports downstream. Barges destined for each port are dropped accordingly.

In addition, at New Orleans, those barges destined for the Gulf ports of Pascagoula (P) and Orange (O) are transferred to another barge line and then the tug turns upstream and picks up available empty barges from the ports as it goes. These empty barges are available after a turnaround time for unloading, which is a random event. Finally, once back at the home port, the tug returns to the available tug queue and the barges go to the empty barge queue.

Now, a simulation model of this system would include the various steps shown in Figure 11-6. Specifically, it would simulate the operation of the barge line over time, drawing randomly for the uncertain events in the diagram, that is, the frequency of arrivals and destinations and the barge turnaround times. The model would also measure how well the barge line performed in terms of barges hauled and barges lost to competitors.

Note that because the barge company has a limited number of barges and tugs, it is considering adding more equipment. It is also considering new policies about the scheduling departures of tugs. For example, should a tug wait for a full tow before leaving? Alternatively, should tugs be scheduled to leave on a regular basis regardless of tow size?

A number of different simulation runs would be necessary to evaluate these alternatives. And each run would have to cover many periods of time in order to get the long run effect of the possible change.

Note that building a simulation model for something even as simple as this barge line is nonetheless a significant task. Fortunately, there is now outstanding software available for constructing and analyzing such models.

CONCLUDING REMARKS

Well, that concludes our overview of the big questions and key concepts in the three major areas of management analysis—statistical analysis, decision and risk analysis, and model building. As I indicated at the outset of this effort, these topics may be covered in various ways in different MBA curricula. They may be in one or two basic courses, and parts may be included with other courses such as Operations Management or Managerial Economics.

As this chapter comes to its close, it is well worth repeating that it was not my intention to cover all the techniques of management analysis in detail. Rather I have simply provided as a big picture overview some illustrations and examples of real applications of practical tools that you will encounter. These key concepts and tools have proven to be very valuable in the practice of sound managerial decision making.

CHAPTER 12

Managerial Economics— Microeconomics for Managers

Peter Navarro*

INTRODUCTION

* A CEO desperate to pump up the bottom line of his failing company raises product prices to boost profits. Instead, profits plunge, and the bewildered CEO has no idea what microeconomic truck just hit him.

* The CFO of a major bank wants to become the low cost industry leader. So he goes on a major acquisition binge in the hopes of dramatically cutting costs through the realization of economies of scale. To his chagrin, he winds up with exactly the same unit cost structure—and a dismal profit outlook.

* A charismatic entrepreneur at the helm of a small, upstart startup decides to enter a market dominated by a few deep-pocketed, well-branded oligopolists. This budding "war" is over almost before it starts as the market leaders soon bury the startup with a retaliatory advertising blitz and deep price cuts.

These are just some of the many mistakes business executives make when they fail to learn the incredibly valuable lessons of *managerial economics*. Managerial economics is the MBA version of the standard *microeconomics* course taught to college undergraduates. It weds the standard key concepts

*Peter Navarro is a business professor at the University of California-Irvine. This chapter is based upon his multimedia CD-ROM textbook *The Power of Microeconomics*, McGraw Hill, and his book *The Well-Timed Strategy: Executing Strategy Through the Business Cycle*, Financial Times/Prentice Hall, 2005.

and tools of microeconomics with intensive business applications and extensive case analysis to answer the kind of big questions illustrated in Figure 12-1.

As you look this figure over very carefully, it should become obvious that managerial economics is very much an *integrative* discipline with very broad business applications across functions. For example, a better understanding of how prices are set in markets will help those executives and managers in charge of marketing while learning about the economics of production helps those in charge of operations management. In a similar vein, understanding the various elements of market entry and exit can greatly improve the performance of any management strategy team.

With Figure 12-1 as our organizational guide, let us now plunge into the major lessons of managerial economics.

F I G U R E   12-1

The Big Questions and Key Concepts of Managerial Economics

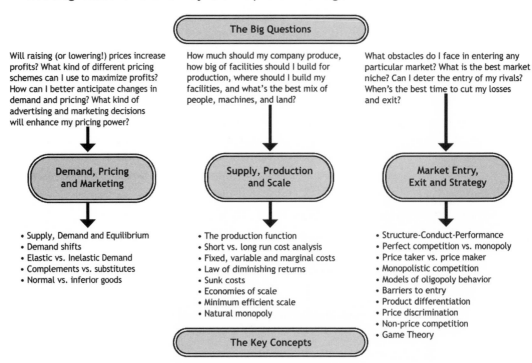

DEMAND, PRICING, AND MARKETING

I will begin by introducing you to the most important graph in all of microeconomics—the big picture that illustrates how the equilibrium price in a competitive market may be found at the intersection of the supply and demand curves. We see such a graph in Figure 12-2, which illustrates the determination of price in the highly competitive semiconductor market.

Note in the figure, that the *supply curve* slopes upward. As the offered price goes up, suppliers are willing to offer more chips in the market. This, of course, is a highly intuitive result since at higher prices, more inefficient and costly chip founders are able to make a buck by producing more chips.

By the same token, the *demand curve* slopes downward. This means that the lower the price, the more chips consumers will be willing to buy. This makes a lot of sense, too. In this case, manufacturers that can buy cheaper chips for their electronic products can sell the products at a cheaper price and therefore sell more of the products. That drives their demand for chips up.

F I G U R E   12-2

Supply, Demand, and Equilibrium

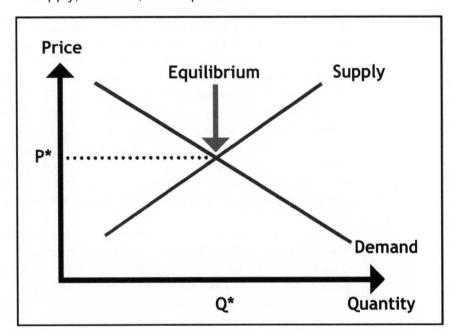

As for the equilibrium price in the market, that may be found at the intersection of supply and demand at a price of p*. At a higher price, suppliers will produce more than consumers will demand so the price will be bid back down to p*. At a price lower than p*, demand will be greater than supply and consumers will bid prices up.

Demand

Okay, that is pretty elementary stuff so far. But now let us make things a bit more interesting by looking more closely at the demand side of the equation. In particular, let us see if we can explore two key concepts—*demand shifts* and *price elasticities*—that are critical to the pricing decisions of your firm.

Demand Shifts

Let us start with the whole notion of *demand shifts*. Suppose you open up your morning newspaper and see on the front page these stories: (1) A large number of U.S. troops will be sent to the Middle East to combat a dramatic rise in urban guerrilla warfare and terrorism; (2) a new study on the health effects of red wine indicates it is a powerful aphrodisiac when combined with Korean ginseng; and (3) ground water contamination is now a pervasive threat to drinking water supplies. In the wake of this news, what do you think will happen to the demand for ceramic body armor, red wine, Korean ginseng, and home water filtration systems?

Of course, demand will go up. But how can this increase in demand be represented in the standard supply–demand figure? Precisely by the outward *shift* in of the demand curve in Figure 12-3A in the body armor, red wine, Korean ginseng, and home filtration systems markets.

By the same token, bad news about a product can shift the demand curve inwards, as in Figure 12-3B. Such a shift might, for example, represent what happened to the demand for air travel in the wake of the 9/11 terrorist attack or the demand for eggs after research indicated that they increased cholesterol levels.

The importance of these shifts is simply that the equilibrium price in the market will change. If you are in one of the affected businesses, you must learn to anticipate such shifts and quickly change your prices accordingly. But what about the actual *slope* of the demand curve? How might it affect your pricing and marketing decisions? Here the key concept of the *price elasticity of demand* comes in.

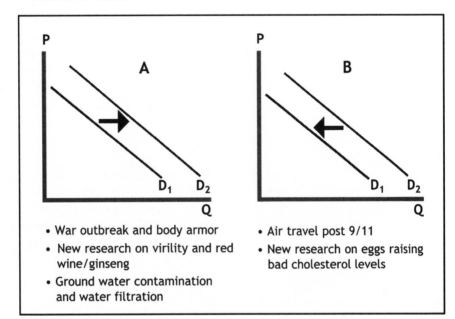

F I G U R E   12-3

Demand Shifts

• War outbreak and body armor
• New research on virility and red wine/ginseng
• Ground water contamination and water filtration

• Air travel post 9/11
• New research on eggs raising bad cholesterol levels

Price Elasticity of Demand

To master this key concept, let us start out by just thinking about the word itself—"elasticity." If you pull back on a rubber band and then let it go, it snaps forward pretty smartly. That is because it is quite elastic. But if you pull back on a piece of string, it only snaps back a little bit. It is quite inelastic.

Well, the price elasticity of demand simply measures how much consumers will increase or decrease their quantity demanded in response to a price change. A big change means demand is elastic like the rubber band and a small change means demand is inelastic.

This idea is important because it lies at the very heart of determining whether a price hike is likely to lead to higher total revenues and profits. In fact, *if demand is elastic, a price hike will lead to just the opposite result that is desired—not higher, but rather lower total revenues and profits.* And that is exactly what happened to our fictional and desperate CEO in the opening vignette of this chapter. To see why this is so, take a look at the two demand curves in Figures 12-4A and B and study the slopes very carefully.

The graph on the left depicts the case of very *inelastic demand*—the curve is nearly *vertical*. In this case, consumers respond to an increase in price by continuing to buy almost the same amount of product.

Such inelastic demand more or less fits the description of products ranging from illegal drugs like cocaine and heroin to legal drugs like cigarettes, alcohol, and heart medication. The idea is simply that "people gotta have it no matter what" so they will continue to buy as much or almost as much of the product if prices are jacked up. Of course, *because the firm is selling almost the same amount of the product but at a higher price, profits must go up!*

At the other end of the spectrum, and as represented in the almost horizontal demand curve in the right side figure, you have highly *elastic demand*. In this case, if a firm raises the price of its product—in this case, beef—people reduce their beef buying substantially (and start buying more chicken or pork). *The result of a price hike in the face of highly elastic demand is to drive profits significantly down!*

F I G U R E   12-4

Demand Elasticities and the Slope of the Demand Curve

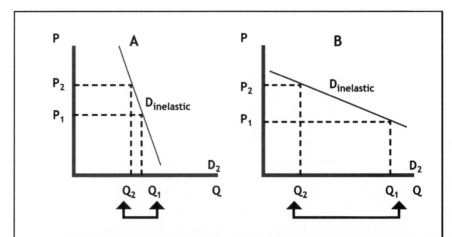

An increase in price from P1 to P2 results in a small reduction in quantity demanded for inelastic goods and a big reduction for elastic goods.

The point of this key concept, of course, is that when a company designs its pricing policies, executives must take into consideration factors such as the price elasticity of demand in order to find that set of prices that will maximize the company's profits. But note this. It is not just *pricing strategies* that the concept of elasticity of demand can help. It is also broader *marketing strategies*. For example, why do you think many airlines offer fare discounts to people who stay over on a Saturday night?

It is because airlines are trying to sort out two different kinds of customers: business people with more inelastic demands who want to fly home on the weekends and be with their families versus pleasure travelers who do not mind staying over on a Saturday night. By making this separation, the airlines can effectively charge two prices: a higher one to business travelers and a lower one to pleasure travelers. This means more total passengers and more total revenue.

Okay, here is another one: Why do most new cars not sell at their sticker price? Put another way, why do you have to go in and haggle when you buy a car whereas if you go to buy a gallon of milk, you just pay the sticker price?

It is because car salespersons are trained to sort out "comparison shoppers" with more elastic demands from "impulse buyers" who have inelastic demands. By not listing the selling price of cars, the salespersons can charge the impulse buyers more. Table 12-1 illustrates a number of other pricing strategies that are elasticity dependent. See how many you recognize.

Determinants of Demand Price Elasticities

Of course at this point, inquiring business minds may want to know what exactly determines the price elasticity of demand for a product? In fact, there are really four factors at work. As a preface to our explanation, take a look at Table 12-2, taken from my CD-ROM textbook, *The Power of Microeconomics*. This table lists the price elasticities for a variety of products. As you scan it, try to develop intuitive reasons as to why some of the products are elastic, with elasticities above 1, and why some are inelastic, with elasticities closer to 0.

Now let us test your intuition. In the table, did you notice that *necessities* like housing, electricity, and bread are very price *inelastic* (see bold)? On the other hand, goods that tend more towards being *luxuries* like restaurant meals and glassware are very price elastic (see bold). Besides luxuries versus necessities, other important determinants of elasticity include: substitutability, proportion of income, and time.

T A B L E   12-1

Pricing Strategies with Market Power

Block pricing	When consumers purchase multiple units, firms offer two or more of the product in a package at less than the single unit price. *Example: Jockey shorts sold in packs of three.*
Bundling	Retailers offer free parking with purchase, fixed price meals in restaurants, and season tickets for sporting events. *Example: You buy front row season tickets to the Lakers and get your own monogrammed parking space.*
Coupons and rebates	Used to attract new customers as well as sell to consumers with a relatively low opportunity cost of time. *Example: Grocery stores.*
Price discrimination: first degree	Extract the maximum value each consumer is willing to pay. *Example: College tuition where financial aid packages match preferences.*
Price discrimination: second degree	This is called "menu pricing," where all customers are offered the same menu of options. *Example: Phone plans.*
Price discrimination: third degree	Different prices for different groups depending on price sensitivity. *Example: Utilities charge different rates to different classes of users like residential versus industrial.*
Two-part tariffs	Pay an upfront fee for the right to buy the product and pay additional fees for each unit consumed. *Example: Pay to enter a county fair and then pay for each ride.*

Suggested by: James Brickley, Clifford Smith, Jr., and Jerold Zimmerman, *Managerial Economics and Organizational Architecture*, Irwin-McGraw Hill, 2004.

T A B L E   12-2

Representative Demand Price Elasticities

Product or Service	Elasticity of Demand	Product or Service	Elasticity of Demand
Housing	**0.01**	Milk	0.63
Electricity (household)	**0.13**	Household appliances	0.63
Bread	**0.15**	Movies	0.87
Telephone service	0.26	Beer	0.90
Medical care	0.31	Shoes	0.91
Eggs	0.32	Motor vehicles	1.14
Legal services	0.37	China, glassware, etc.	**1.54**
Automobile repair	0.40	Restaurant meals	**2.27**
Clothing	0.49	Lamb and mutton	2.65

The more substitutes for a good, the more elastic its demand. For example, beef has a lot of substitutes—poultry, fish, and soy products. In contrast, crack cocaine has few or no substitutes. That is why a drug addict's demand is much more inelastic than a beef eater's—as we saw in the graphs above.

A third factor determining elasticities is the proportion of income. Other things equal, the higher the price of a good relative to your budget, the greater will be your elasticity of demand for it.

For example, a 10 percent increase in the price of pencils will amount to only a few pennies, with little response in the amount you demand. But a 10 percent increase in the price of housing would have a significant impact on the quantity of house you would purchase.

The fourth factor is time. In general, demand will tend to be more elastic in the longer run than in the short run. For example, during the energy crisis of the 1970s, the demand for oil was very inelastic in the short run. However, over time, businesses invested in energy-saving technologies while people started driving more fuel-efficient cars, and the demand elasticity increased.

SUPPLY AND PRODUCTION THEORY

Let us turn now to the supply side of the market equilibrium equation—that part of MBA managerial economics that teaches *production theory*. To begin, let us suppose that tomorrow morning you wake up and find yourself as the main character in a Steven Spielberg movie called "Back to the Business Future." You are a refugee from the new millennium, circa AD 2010, and you find yourself smack dab in the middle of 1972 shortly before the OPEC oil cartel slapped an embargo on the American economy.

Your only possessions are the design and engineering blueprints of a highly energy-efficient automobile—blueprints that your mad scientist buddy stuffed in your hands just before he accidentally catapulted you back to one of the worst decades in American economic history. Some friend, uh?

Now to round out this plot, let us assume that the only way you can save the planet from a rapacious foreign cartel—and also get back home to your family and friends—is to make a hundred million bucks producing these energy-efficient cars. How do you do it?

The Production Function

Well, the first thing you have to settle upon is your "recipe" for producing the car. This recipe is called the *production function*, and in technical terms, it specifies the maximum output that can be produced with a given quantity of inputs for a given state of engineering and technical knowledge. Algebraically, it looks like this:

$$Q = F(K, L, R)$$

where Q is the quantity of cars you want to produce, K is the *capital* or plant and equipment that you will need for the production, L is the number of employees or quantity of *labor*, and R is a catch-all term for other things like *raw materials* and *energy*.

As for that "*F*" term, that is very important. It stands for "a *function* of" and it summarizes the state of the current technology. The more advanced the technology, the more output you will be able to produce for a given mix of labor, capital, and resource inputs.

Now the questions facing you are: *What combination of inputs are you going to choose and, by implication, what will be the size of your automobile plant?* To answer these questions, we first have to distinguish between the *short run* and the *long run*.

The Short versus Long Run

To illustrate the *short run*, suppose the factory for your energy-efficient auto is already up and running and producing 10,000 cars a year. Further suppose that the Organization of Petroleum Exporting Countries—that nasty OPEC cartel—slaps an embargo on the United States and quadruples the price of oil—just as it did in 1973 and 1974. At this point, demand starts to increase dramatically for your cars as consumers seek to substitute your Gas Miser for their gas guzzlers. What do you do?

In the short run, you add two more shifts, hire more workers and use more energy and raw materials as you try to run your plant around the clock to meet increased demand. In fact, in the short run, this is your only option because it would take over a year to build a new factory. And that is the definition of the short run! *The short run is the period in which firms can adjust production only by changing variable factors such as materials and labor but cannot change fixed factors such as capital.*

In contrast, the *long run* is a period sufficiently long enough so that all factors in the production function, including capital, can be adjusted. In this case, it is the time it would take for you to expand your existing factory or build a new one. This distinction between the short and long run is important in production theory because each period has its own kind of cost analysis.

Short Run Cost Analysis

To get a handle on short run cost analysis, please now take a look at Table 12-3, which details the fixed, variable, and marginal auto production costs at your factory. The first column is the quantity of cars your factory can produce in thousands and the second column simply represents your firms' *fixed costs*. As you learned in the chapter in this book on financial accounting, these fixed costs are sometimes called *overhead*, and fixed costs are those costs that do not change with the level of output.

Examples of fixed costs include rent, interest on the bonds you issued to get money to build your factory, insurance premiums, the salaries of top

T A B L E   12-3

Fixed, Variable, and Marginal Costs

1	2	3	4	5	6	7	8
				Marginal Costs (MC)	Average Fixed Costs (ATC)	Average Variable Fixed Costs (AVC)	Average Total Costs (ATC)
Output	Fixed Costs (FC)	Variable Costs (VC)	Total Costs (TC)	(Change in Total Costs)	(AFC) FC/Output	VC/Output	AFC + AVC
4	50	50	100	10	12.50	12.50	25.00
5	50	60	110		10.00	12.00	22.00
10	50	100	150	6	5.00	10.00	15.00
11	50	106	156		4.54	9.64	14.18
17	50	150	200	7	2.94	8.82	11.76
18	50	157	207		2.78	8.72	11.50
21	50	182	232		2.38	8.67	11.05
23	50	200	250	10	2.17	8.70	10.87
24	50	210	260		2.08	8.75	10.83
28	50	250	300	15	1.79	8.93	10.72
29	50	265	315		1.72	9.14	10.86
32	50	350	400		1.56	10.94	12.50

management, and so on. Note that all of the rows in this column are all equal to the same thing—50. *Fixed costs are fixed, and that is the point!*

The second and third columns represent *total variable costs* and *total cost*. *Variable costs* are simply those costs that change with the level of output. For example, when you increase production to meet demand, you have to pay for more raw materials and fuel. You also have to pay more in wages to cover the increased overtime and additional workers. Those are all variable costs. Now in the table, note that *total cost is simply variable costs plus fixed costs*.

The fifth column represents a very important concept in economics—*marginal cost*. Marginal cost is simply the additional cost incurred in producing one extra unit of output. Thus, in the table, when we increase output from, say, 10 to 11, we observe that total cost increases from 150 to 156. In this case, the marginal cost of that additional unit of production is six.

At this point, the astute reader will notice an interesting pattern: *while fixed costs stay the same in column two and both variable and total costs rise, marginal costs first fall and then rise.* How would you explain this pattern?

The Law of Diminishing Returns

The answer lies in one of the most important key concepts in all of economics: *The law of diminishing returns.* What is this law? In the context of production theory, we have to first remember that in the short run, capital is fixed but factors like labor are variable. In such a situation, adding more workers means that each additional unit of labor has less capital to work with. At some point, however, as the factory floor gets crowded with workers, the extra or marginal product of each additional worker must begin to decrease so production per unit becomes costlier. That is the law of diminishing returns!

Average Fixed, Variable, and Total Cost

Now let us complete our short run cost analysis table by introducing the final three columns in our table for *average fixed cost* (AFC), *average variable cost* (AVC), and *average total cost* (ATC). Columns six, seven, and eight are simply derived by calculating averages using columns one through four and the formulas in the table.

The interesting thing about these three columns is the graph we can draw from them and our now old friend marginal cost. Look at Figure 12-5 carefully and use your intuition to try to answer these questions: Why does

F I G U R E   12-5

The Big Cost Curve Picture

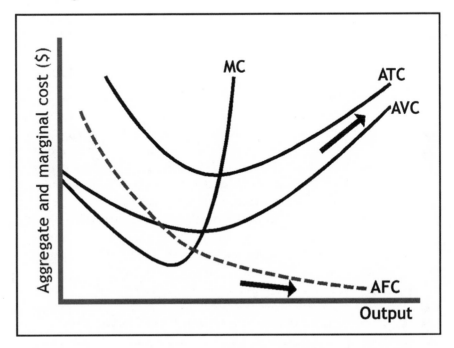

the AFC curve slope downward and approach zero on the horizontal axis while the AVC curve approaches the ATC curve?

The AFC curve approaches zero because as a firm's output increases, it spreads its fixed costs over a larger number of units so average fixed costs must fall. For the same reason, the AVC curve must approach the ATC curve as output increases. *These are important insights in business because the name of the game is often to spread your fixed costs over as many units as possible.*

Now here is a trickier question. We know why the ATC, AVC, and MC curves slope first down and then up—it is the law of diminishing returns. Remember? *But why does the MC curve intersect both the AVC and AC curves at their minimums?*

The answer is simply that if MC is greater than ATC, then the ATC must be rising, and vice versa. Think of it this way. If the production of an additional unit has a marginal cost greater than the average cost, then production of that unit must drive the average up, and conversely. Thus, it must be that only when MC = ATC that the ATC is at its lowest point.

This is a critical relationship. *It means that a firm searching for the lowest average cost of production should look for the level of output at which marginal cost equals average cost.*

Long Run Cost Analysis

Now let us turn to *long run cost analysis*. Recall that the long run is when all factors are variable, including capital. Let us put this in plain terms by going back to our example and your Back to the Business Future auto plant.

Remember that in the beginning, we assumed that you started off with a relatively small plant. Then, as demand expanded, you built more plant capacity. Now suppose that this pattern kept repeating itself and that you kept building larger and larger plants. What do you think would happen to your firm's average cost as plant scale increased?

It is a good question, but it is also a trick question because there are a number of possible answers. Figure 12-6 represents the first answer.

F I G U R E   12-6

The Long Run Average Cost Curve

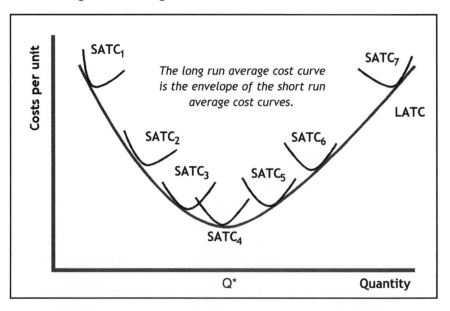

It illustrates an important mantra that I want you to remember. The long run average cost curve is the *envelope* of the short run average cost curves.

Think of this envelope concept this way. For any given plant scale, two things are certain: capital inputs are fixed in the short run AND there is a point on the ATC curve where average cost is minimized. Now, if you build a bigger plant, output will increase, and there will be another short run ATC curve created. Each point on this bumpy planning curve shows the least unit cost obtainable for any output when the firm has had time to make all desired changes in plant size.

Now there is something very important I want you to notice about this long run cost curve: its obvious broad U-shape. The U-shape of the long run average cost curve suggests that, at least up until point Q*, a larger and larger plant size will mean a lower and lower unit cost. However, beyond Q*, successively larger plants mean *higher* average total costs. The reason for this is *not* the law of diminishing returns, which explained our U-shaped short run average cost curves! That is because in the long run, the law of diminishing returns does not apply because all factors are variable. Instead, the explanation lies in understanding the key concept of *economies of scale.*

Economies of Scale

Economies of scale exist when the per unit output cost of all inputs decreases as output increases. For example, if producing 40,000 VCRs costs the firm $16,000 or $400 each but producing 200,000 VCRs costs the firm $40,000 or $200 each, there are significant economies of scale associated with the higher output level. Such economies of scale may be traced to such factors as increased labor and managerial specialization and more efficient capital use.

Increased labor specialization means dividing and subdividing jobs as plant size increases. Instead of performing five or six jobs, a worker can focus on one. For example, in a small plant, a skilled machinist might spend half the time performing unskilled tasks leading to higher production costs. Greater specialization also eliminates the loss of time that occurs when workers shift between jobs.

Similarly, with managerial specialization, a supervisor who can handle 20 workers will be under-used in a small plant as will a sales specialist who may have to divide his or her time between other managerial functions such as marketing, personnel, and finance.

Larger plant size also facilitates the most efficient capital use. For example, in the auto industry, the most efficient production method involves robotics and sophisticated assembly line equipment. But effective use of such machinery and equipment requires an output of at least 200,000 cars.

Four Cost Curve Possibilities

Now take a look at Figure 12-7. It shows four very different possible long run cost curves for a given industry. The first graph on the top left shows the broad U-shaped curve we observed earlier. But in the second graph on the top, note that the U-shape is much more pronounced—in fact, it is more like a V-shape. Note also the flat segment in the third graph—bottom left. And finally, note the downward slope in the fourth graph—bottom right. Intuitively, how would you explain the shapes of each of these curves?

Let us start with the second graph. Here, the narrow and steep U-shape indicates that economies of scale are exhausted quickly so that minimum unit costs will be encountered at a relatively low output. The typical profile

F I G U R E   12-7

Four Possible Shapes of the Long Run Cost Curve

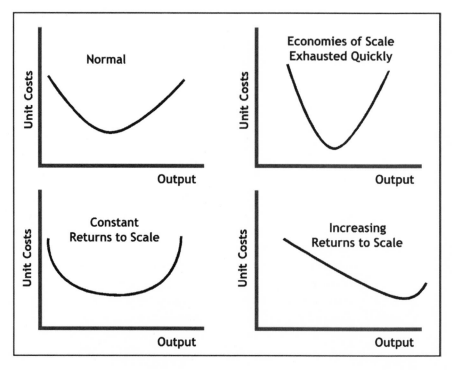

of an industry characterized by this normal kind of curve is numerous sellers and healthy competition. Examples include many retail trades and some types of farming as well as certain types of light manufacturing such as baking, clothing, and shoes. In such industries, a particular level of consumer demand will support a large number of relatively small producers.

In the third graph, we have *constant returns to scale*. That is, rather than a smooth U, there is a long flat spot in the middle of the curve over which unit costs do not vary with size. This is the case of constant returns to scale, and it is has important implications for business executives contemplating strategic decisions such as mergers and acquisitions.

For example, during the 1980s, there were a lot of mergers in the commercial banking industry. At the time, most analysts thought that unit costs would fall dramatically. After all, banks could close some of their branches in overlapping markets and combine support services such as computer processing, advertising, auditing, and legal work. However, the mergers did not significantly reduce costs. *The likely culprit was constant returns to scale over a broad spectrum of output—as our fictional CFO in the second opening vignette to this chapter found out the hard way.*

Now take a look at the fourth graph. This is one of the most famous pictures in economics because it is the signature of *natural monopoly*. Because unit costs steadily fall, we have *increasing returns to scale* over the relevant range of output. This means that over time, bigger producers will drive out smaller producers until there is only one producer left—the infamous monopolist.

The result of this so-called *market failure* is that price will be set too high and output too low for market efficiency, and government regulation may be warranted. That is why we see *regulated* natural monopolies such as the railroads and electricity and gas distribution.

The case of natural monopoly allows us to introduce yet another important key concept in production theory—*minimum efficient scale* (MES). This is defined as the smallest level of output for which a firm can minimize long run average costs.

In our constant returns to scale figure, this point is reached where the curve first flattens. However, note that because of the extended range of constant returns to scale, relatively large and relatively small firms can coexist and be equally viable. This, in fact, is the case in industries such as apparel, food processing, furniture, wood products, and small appliances.

In contrast, in the case of natural monopolies such as the railroads and utilities, small firms cannot realize the MES—the minimum efficient scale—so there is only one seller. At the same time, a large MES can also give rise to another type of industry structure known as oligopoly, which is characterized by a small number of large sellers. Examples include automobiles, aluminum, steel, and cigarettes.

The broader point here is that the shape of an industry's long run average cost curve has an enormous influence on the structure of that industry. Will it be competitive, oligopolistic, or monopolistic? And that would seem to be an excellent segue to our next set of managerial economics decisions—those involving market entry, exit, and broader strategic issues.

MARKET ENTRY, EXIT, AND STRATEGY

To help analyze entry and exit decisions, I am going to introduce a key concept known as the *Structure–Conduct–Performance paradigm*, which is illustrated in Figure 12-8. The powerful idea behind this paradigm is that the *structure* of a market—for example, whether it is highly competitive or monopolistic—will determine market *conduct* with respect to both strategic and tactical decisions regarding pricing, output, and entry. Moreover, conduct and strategy will, in turn, determine market *performance* with respect to the industry's level of profits and rates of return, the rate of technological change and innovation, and the level of capital investment as well as broader public policy yardsticks related to market efficiency and equity.

As I discuss this Structure–Conduct–Performance paradigm, note that we will revisit a number of the same themes and ideas to which you were

F I G U R E   12-8

The Structure–Conduct–Performance Paradigm

How many firms in the industry? Are firms big or small? What is the cost structure? What is the distribution of market share and market concentration?

Are the firms price takers or price makers? Are prices set closer to the competitive or monopolisitc outcome? Do firms collude to restrict output? Do firms deter the entry of rivals?

How will consumers, producers, and the broader society fare given the market structure and the conduct that flows from it?

Market Structure → **Market Conduct and Strategy** → **Market Performance**

- Perfect Competition
- Monopolistic Competition
- Oligopoly
- Monopoly

- Pricing
- Output
- Entry
- Exit

- Level of profits & rates of return
- Rate of technological change and innovation
- Level of capital investment
- Market efficiency
- Market fairness

introduced in Chapter 3 on management strategy. In fact, the field of management strategy is, in many ways, highly derivative of the kind of industry analysis featured in managerial economics. So let us see if we can help connect the dots now between strategy and economics.

Market Structure

Market structure refers to how many firms are in an industry, whether the firms are big or small, what the firm's cost structures look like, and how market share is divided among the firms. The four major types of market structure include *Perfect competition*, *monopolistic competition*, *oligopoly*, and *monopoly*.

Figure 12-9 illustrates the four basic forms of market structure, their underlying assumptions, the types of conduct one is likely to observe, and the performance business executives can expect.

From the business executive's point of view, the most important feature of each form of market structure is the degree of pricing and market power

FIGURE   12-9

The Four Forms of Market Structure

Grains like wheat and corn Commodities like copper	Book publishing Paperboard boxes Men's suits Upholstered furniture	Chewing gum Diapers Cigarettes Car rentals Razors Soda	Electricity Gas Water Cable TV
• Numerous buyers and sellers • Homogeneous product • Free entry and exit • Complete information	• Relatively large number of sellers • Easy entry and exit • Market concentration low • Product differentiation	• Small number of large firms • Barriers to entry • Market concentration low • Product differentiation	• One seller • Barriers to entry • Economies of scale for natural monopolies • Often regulated
Perfect Competition	**Monopolistic Competition**	**Oligopoly**	**Monopoly**
• Price takers • P=MC • Consumers receive most goods at lowest price • Allocatively efficient	• Heavy advertising to increase product differentiation • Pricing power rises with product differentiation • Non-price competition common	• Level of strategic interaction high • Explicit or tacit collusion on price and output • Entry deterrence • Price closer or equal to monopoly outcome	• Price maker • P=MR • Price higher and output lower than perfect competition • Allocatively inefficient

that each endows upon participants in that market. Put simply, if you are stuck in a perfectly competitive market, you will not have a lot of room for strategic maneuvering and will spend the bulk of your time minimizing your costs. But find yourself in an oligopolistic or monopolistic position, and let the strategic games begin!

Let me show you why this is so by delving a little deeper into the question of what exactly determines a market's structure. And let us begin with the left-hand side of Figure 12-9 and the basic assumptions underlying the polar case of perfect competition.

Perfect Competition

Arguably the most important requirement of *perfect competition* is *numerous buyers and sellers*. When this assumption is met, any one firm's output is miniscule compared to the market output—like a grain of sand compared to a beach. Therefore, what one firm does has no influence on what other firms do. This condition is important because it is one of the primary reasons why perfectly competitive firms are *price takers* rather than price makers in the market.

A second important assumption of perfect competition is that of a *homogenous product* where each firm's output is indistinguishable from any other firm's output. Examples include commodities such as wheat and coal. In contrast, you can buy 30 different brands of differentiated products. Soda is not soda, it is 7-Up or Coke. Cars are not cars, they are Fords and Volvos. And so on.

The homogeneous product assumption is important because it means that every firm in the industry is selling exactly the same product so that *the only thing that firms can compete on is price* and not on other things such as product design and product quality. As we shall see, a key difference between perfect competition and monopolistic competition is that with monopolistically competitive firms, products are differentiated and nonprice competition is common.

Still a third important assumption is that of *free entry and exit*: additional firms may freely enter an industry when prices and profits rise and just as easily exit the industry in the presence of losses. In order for this free entry condition to hold, there must be no barriers to entry. Such barriers range from exclusive patents and the large capital requirements symptomatic of natural monopolies, to the ownership of valuable resources such as the bauxite reserves owned by Alcoa, the world's largest aluminum producer.

Now, given a market structure of perfect competition, what kind of conduct with respect to pricing can we expect? The answer is that price will be set to a firm's "marginal cost" of production, that is, P = MC. Moreover, this pricing scheme will be economically efficient because the market is allocating resources efficiently and consumers will receive the most output at the best price.

Monopoly

We do not get such a happy result for consumers and society, however, at the other end of the spectrum in Figure 12-9 where *monopoly* exists. This is when there is only one seller in the market selling a product for which there are no close substitutes. In such a case, the monopolist is a *price maker*, meaning that he or she exerts considerable control over what the market price will be. And please note, the monopolist wields this power by controlling the quantity supplied in the market.

In this regard, the monopolist has a quite different pricing rule. The monopolist will not set price equal to its marginal cost but rather to its higher *marginal revenue*, where marginal revenue is simply the amount of revenue obtained by selling the last unit and higher than marginal cost. *The result is that consumers pay a lot more for a lot less—while the monopolist earns profits well above that of the perfect competitor.*

Oligopoly

While perfect competition and monopoly are useful to study to fix our ideas about market structure, they are more the exceptions, rather than the rule, in most global economies. Indeed, most industries fall somewhere between these two extremes and can be classified either by monopolistic competition or oligopoly.

To analyze the strategic implications of *oligopoly*, let us begin with this question: What do these American industries have in common: tennis balls, disposable diapers, chewing gum, cigarettes, baseball cards, electric razors, car rentals, batteries, soft drinks, credit cards, razor blades, toothpaste, beer, soap, coffee, canned soup, canned tuna, and spaghetti sauce. If you guessed that all of them are oligopolies, go to the head of the class.

Oligopoly exists when a small number of typically large firms dominate an industry. The central element of oligopoly is the *strategic interactions* that might arise through either explicit or tacit *collusion* over price, output, and market entry and exit.

Strategic interaction is a term that describes how each firm's business strategy depends on their rivals' strategies. Put simply, as the number of firms in an industry shrink and industry concentration grows, the executives of each firm are more likely to base their pricing and output decisions more on how other firms in the industry are likely to respond.

With this mutual interdependence recognized, the executives of each firm are more likely to want to collude when setting price and quantity—where *collusion* may be defined as the concerted actions by such executives to restrict output and fix price.

Now, here is the important point: *Because of the small number of firms in an oligopoly, collusion is possible.* To understand when such collusion might take place, we first must explain the sources of oligopoly.

As with monopoly, one such source is the presence of the previously discussed *economies of scale* in production. There is an important difference here, however. In the case of monopoly, the minimum efficient scale is so big that there is room for only one player. With oligopoly, it is simply a variation on this theme: *A few large firms win the race to achieve their minimum efficient scale and drive every one else out.*

To see why scale matters, consider this typical *market entry* problem. Assume you want to enter an industry in which there are already three big firms. Each currently produces at their minimum efficient scale, and each has an equal share of the existing market. If your new firm tries to enter the industry at a plant size less than the minimum efficient scale of the existing players, your firm will be a higher cost producer than your three rivals and at a severe strategic disadvantage. In fact, all your rivals need to do to bury you is to set price below your new firm's costs, inflict heavy losses upon you, and eventually, you will withdraw. In fact, that is exactly what happened to our upstart entrepreneur in the third opening vignette to this chapter. Alternatively, if your firm decides to build a plant big enough to achieve the minimum efficient scale, it will have to seize a sizeable market share from its rivals to achieve efficient production. In this example, it would have to grab enough market share to cut each of the other Big Three rivals down from a third to a fourth of the national market. *The likely result would be losses for all four firms.* Given this dilemma, it is perhaps not surprising that scale-economy barriers deter entry into the industry and preserve the oligopolistic structure.

Of course, there are other important barriers to entry beyond mere economies of scale. One such barrier is the large capital requirements that characterize industries like cigarettes, autos, steel, and petroleum refining.

In each of these industries, it simply requires a lot of capital investment to set up the elaborate plant and equipment necessary to produce. In this case, the broader problem is that established firms with a track record may have better access to lower cost capital than new entrants.

Still a third important barrier has to do with absolute-cost advantages derived from valuable know-how in production or so-called trade secrets. For example, one of the best-kept secrets in the industrial world is the secret ingredient in Coca Cola. Only a few executives in the company know what it is.

The bottom line here is that barriers to entry play a very important role in creating and sustaining oligopolistic industries. An obvious next question is: What does this imply for management strategy? Before we answer that, let us turn to our fourth major form of market structure, namely, the seemingly oxymoronic *monopolistic competition*.

Monopolistic Competition

The defining characteristics of *monopolistic competition* are: (1) a relatively large number of sellers; (2) easy entry to, and exit from, the industry; and (3) product differentiation. The first and second characteristics provide the "competitive" aspect of monopolistic competition while the third characteristic contributes the "monopolistic" aspect.

In fact, monopolistic competition is one of the most prevalent market structures in the American economy. From mattresses to men's suits, from book publishing to paperboard boxes, and from upholstered furniture to fur goods, all these industries are monopolistically competitive just as are the industries producing the several hundred magazines on a newsstand rack and the 50 or so competing brands of personal computers. Perhaps the best way to understand monopolistic competition and what this market structure implies for the management of your company is to focus on the differences between monopolistic competition and oligopoly on the one hand and monopolistic competition and perfect competition on the other hand.

Monopolistic Competition versus Oligopoly and Perfect Competition The biggest difference between oligopoly and monopolistic competition is that monopolistically competitive industries are relatively unconcentrated. That is, each firm has a comparably small percentage of the total market so that each has limited control over market price. *This relatively large number of firms in a monopolistically* *competitive industry ensures that collusion is all but impossible.* In contrast, market concentration in an oligopoly is relatively high and so, too, is the oligopolists' price-making power.

As for the connections between monopolistic competition and perfect competition, monopolistic competition resembles perfect competition in three ways: there are numerous buyers and sellers, entry and exit are easy, and firms are price takers. *The big difference, however, is that with monopolistic competition, there is product differentiation—one of the most important key concepts in all of economics, strategy, AND marketing.*

As we said earlier, purely competitive firms produce a standardized or homogeneous product. This means that consumers will have no basis other than price for preferring one firm's product over another's, and price competition is the norm. But monopolistically competitive producers turn out many variations of a particular product. To get a really graphic picture of this phenomenon, just walk down the cereal aisle of any grocery story and see how many different ways that Kellogg's can package up a flake of grain.

Because of such product differentiation, consumers have reasons other than price to prefer one product over another so that economic rivalry typically takes the form of *nonprice competition*. Such nonprice competition can come in the way that firms differentiate their products, and such differentiation can be accomplished in many ways—from product quality and conditions of sale and service to location and advertising and packaging.

For example, in the realm of product quality, personal computers can differ in terms of hardware capacity, software, graphics, and how "user friendly they are" while that big burger served up at any one of a number of fast food restaurants may differ on the leanness of the beef, the size of the bun, and whether it is broiled or fried.

In a similar vein, plain old aspirin may be enhanced by buffered compounds to prevent stomach aches or caffeine to keep you awake, detergents may be specially formulated for use in cold or hard water, and beer might have less alcohol or more malt. Moreover, when it comes to durable goods like automobiles, different brands can differ in hundreds of ways—from styling and horsepower to airbags, gas mileage, and stereo systems. Indeed, while a rose may be a rose may be a rose, a Ford is not a Chevy is not a Toyota.

Beyond physical characteristics and product quality, products may also be differentiated in other ways such as the amount of service and the conditions of sale. For example, one auto dealer might offer low-interest financing and free service while another might feature multiyear warranties.

One grocery store may stress the helpfulness of the clerks that bag your groceries while a "warehouse" may leave the bagging and carrying to you but offer lower prices. And one pizza restaurant might tout its fast delivery while another touts its fat mushrooms and thick crust.

Note that while product quality and conditions are based on real differences between products, such is not always the case with a third major source of product differentiation: advertising and packaging and the use of brand names and trademarks.

For example, while there are many aspirin-type products, promotion and advertising may convince headache sufferers that Bayer or Bufferin are superior and worth a higher price than a generic substitute.

Similarly, a celebrity's name associated with jeans or perfume may enhance those products in the minds of buyers while a tobacco or an auto company that can successfully associate their product with greater sex appeal may get a leg up on its competitors.

Now, with a large blow of the trumpet, let me now announce the punch line to this discussion: *From the business executive's perspective, product differentiation in general and advertising in particular have two strategic goals in mind.* As illustrated in the left side of Figure 12-10, the first goal is to increase consumer demand and thereby shift the firm's demand curve outwards and increase the firm's market share.

F I G U R E   12-10

The Goal of Advertising from the Managerial Economist's View

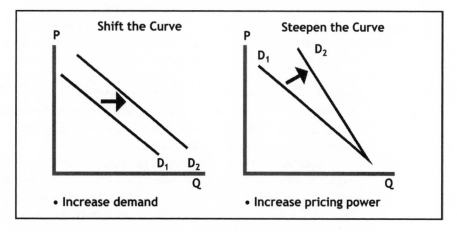

• Increase demand   • Increase pricing power

As illustrated in right-hand side of Figure 12-10, the second goal is to increase the inelasticity of the demand curve for its product, which, as we have already learned, is a handy-dandy way to increase one's profits through price hikes.

Of course, one of the ways a company can increase a product's demand inelasticity is by creating *brand loyalty* among consumers through advertising, thereby creating a stronger preference for the firm's product—and thus we close here one of the many integrative loops between economics and marketing.

Note, also, that this increased inelasticity increases the *strategic* opportunities of business executives. For starters, rather than being a *price taker*, executives running the monopolistically competitive firm becomes more of a *price maker*, albeit with less flexibility than a pure monopolist. At the same time, because executives can now react to changing market conditions by changing the traits of its product, they can also engage in more nonprice competition.

Structure and Strategy

In discussing the various forms of market structure, we made repeated references to how the executive teams at different organizations are likely to formulate strategy based on the particular industry in which they operate. For example, business executives in oligopolies and monopolies can tacitly collude to increase prices and restrict entry while executives operating in a monopolistic competition world must focus on nonprice competition and product differentiation.

To flesh these ideas out a bit more and finish this chapter, I would like to take a slightly deeper cut at this important interaction between market structure and market strategy. To do so, we first have to get a better handle on the key concepts of *market power* and *market concentration*.

Market Power and Market Concentration

Market power is what every business executive worth his or her salt seeks. It signifies the degree of control that a firm or a small number of firms have over the price and production decisions in an industry.

A common measure of market power is the *four-firm concentration ratio*, which is simply defined as the percent of total industry output accounted for by the four largest firms. Table 12-4 illustrates the four-firm concentration ratios for a sampling of some of the most highly concentrated of American

T A B L E   12-4

Industry Concentration in America

Product	Largest Firms	Four-Firm Concentration Ratio
Instant breakfast	Carnation, Pillsbury, Dean Foods	100
Disposable diapers	Proctor & Gamble, Kimberly-Clark, Curity, Romar Tissue Mills	99
Video game players	Nintendo, Sega	98
Cameras and film	Eastman Kodak, Polaroid, Bell & Howell, Berkey Photo	98
Telephones	Western Electric, General Telephone, United Telecommunications, Continental Telephone	95
Car rentals	Hertz, Avis, National, Budget	94
Telephone service (long distance)	AT&T, MCI, Sprint	94
Batteries	Duracell, Eveready, Ray-O-Vac, Kodac	94
Soft drinks	Coca-Cola, Pepsico, Cadbury Schweppes (7-UP, Dr. Pepper, A&W), Royal Crown	93
Credit cards	Visa, MasterCard, American Express	92
Razor blades	Gillette, Warner-Lambert (Schick; Wilkinson), Bic	91
Greeting cards	Hallmark, American Greetings, Gibson	91
Toothpaste	Procter & Gamble, Colgate-Palmolive, Lever Bros., Beecham	91
Automobiles	General Motors, Ford, Chrysler, Honda	90
Beer	Anheuser-Busch, Phillip-Morris(Miller), Coors, Stroh	90
Canned tuna	Heinz (Starkist), Unicord (Bumble Bee), Van Camp	82
Spaghetti sauce	Unilever (Ragu), Campbell Soup (Prego), Hunt-Wesson (Health Choice)	80
Aspirin	Johnson & Johnson, Bristol-Myers, American Home Products, Sterling Drug	78
Records and tapes	Time Warner, Sony, Thorn, Matsushita	77

industries—from instant breakfast and disposable diapers to canned tuna, spaghetti sauce, and aspirin. Take a very careful look at this table because it contains many of the titans not just of American industry but also of the international marketplace.

Now the reason why concentration ratios are so important is that they help serve as an indicator of the degree of strategic interaction that might occur in an industry. As I indicated earlier, strategic interaction is a term that describes how each firm's business strategy depends on their rivals' strategies.

In particular, as the number of firms in an industry shrink and industry concentration grows, the executives of each firm are more likely to base their pricing and output decisions on how other firms in the industry are likely to respond. Moreover, once this mutual interdependence is recognized, firms—and the executives that run them—have a choice between pursuing *cooperative* versus *noncooperative behavior.*

Cooperative versus Noncooperative Behavior

On the one hand, business executives act noncooperatively when they act on their own without any explicit or implicit agreements with other firms. That is the kind of market conduct that typically characterizes monopolistic competition. On the other hand, business executives operate in a cooperative mode when they try to minimize competition by explicitly or tacitly colluding on price and output and other market issues.

Perhaps the most famous historical example of explicit collusion—which is illegal in most countries—involves the so-called "phases of the moon" conspiracy. In 1960, executives at General Electric, Westinghouse, and Allis-Chalmers cooked up a scheme to fix prices in the market for heavy electrical equipment. Each company submitted sealed competitive bids, but it was arranged beforehand that the work would be allocated to a particular company based on which phase the moon was in. This allowed all the companies to submit bids higher than would have prevailed without this collusion. It also allowed the prearranged winner to submit an only slightly lower bid—one well above the competitive outcome. The eventual outcome of this conspiracy was that 29 manufacturers and 46 company officials were indicted, substantial fines were levied, and many of the executives went to jail.

Because explicit collusion is illegal, business executives have figured out a variety of ways to collude *tacitly. Tacit collusion* occurs when firms in an industry are able to voluntarily refrain from competition without explicit agreements.

One common vehicle for such tacit collusion is public speeches given by leading executives. In some of those speeches, when executives are talking about, say, how costs are rising in an industry and why it might be time to raise prices, they are not just talking to who is in the room. They are talking through the media to the other top executives in the industry—and it is all quite legal.

Similarly, industry trade associations can play an important role in tacit collusion. This is because such trade associations can act as a conduit and clearing house for information about prices and costs in an industry. And from such information, executives can better glean what their rivals are doing and, in some cases, then coordinate their activities.

The upshot of all of this is that when firms tacitly collude, they often quote identical high prices that push up profits and decrease the risk of doing business. It is all quite legal, and frankly, as a CEO, you will need to be aware that such kind of communication regularly occurs.

Models of Oligopoly Conduct

To better understand how both explicit and tacit collusion can shape your firm's market strategy, I am going to give you a quick sampling of two common models of strategic behavior: the *cartel model* and *price leadership*.

The Cartel Model

To understand the cartel model, consider a four-firm oligopoly in which each firm has grown tired of ruinous price wars. So during the industry's annual trade show in Las Vegas, the CEOs of all four companies ignore antitrust laws against explicit collusion and risk a possible jail sentence as they slip off to a secret rendezvous. During that rendezvous, they then negotiate what price should be charged for the product. And, of course, as part of their secret cartel agreement, each firm will also have to agree to restrict its output so the price can be maintained in the market. So where do you think these oligopolists will set price?

If you think about it, the answer is really simple. If the oligopolists can truly coordinate their activities, the obvious price to set is the same as that which would be set by a single monopolist. That means, of course, that price will be set by the profit-maximizing rule of marginal revenue equals marginal cost; and if price is set at that point, *the oligopolists will jointly maximize their profits*, which is why this model is often called the joint profit maximization model.

Price Leadership

A second model, the price leadership model, provides insight into how firms in an industry might tacitly collude as well as how firms that refuse to collude might be punished. In the price leadership model, the policing or enforcement mechanism used is often punishment by the price leader—usually the biggest or dominant firm in the industry.

With price leadership, executives within the industry do not have to slip off to a secret rendezvous in Vegas to set prices. Rather, a practice evolves where the *dominant firm*—usually the largest firm—becomes the *de facto* price leader. It will initiate a price change and all other firms more or less automatically follow that price change. Moreover, if one or more firms refuse to follow suit, the price leader may choose to back down. Alternatively, it may "punish" the noncooperative firms by significantly lowering prices for a while, forcing the followers to incur losses. In this way, the oligopoly can maintain price discipline.

A classic case of such price leadership involves the cigarette industry. The Big Three firms—Reynolds, American, and Liggett and Meyer—evolved a highly profitable practice of price leadership that resulted in virtually identical prices over the entire period between 1923 and 1941. During that period, the companies averaged a whopping 18 percent rate of return after taxes—roughly double the rate earned by American manufacturing as a whole at the time.

In more recent times, other industries such as farm machinery, anthracite coal, cement, copper, gasoline, newsprint, tin cans, lead, sulfur, rayon, fertilizer, glass containers, steel, automobiles and nonferrous metals have likewise practiced some type of price leadership.

Game Theory

You can see from this sampling of the traditional models of oligopoly behavior how important the strategic behavior of rivals can be in determining the eventual outcome in an industry. However, far more subtle models of strategic behavior have been advanced under the flag of *game theory*.

Game theory is important for business executives for an obvious reason. The many different possible games articulated by the theory help capture the essence and complexity of strategic conduct. This is because, with mutual interdependence recognized between firms, strategic conduct becomes a game of strategy such as poker, chess, or bridge. And the best way to play your hand in a poker game depends on the way rivals play theirs.

My point is simply that understanding game theory will help you better understand not just your own actions but your rivals' actions as well. That said, since game theory was discussed in Chapter 3, I am not going to belabor the topic here. All I will do is remind you that the guiding philosophy in game theory is this: *You will choose your own strategy under the assumption that your rival is analyzing your strategy and acting in his or her own best interest.*

In closing this chapter on managerial economics, let me emphasize that this is a highly integrative subject that can help you manage in many other functional disciplines—from operations management and strategy to marketing. That is why it has an important place in the "toolbox" of every MBA curriculum.

CHAPTER 13

Concluding Thoughts

I hope you have truly enjoyed this book. I also hope that this book will assume a permanent position in your bookshelf as a very handy reference guide that you can turn to again and again. In closing, I would like to offer several final reflections on the relationship of this book to the MBA experience.

First, I want to strongly reiterate a point that I made in the opening chapter, namely, that this book can *never* be a perfect substitute for the MBA *experience*. As I stated in that opening chapter, there are really *two* main benefits that every great business school serves up to its students. One benefit is the set of key concepts, tools, and skills that I hope have been conveyed to you quite ably in this book. The second benefit, however, is the *invaluable set of networks* that students develop as part of their MBA experience. Indeed, for many MBA graduates, these networks turn out, over time, to be almost as valuable as the knowledge embedded in the degree itself.

As for the second reflection, this has to do with the business school courses that were purposefully *not* covered in this book. In this regard, you may recall from Chapter 2 in our survey of the MBA core curriculum, that there are a number of courses like finance, marketing, and financial accounting that are required in virtually every Top 50 business school. However, there are other courses ranging from business and government and corporate ethics to information technology and human resource management that are taught at only *some* of the Top 50.

Because of space constraints and because I did not want to overwhelm you with an encyclopedia of information, I used a cut-off point of 50 percent for a subject's inclusion in this book. That is, unless more than half of the Top 50 schools require the subject in the core, the topic was not covered in this book. Of course, lost in this triage were *some* very interesting courses that are worth a brief comment.

Let us start with *Information Technology*. At 50 percent, this one just missed the cut, but there was another important reason to exclude it other than coverage. In the go-go days of the 1990s, IT became a very popular and trendy course. In fact, some business schools—including my own at UC-Irvine – chose to market themselves with an "IT focus," seeking to capitalize on the then emerging trend. Interestingly, however, only one of the Top 10 ranked schools fell into this trendy trap.[1] I believe this is for a very good reason.

While IT may be worth studying separately as an *elective* course, the trend nowadays is to simply integrate an IT component into each of the more traditional courses. Thus, for example, courses on operations management now stress how IT applications can improve supply chain efficiency while we saw in Chapter 8 on marketing how Customer Relations Management is a phenomenon almost totally driven by very powerful computer software.

The broader point is that you do not really need to learn IT separately. Instead, you really do need to learn it as part of your other courses, and any business school that has failed to so integrate IT into their core courses is one doomed to fail you.

In a similar vein, I would also like to say that the same kind of integrative approach likely applies to the subject of *Business Communications*, which also missed the cut in this book.[2] This is a subject that is likely much better integrated into the other courses in the curriculum. One way that this can be done is by providing students with greater opportunities to write papers and present their ideas in formal class settings. Alternatively, it is to present to the local business community through integrative projects.

Now how about two other courses that missed the cut in this book— *Corporate Ethics* (40 percent) and *Business and Government* (24 percent). It was particularly painful for me not to cover these courses because in addition to holding a Ph.D. in economics from Harvard University, I also have a Master's degree from Harvard's Kennedy School of Government. As to why that is a relevant observation, it is simply that I know just how important the legal and regulatory environment can be to achieving success in business.

In this regard, in the many courses in business and government that I have taught at UC-Irvine, the first thing I always tell my students is "get into politics or get out of business." What I mean by that is if business executives

---

1. Arguably, the one school in the Top 10 that has IT in the core is not in a "trap" at all but simply doing one of the things it does best. That Top 10 school would be the Massachusetts Institute of Technology's Sloan School.

2. While about 60 percent of the Top 50 schools require some type of course in this subject—well above our cut line—many of these courses are not full courses but rather "mini-courses." Therefore, the topic was excluded.

fail to understand how legal, regulatory, and tax policies shape the business climate, they will invariably fail in their mission to maximize shareholder value.

As for corporate ethics, there are some academics who take the view that the teaching of ethics in business schools has no place. In a post-Enron era in which we have seen a parade of top executives accused—and often convicted!—of the most heinous of white collar crimes, I remain puzzled by the lack of this course in the core of every Top 50 school.

As a final comment, the last course I regret not being able to include in this volume is that of *Human Resource Management* (28 percent). This subject is required in only a quarter of the Top 50 schools. Yet in working with Professor Raymond Noe at Ohio State on a chapter on this subject (which later had to be excluded for space constraints), I came to the conclusion that this topic is every bit as useful and interesting as *organizational behavior,* which was covered in Chapter 10.

In closing, I would especially like to thank Stephen Isaacs at McGraw-Hill who inspired this book and Larra Coyle for her usual fine artwork. I would also like to thank Chris Bergonzi, editor of the *Sloan Management Review,* for his keen insights and occasionally quite sharp editing pencil as he reviewed a late draft of this book. For those of you who want to make the study of management a lifelong endeavor, subscribing to *SMR* is a great first step in staying abreast of the latest developments in management theory and practice.

And as my final word: Now that you have heard from me on the MBA experience, I really hope that over time, I will hear from you. I would particularly like to know if this book has been helpful to you either in your business career or in your MBA studies. So feel free to contact me at the Web site below.

I wish you the greatest luck in your career and life!

Peter Navarro
www.peternavarro.com

I N D E X